Building Popular Power

BUILDING POPULAR POWER

Workers' and Neighborhood Movements
in the Portuguese Revolution

John L. Hammond

Monthly Review Press
New York

Library of Congress Cataloging-in-Publication Data
Hammond, John L.
   Building popular power : workers' and neighborhood movements in
the Portuguese Revolution / John L. Hammond
      p.   cm.
   Bibliography: p.
   Includes index.
   ISBN 0-85345-740-9.   ISBN 0-85345-741-7 (pbk.)
   1. Portugal—History—Revolution, 1974.   2. Government, Resistance
to—Portugal—History—20th century.   3. Political participation—
Portugal—History—20th century.   4. Middle classes—Portugal—
Political activity—History—20th century.   I. Title.
DP681.H36   1988
946.9′044—dc19   88-9218   CIP

Monthly Review Press
122 West 27th Street
New York, N.Y. 10001

Manufactured in the United States of America

10 9 8 7 6 5 4 3 2 1

To my *Apoio* comrades

Contents

Abbreviations

AOC	Worker-Peasant Alliance
BR	Revolutionary Brigades
CDE	Democratic Electoral Commissions
CDS	Democratic Social Center
CIL	Secretariat of Workers' Commissions, Lisbon Industrial Belt
COPCON	Continental Operational Command
CR	Council of the Revolution
CRAMOs	Autonomous Revolutionary Dwellers' and Occupiers' Commissions
CRAOs	Autonomous Revolutionary Occupiers' Commissions
CRMP	Revolutionary Dwellers' Council of Oporto
CUF	Union Manufacturing Company
ELP	Portuguese Liberation Army
FNLA	National Front for the Liberation of Angola
Frelimo	Mozambique Liberation Front
FSP	Popular Socialist Front
FUR	Revolutionary Unity Front
LUAR	League for Revolutionary Unity and Action
MDLP	Democratic Movement for the Liberation of Portugal
MDP	Portuguese Democratic Movement
MES	Left Socialist Movement
MFA	Armed Forces Movement
MPLA	Popular Movement for the Liberation of Angola
MRPP	Movement to Reorganize the Proletarian Party
PAIGC	African Party for the Independence of Guinea and Cape Verde
PCP	Portuguese Communist Party
PCP(ML)	Portuguese Communist Party (Marxist-Leninist)
PCP(R)	Portuguese Communist Party (Reconstructed)
PDC	Christian Democratic Party
PIDE	International and State Defense Police (pre-1974 secret police)
PPD	Popular Democratic Party
PRP	Revolutionary Party of the Proletariat
PS	Socialist Party
RALIS	Lisbon Artillery Regiment (originally First Light Artillery Regiment)
SAAL	Mobile Local Support Service
SUV	Soldiers United Will Win
UDP	Popular Democratic Union
UNITA	National Union for the Total Independence of Angola
UPA	Union of the Peoples of Angola

Preface

The Portuguese revolution brought a tremendous upsurge of political activity. Though it was brief, it gave rise to a dynamic mass movement involving people from all levels and sectors of the society. Revolutions must not only bring changes in political structures; transforming a society requires transforming the lives of ordinary people too. In Portugal in 1974 and 1975, ordinary people challenged the social order forcefully, turning a military coup into an attempted revolution.

Their political activity arose in the context of their everyday lives. People created movements to improve their immediate living and working conditions. So the experience was different for someone who worked in a bank, on a farm, or in a textile factory; for someone who lived in a shantytown, a middle-class suburb, or a village; for a soldier or a student. The movements were concrete in their demands and their actions; people did not act in response to an abstract ideology. This was the revolution's strength: because it was directly related to the lives of individual participants, they could appropriate the revolution and make it their own.

This also makes the revolution a much more exciting story, a story of real people. In this book I have tried to convey their individual experiences. Still, their stories have something in common: a sense of empowerment. People were empowered, first of all, by their participation in the mass movement itself. It drew them in, lifted the repression which had held them down, and opened up new opportunities to act. But they were empowered even more because participation became a conscious goal. They tried to make their experience the basis of a new society.

Adopting that goal, they developed a model of revolution which I call the popular power model. It was not unique to Portugal—similar ideas have developed in other revolutionary situations. But while activists in Portugal drew on previous experiences, they also went beyond them. Their own development of popular power was profound and sustained.

The Portuguese revolution was defeated politically. But it left an important heritage: the experience of popular power and the ideal of a political system which will expand and deepen the value of political participation for the people as a whole, guaranteeing them the power to rule their society.

Today when people speak of transforming societies, in both capitalist and socialist countries, they usually do not look to experiences of popular power or broadened participation for their models. Rather, they rely on market-oriented individualism and technological solutions. But such measures can hardly assure that a transformed society will provide a good life for its members. Portugal offers a different ideal. Even though it was not achieved, that ideal demonstrated that it could inspire people to act, and it is still worth aspiring to: a society based on equality and full participation, and organized around cooperation, community, and empowerment in collective action.

In writing this book over many years, I have incurred debts to a large number of people on both sides of the Atlantic. It is a pleasure to acknowledge their contributions now, though I fear that that will hardly repay the debts.

Of the many friends who welcomed me in Portugal, special thanks to Agostinho da Silva, Fernando and Teresa Nunes da Silva, José Branco Rodrigues, Julieta Rodrigues, Margarida Silva Dias, and Maria Violante Vieira. João Bernardo, Jorge Abegão, Jorge Almeida Fernandes, José Manuel Rodrigues da Silva, Luis Castanheira Lopes, Pulqueira, and Vasco Massapina generously shared documents and resources with me. Thanks above all to the dozens of informants who allowed me to interview them and attend their meetings, who of course remain anonymous.

Two groups of people, for many years, have offered intellectual and personal sustenance and encouragement which helped me in essential ways. The first was a study group whose members have included Gordon Adams, Nelly Burlingham, Woody Franklin, Paul Hoeffel, Tom Kappner, George Martin, Pat Peppe, and Hoby Spalding. *Apoio* (the American-Portuguese Overseas Information Organization) published a newsletter about the Portuguese popular power movement, and its members have stayed together as friends for a long time afterward. My thanks to Chip Downs, Florence Dinerstein, Gloria Jacobs, Mimi Keck, Dee Knight, Patty Parmalee, David Ruccio, Jon Steinberg, Carol and Jonas Woolverton. (The other contributions of some of these people are mentioned elsewhere.) Dan Jones offered general and continuing support.

Many people read the book or parts of it and their comments have made it much better. Keitha Fine, Ken Maxwell, Jim Mittelman, and Michael Perna commented on the entire manuscript. Lourdes Benería, Nancy Bermeo, Luis Costa Correia, Marty deKadt, Paul Goldman, Ann Kinney, Jon Kraus, George Martin, Mario Murteira, and Douglas Wheeler read some of the earlier papers which have been incorporated into the book. Chip Downs and Mimi Keck not only were friendly and severe critics of the book and of earlier pieces; they shared their unpublished writings and their knowledge in many discussions. Mark Kesselman and Pat Peppe have given time, thought, and constant encouragement. I appreciate my ongoing intellectual exchange with both of them, not only about this book. Sara Friedman's eagle eye and sharp pencil penetrated my often dense prose and pointed out to me in many places what I was really trying to say. I of course did not always follow these friends' advice, so none of them can be blamed for the result.

A generous grant from the National Science Foundation enabled me to spend six months in Portugal in 1980 to complete the research and provided further time for writing.

With sadness I must pay tribute to the memory of two friends: Alexandre Oliveira, editor of *Republica* under worker control, friend and comrade, helped me to understand much about the uniqueness of the Portuguese process. Joyce Riegelhaupt, one of the first U.S. scholars to work in Portugal, was my friend and tutor when I started to learn about things Portuguese, and was generous and helpful not only in scholarship but in many other ways. Often while writing I have thought of one or the other and wanted to ask a question or seek a reaction, and then realized that I could not. Both of them, gone before their time, are sorely missed.

Jon Steinberg not only read and commented on the manuscript and some of my earlier work, but also brought me together with Monthly Review Press. Thanks also to Karen Judd and Susan Lowes of MR.

Finally, I want to thank all the people, most of whose names I never knew, who made my first trip to Portugal in 1974 such a pleasure that I had to find an excuse to go back.

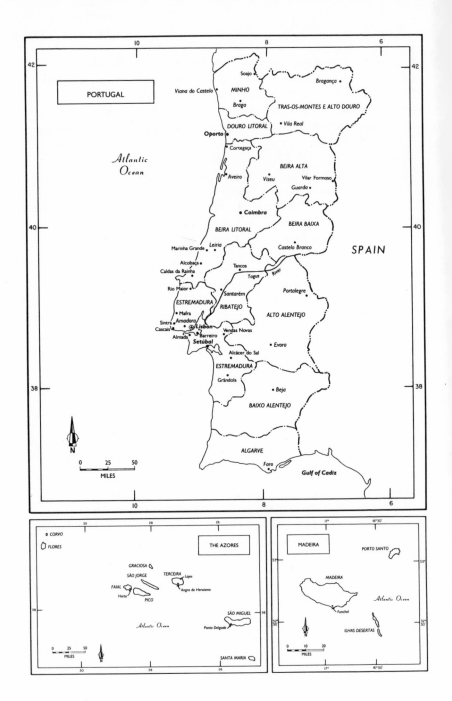

O governo provisório lançará as bases duma nova política económi-ca, posta ao serviço do Povo português, em particular das camadas da população até agora mais desfavorecidas.

—Programa do Movimento das Forças Armadas

The provisional government will lay the bases for a new economic policy, in the service of the Portuguese people, especially of the heretofore least privileged sectors of the population.

—Program of the Armed Forces Movement

Qualquer coisa como isto aconteceu depois de Abril quando as formigas despertaram, quando o sorriso foi permitido aos pobres e Portugal aprendeu a dizer tu. Era o prenúncio. Mas a mão pesada do bom senso burguês domou a Revolução, pôs-lhe um colete-de-forças.

—Urbano Tavares Rodrigues

Something like this happened after April when the ants woke up, when poor people were allowed to smile and Portugal learned to say *tu*. It was the foretaste. But the heavy hand of bourgeois good sense tamed the revolution, put it in a straitjacket.

—Urbano Tavares Rodrigues

O que faz falta é avisar a malta
O que faz falta
O que faz falta é dar poder à malta
O que faz falta
—José Afonso

What's needed is to let the folks know
What's needed
What's needed is to give the folks power
What's needed
—José Afonso

A Note on Names and Ranks

A Portuguese man may use a given name and surname, a given name and two surnames, only two surnames, or, in rarer cases, only given names. (Naming customs for women are less varied.) Introducing each man in this book, I use his given name and whatever surnames he generally uses; in subsequent references I try to use the form by which he was most commonly known. In the index and references, however, I follow the usual bibliographic practice of alphabetizing according to the last surname. This may cause an unavoidable confusion since, for example, President Costa Gomes is referred to by that name in the text, but he appears in the index and references as "Gomes."

A Portuguese officer assigned to a command higher than one to which his rank entitles him may be "graduated" to a higher rank, ex officio, with the presumption that he will return to the lower rank when he leaves the command if he has not meanwhile been promoted. With the frequent shuffling of commands in 1974 and 1975, many men were "graduated," and I have not tried to keep track of the changes in rank. I normally mention the rank only when first mentioning a person, and I have tried to use the rank he held at the time to which the first mention refers.

I have generally referred to communities and business firms by their real names, even when my information came from an interview with a confidential source. Because there are many locations to which I refer repeatedly, pseudonyms would have been cumbersome and most locations would be easily recognized anyway.

1

Introduction

Grândola, Vila Morena
Terra da fraternidade
O povo é que mais ordena
Dentro de ti, ó cidade

April 25, 1974, 12:25 a.m.: the young officers of the Armed Forces Movement (MFA) had chosen José Afonso's song "Grândola" as their signal to move. It tells of a town of brotherhood, where the people rule, where one meets a friend on every corner. A sympathetic radio announcer agreed to play it at the chosen moment, and when it came across the airwaves the officers launched a carefully planned coup against the Portuguese government. Virtually without bloodshed, they brought down the longest-established fascist regime in the history of the world and the only remaining colonial empire.

Taking power, the MFA promised a full restoration of civil liberties, including freedom of speech, abolition of censorship, and freedom for political parties; the democratic election of a constituent assembly within a year; the abolition of the secret police and paramilitary Portuguese Legion; and a "political, not military" solution to the wars in Portugal's African colonies. By themselves, these promises, which were all kept, portended radical changes for Portugal. But the MFA went even further, promising an economic policy "in the service of the Portuguese people, especially of the heretofore least privileged sectors of the population" and an "antimonopoly strategy" (quoted in A. Rodrigues et al., 1976: 299–302).

The public response was overwhelming. Within hours after the news was broadcast, civilians stormed the streets of Lisbon to greet the soldiers who had liberated them. Within weeks, people drove suspected fascists and sympathizers from office in local governments, unions, and other institutions; workers in hundreds of firms went on strike to demand—and win—higher wages.

They formed a sweeping popular movement. At first it was spontaneous and not very coherent, but it came together quickly. In workplaces and neighborhoods, people united in organizations to press their claims. During the next year and a half, workers pushed to have their factories nationalized or took them over themselves while people in all walks and areas of life organized to demand power to run the institutions that affected them.

People felt freer to act than they had for many years. A man who took part in it explained to me: "What we saw after April 25 was an explosion of the working masses which convinced them that they could run political and economic affairs: and they took initiatives in the countryside, in the factories, in the neighborhoods, in the workplace, in the schools. . . . That experience proved that the working masses had a deep aspiration to influence their own fate . . . [even if] it was a little idealistic, utopian, to create islands in the middle of a heritage of fascism."

They were free to act not just because the forces of repression were dismantled, but because the immediate outpouring of rejoicing was contagious. They broke the habits ingrained during a lifetime of submissiveness and transcended the confines of ordinary consciousness. Just such a break with normality must occur if a mass movement is to take hold. People must reject the structures of thought which define their ordinary experience and regulate their behavior; they must recognize possibilities which normally seem out of reach, or are not even conceived (Ash 1972: 20–22; Piven and Cloward 1979: 6–12).

The transcendence of the normal can reach extraordinary proportions, creating what Zolberg calls "moments of madness" in which it appears that "all is possible," moments of "immense joy, when daily cares are transcended, when emotions are freely expressed, . . . when the carefully erected walls which compartmentalize society collapse" (1972: 183–86). The April 25 coup and the months which followed it were such a moment. Beliefs and perceptions formerly taken for granted, which had made the capitalist social order seem acceptable and deprivation and subordination inevitable, no longer held people down.

The popular movement had three main centers: in industrial workplaces, in urban neighborhoods, and on large farms worked by day laborers. Soldiers and students also organized. At first workers or residents gathered locally to solve immediate problems and achieve limited goals—raises, job security, housing, neighborhood amenities. But in each case, as they won minor victories—and the fact of acting was itself the first victory—they demanded even more. They began locally and independently of each other, but as the scope of their goals expanded so did their horizons, until they came to see themselves as part of a single movement with a common objective: a new way of life and a new kind of society. The movement itself became their model for the institutions of mass popular democracy which they would create and which would allow everyone to participate equally and directly.

Many view movements which demand the expansion of participation as the product of growing affluence. The May 1968 events in France provide the most widely recognized example. In a society where basic economic needs are met, progressively better educated workers raise new, "qualitative" demands, and many reject the growing instrumentalism of political life (Bornstein and Fine 1977; Gombin 1975: 76; Gorz 1973: 27–29, 89–97; Zolberg 1972: 202). By that standard, Portugal would seem an unlikely place for such a movement. It is the poorest country in Western Europe, has the highest illiteracy rate, and suffered five decades of repression—an improbable breeding ground for the politics of affluence.

The revolution was also unusual for the role of the military. The Armed Forces Movement which unseated the government had come together only to end the seemingly interminable colonial war; within little more than a year the military government not only found a "political solution" but granted independence to all of Portugal's colonies (except Macao and East Timor).[1] But it did more than that. Its program was vague, but the MFA moved steadily to the left and began to call for more radical domestic policies, demanding to control the economy and redirect it in the interest of the working class.

The officers' evolution after the coup was due above all to the unexpected strength of the popular movement, which welcomed the MFA's apparently progressive intentions and supported its program from the beginning. As the movement more explicitly called for socialism and its capacity to mobilize grew in late 1974 and early 1975, it provided leftist officers with an ideological definition and a political resource. Though the officers ruled, the popular movement pulled the political process forward. Without its impulse there would have been no revolution.

During the first months after the coup, the MFA needed that support. Its program, though unclear, aroused intense opposition from the senior officer corps and industrial and financial capitalists, who were unwilling to free the colonies. Bolstered by the popular movement, however, the MFA won its early battle with the generals over decolonization and asserted its power to govern. But then disagreements surfaced within the MFA itself. While some officers wanted to assert state power to move rapidly toward socialism, others wanted to limit themselves to short-term measures and leave major decisions to a future democratically elected government. For nearly a year after the coup, while the popular movement gathered strength, the MFA hesitated.

The MFA's left wing was decisively strengthened, however, by a bungled rightwing countercoup attempt on March 11, 1975. Leftists seized the opportunity and moved rapidly to implement their radical program. Soon they declared that the MFA was a national liberation movement and that Portugal was on the road to socialism. In short order they nationalized banks, insurance companies, and basic industries; encouraged the movements for direct democracy in neighborhoods and worker control in industry; gave land to farmworkers; and began to call for the internal democratization of the armed forces. People now called what was happening the "Portuguese revolution."

But what kind of revolution, and what kind of socialism? While the West interpreted the Portuguese events purely as a battle between capitalism and communism, they also represented a confrontation between two models of socialist revolution. One was similar to the model which inspired the creation of socialism in the Soviet Union and elsewhere. The other was more libertarian, based on the unexpected example of the popular movement. These two models, which I call the centralist and popular power models of revolution, envision different forms of socialism and different processes for arriving at it.

The division between these two models came to be mirrored in the MFA. Some of its leftwing officers, generally allied with the Portuguese Communist Party (PCP), wanted to create a centralized socialism in which the state would take the leading role. Other leftists followed the popular movement in wanting to give people the power to govern themselves directly in organizations of mass democracy. More moderate MFA officers sought only to establish parliamentary democracy; they were frightened by proposals for popular power and alienated by the centralists' imposition of socialism without regard for democratic decisionmaking, and since the MFA itself comprised only a small fraction of the officer corps, there were many in the military who did not share the goals of the revolution at all; as the growing challenge by the popular movement threatened to tear Portuguese society apart, these rightwing officers allied with the moderate MFA members to put a halt to the revolution.

Events moved rapidly; tension and confrontation grew. Officers who called for the restoration of order gained the upper hand in a coup on November 25, 1975. They established their power over the armed forces and demobilized leftwing military units, leaving the popular movement demoralized and disoriented. After only nineteen months, the revolution was defeated.

In fact, the period of rapid structural change and the peak of the popular movement lasted only from March to November 1975. Can this brief and ultimately unsuccessful episode be called a revolution? Not on the basis of its outcome, certainly: the major lasting effect was parliamentary democracy, facilitating the ascendance of a new segment of the capitalist class. But the movement itself was revolutionary in two respects: it attempted to transform society and to transfer power to a completely new class, and it based that attempt on the power of the popular movement. Like the Russian revolution of 1905, it failed; but it still deserves the name "revolution."

Two Models of Socialist Transition

Contending forces in Portugal offered two models for building a socialist society: centralism and popular power. These models embrace different concepts of socialist society—how the new society is to be governed and how production is to be organized—and of the process of creating it—how the transition to socialism will be accomplished and the part that the consciousness and activity of workers will play.

The centralist model is consistent in its methods for taking power and organizing the new society: the socialist economy, like the party which wages the revolutionary struggle, is viewed as a command structure in which people's participation consists largely in supporting decisions made in their name by a central authority. The process of transition is likewise centrally directed: socialists are to assume power and carry out the transformation from above by expropriating the centers of economic power and abolishing private ownership of the means of production, thereby ending exploitation.

The level of popular political consciousness is not important in this model, because once scarcity disappears so will acquisitiveness and competition. The model is governed by the view that "raising material living standards of the masses will by itself foster socialist consciousness," enabling people to participate conscientiously and cooperatively in socialist society (as Sweezy characterizes Soviet ideology in Sweezy and Bettelheim 1971: 118).

The popular power model represents a reaction to what it sees as excessive central direction and the lack of democracy in existing socialist societies. It denies that a transition to socialism can be undertaken from within the existing capitalist state; rather, the state must be transformed by the activities of workers. It also rejects the idea that seizing the commanding heights of the economy and raising living standards will be enough to assure social transformation. Private property in the means of production must be abolished, to be sure, but not by government decree; rather, through a process of struggle in which workers come to control the means of production directly and collectively. Finally, the popular power model rejects centralized and representative governing structures, even if democratically chosen, and insists on direct participation by all in both economic and political decisions.

These two models have different concepts of power. The centralist model assumes that power exists in a society in a fixed quantity and that a class wanting to take power must expropriate it from those who hold it. The popular power model argues that the exploited must—and can—*create* power by organizing collectively to assert their demands and challenge the dominant classes.

Both models present mass movements as the vehicle through which otherwise powerless people achieve unity and organization. But for the centralist model, mass mobilization is important only as a tactical tool for the revolutionary leadership, while for the popular power model such movements empower people: participation transforms their consciousness and creates the collective strength they need to challenge capitalism.

Corresponding to these different views of the state and of power are different political practices. While centralists, fearing the loss of leadership initiative, discourage autonomous mobilization from the base, the popular power model holds that the democratic and collective participation that are to characterize socialist society must be anticipated in the transition. This model has been embraced by people who have themselves had empowering experiences of political participation. Extending that participation to society as a whole, they argue, will build support during the revolution and prevent leaders from monopolizing power afterward.

Proponents of the popular power model argue that active participation will also shape people's consciousness and behavior, preparing them to govern the future society: it will help them to free themselves of the competitiveness, individualism, and passivity into which they have been socialized in a capitalist society. The discipline, autonomy, cooperation, and the skills necessary to rule can develop only through practice in popular struggles. Boggs points out that such struggles are important in revolutionary as well as in nonrevolutionary situations because they are prefigurative:

they try to embody "within the ongoing political practice of a movement . . . those forms of social relations, decision-making, culture, and human experience that are the ultimate goal" (1977: 100). Workers cannot wait until capitalist ownership has been expropriated to learn how to govern; they must begin during the struggle itself.

Perhaps most important, the exercise of popular power in the transition will protect against bureaucratization and centralized rule afterward. A centrally directed transformation conflicts in principle with what this model holds to be an integral goal of socialism: the extension of democracy to more people and more areas of social life, providing for the collective exercise of power by the working class. Unless people win that power by their own efforts during the struggle, they are unlikely to gain it later.

Worker control of industry is the concrete expression of abolition of private property in the means of production. Powerful movements for worker control have burst forth in every revolutionary struggle in an advanced capitalist country since the Paris Commune of 1871. In Russia in 1905 and 1917, Germany in 1918–19, Italy in 1919–20, Spain in 1936, and Chile in 1970–73, to name the most important examples, workers' efforts to take over, own, and run their workplaces were an integral part of the challenge to capitalist domination.[2] These takeovers claimed to be the basis for a new form of organization of society, in which the elimination of capitalist exploitation would give all workers the opportunity to control their work. They were also an example: proving that workers *could* manage production, they validated the ideology which inspired the revolutions.

Workers have rarely seized control outside of revolutionary situations, because capitalist relations of production are normally protected both by repression—police forces defend the right of property—and by ideological hegemony—workers accept as natural, or at least inevitable, the private appropriation by others of the means of production and the products of their labor. Worker control is therefore relatively rare either as a demand or as a practice in capitalist societies. Worker control movements arise only when workers break through the restraints of everyday consciousness. Moments of revolution stimulate them by challenging the taken-for-grantedness of capitalist private property, and also by weakening the forces of repression (Mandel 1973: 14–15; Wallis 1978).

Such a movement arose in Portugal. It arose mainly in small, weak firms which capitalist owners abandoned, leaving workers threatened by unemployment. Workers took over the firms to save their jobs. But once in charge, they discovered not only that they could manage without their former bosses but that sharing a common project created bonds of solidarity.

Workers mobilized in other firms as well: in some they demanded that the firms be nationalized; in others they sought more limited forms of self-determination and battled against authoritarian management.

Experiences of worker control have provided the means for putting the popular power model into practice. They have repeatedly given rise to a specific type of organization, the council, which first emerged in the Paris Commune (Arendt 1965: 270–73; Boggs 1977; Gombin 1975: 91–92; Pannekoek 1973). Marx and Engels viewed the council as the vehicle of popular participation, in which representation was abolished and decisions were to be made in assemblies in which everyone voted. Where delegation was necessary, delegates were to receive the same wages as other workers and were subject to recall at any moment (Marx and Engels 1972: 536, 555–56). These goals were not fully realized in the Commune, but revolutions in Europe in this century brought further experiences of council management.

Gramsci, analyzing the Turin factory council movement after World War I, argued that the council is a specifically proletarian form of organization, one through which workers for the first time claim the power which belongs to them as the direct producers of value. The councils therefore differ fundamentally from older forms of working-class organization, the party and the trade union, which in a capitalist society represent workers as commodities in the labor market and attempt to improve their bargaining power but necessarily defer to the power of capital (Gramsci 1977: 98–111).

With the growth of cities, neighborhood-based urban movements have also conducted important political struggles for housing and city services if these are inadequately provided by private capital. Especially since the 1960s, many West European countries have witnessed struggles to demand that the state guarantee collective consumption (Castells 1979: 454–62). Created to meet immediate material needs, urban movements have typically gone on to demand democratic administration of services. Where they have succeeded, they have provided examples of self-management at the local level and often become part of larger political movements for expanded democracy (Coit 1978: 303–10).

Neighborhood organizations in Portugal worked mainly to resolve the housing shortage. With government support, shantytown dwellers organized to build new houses; against government hostility, others took over empty houses and apartments in the central cities and turned them over to needy families. Many of these neighborhood organizations went beyond the housing issue and claimed the authority to govern their localities; they also created a spirit of community and neighborliness among previously anonymous urban dwellers.

Neighborhood struggles have been regarded as secondary to worker movements because they do not challenge capitalist control of the process of production (Castells 1979: 376–77). But their importance goes beyond their immediate aims. Their goals and structure set them more immediately political tasks than is the case for workers' movements. Their target is the state, while for workers it is usually their employers. The neighborhood offers an arena for mobilization of a much broader range of people than does the workplace; this potential for universal participation makes neighborhood organizations a better model for direct democracy. This more explicitly political vocation of neighborhood movements is paradoxical in the light of the priority socialist theory gives to the workplace. Nevertheless, the clearest articulation of the popular power model in Portugal came from the neighborhood commissions.

Council activists have made three political claims for councils (identified by Anweiler 1974: 5): a council is " 'the people' organized to exercise state power"; a "revolutionary committee," the general staff of the revolutionary struggle; and a "workers' committee" to organize worker control of production. In this view, councils institutionalize democratic participation in the revolutionary struggle itself and lay the basis for democracy both in the exercise of state power and in the management of the economy once socialists achieve state power.

How can councils be organized to achieve Anweiler's three aims? Indeed, is it possible that the same organization can achieve them all? The popular power model does not clarify how the activities of the councils are to be coordinated for revolutionary struggle, or what relation they will have to the traditional working-class organizations—the parties and the trade unions.

Council management of an entire economy raises further questions: how is the economy as a whole to be organized and how are the interests of workers in a particular workplace to be balanced against the interests of the whole working class? Decentralized worker control may encourage workers to attend to their own parochial interests. Or (the more common problem) centralized revolutionary leadership may usurp local autonomy, encouraging worker control only to the extent that it strengthens the leaders in the struggle for power.

In principle, councils are supposed to create the forms of organization for a new state and a new society in the course of struggle, and then transform themselves into state structures which replace the existing state once the revolution has triumphed. But one must ask whether these creatures of spontaneous struggle can stabilize themselves to serve the needs of political representation and economic organization in more normal times. There is also a problem of scale: perhaps a workplace or neighborhood can be governed by direct democracy, but it may seem utopian to expect that a nation can.

Councils in Portugal (usually called commissions) embodied all these contradictions. They did not create a new society; the revolution was defeated. So the experience tells us more about the role of councils in the revolutionary struggle than their viability as governing institutions. But mass struggles have been presented as a prefiguration of the postrevolutionary organization of society, so the Portuguese experience should offer at least some evidence about the possibility of a society governed by popular power as well.

The issues which divided the advocates of centralism and popular power in Portugal have arisen in various forms throughout the twentieth century. Lenin's conduct of the Russian revolution exemplified the centralist model; Luxemburg criticized him for assuming "that the socialist transformation is something for which a ready-made formula lies completed in the pocket of the revolutionary party. . . . This is, unfortunately—or perhaps fortunately—not the case."

Luxemburg continued:

> socialist democracy is not something which begins only in the promised land after the foundations of socialist economy are created; it does not come as some sort of Christmas present for the worthy people who, in the interim, have loyally supported a handful of socialist dictators. Socialist democracy begins simultaneously with the beginning of the destruction of class rule and the construction of socialism. . . .
>
> But this . . . must proceed step by step out of the active participation of the masses; it must be under their direct influence, subjected to the control of complete public activity; it must arise out of the growing political training of the masses of the people (1970: 69, 77–78).

Moore (1963) discusses the dispute over centralism and popular power in the context of an armed insurrection, the same context in which Lenin and Luxemburg debated it. But reformism, too, allows for both the centralist and popular power models. The attempted transition to socialism in Portugal was a reformist one: with minor exceptions, advocates of both the centralist and popular power models assumed that they could transform society peacefully. Like most socialists in advanced capitalist societies today, they ruled out armed revolution and proposed to establish socialism through reforms which while gradual would nevertheless completely transform the social and economic system, transfer power from one class to another, and therefore deserve the name "revolution."

According to the popular power model, mass struggle is as essential to peaceful transition as it is to armed revolution. Not all the revolutions mentioned in which worker control movements emerged to challenge capital were armed. Italy after World War I faced a revolutionary situation but not an armed revolt: the government had lost its monopoly over the means of violence and could not exercise complete power. Workers challenged the capitalist state politically and economically, not by military means. Even a reformist transition requires a weakening of the old regime's ideological hegemony and its coercive power. Mass movements heighten a crisis by exposing and exacerbating the weakness of the regime and winning over vacillators.

Mass movements play a different role after a reformist government has taken office. During the Spanish Civil War and in Chile under the Popular Unity government, the mass movements agitated to force their governments to move more decisively. In a state which is still capitalist, pressure from the base can expand a reformist government's power by both forcing and encouraging it to enact its program vigorously rather than to conciliate capital. Workers organized in strategic firms can help enforce a reformist program by denouncing economic sabotage by capitalists and supporting nationalization or other transitional measures that affect their firms. Here again the process will involve both conflict and cooperation, with workers supporting the government when it lives up to its program and prodding it when it does not.

The Portuguese revolution, though it began with a military coup, faced some of the same problems of attempted reformism elsewhere—problems inherent in the nature of the capitalist state, not contingent on whether the reformers achieve office through formally democratic procedures. In the conflict between the centralizers and the popular movement, the Portuguese revolution illustrates the problematic relation between the working class and a state in which it holds significant but incomplete power.

The officers who governed adopted the centralist model of transition, with the encouragement of their allies in the Communist Party. But at first the MFA intended no revolution; and the Communists, following their centralist orientation, deferred to the initial moderate inclinations of the MFA and repeatedly tried to stifle initiatives from the base.

The centralists gained the confidence to take action only after the popular movement showed its strength. And the movement was inspired by the popular power model, at least implicitly. The popular power model was not so clearly spelled out as the centralist model, nor was it so clearly identified with any specific group. Its most self-conscious advocates were found in the far-left parties and among their military sympathizers. But the popular movement was far bigger than the far-left parties or the military faction which identified with it. And its example was crucial: there would have been no revolution at all if the popular movement had not overwhelmed the cautious officers and pulled them to the left by its example.

Like the popular power model, the movement itself was highly amorphous. A social movement by definition has fluid boundaries. It cannot be reduced to specific organizations, though it encompasses organizations (Zald and Ash 1966; Tilly 1978: 8–10). It does not authoritatively endorse an ideology, explicitly adopt lines of action, or leave written records. One cannot point to traces substantiating its past existence.

For this reason, it is hard to establish that supporters of the popular movement held particular beliefs, took particular actions, or strove for particular goals. The organizations most closely identified with it—the political parties of the far left—were much smaller than the movement as a whole, and if one reduces the movement to the parties, their small size and mutual ideological antagonism make it appear that the movement had no coherent program or objectives and was too small to have any impact.

But the popular movement was seen at the time as a single, large, and (at least relatively) coherent movement. And it was the collective actions of that movement which inspired the idea of popular power, even though few people articulated it. The events of 1974 and 1975 went beyond the acts of specific individuals, groups, or parties, and the effect of the movement was out of proportion to the size of the formally organized groups which it encompassed.

What Really Happened?

Many of its supporters saw the popular movement as the key phenomenon of the Portuguese revolutionary process, defining its overall character. So did some others, who were not politically identified with the movement, among them Major Ernesto Melo Antunes. Melo Antunes drafted the MFA Program and became the leader of the moderate faction of the MFA whose major concern was to establish parliamentary democracy even at the cost of suppressing the popular movement. Yet several years later he commented:

A few hours after the start of the coup, on that same day, the mass movements began. This immediately transformed [April 25] into a revolution. When I wrote the Programme of the MFA, I had not predicted this, but the fact that it happened showed that the military were in tune with the Portuguese people (quoted in Ferreira and Marshall 1986: 163).

But not all observers share that view of the popular power movement. Cabral, for example, dismisses it as "nostalgia of those days back in 1974" (1987: 84). Others, too, deny that the movement had any significant scope or consequences, and some claim that the mass political activity which occurred during the period was formless and undirected and cannot properly be described as a single movement at all.

This difference of views is basic to the different interpretations of the Portuguese revolution as a whole. On the tenth anniversary of the 1974 coup, a conference at Columbia University brought together Portuguese officers and civilians who had taken leading roles in the revolution; Portuguese and foreign academics; and diplomats and journalists who had witnessed the events directly. The announced topic, "Armed Forces and Society," was broadened to deal with the whole spectrum of domestic military and civilian politics. As the conference rapporteur summarized the discussion:

Ten years after the MFA coup in Portugal, it is still extremely difficult to carry on a broadly based debate on the causes and consequences of the tumultuous nineteen month period from April 25, 1974 to November 25, 1975. [There are] radically different visions of what actually took place. . . . Within each of these perspectives, different actors and events are analytically relevant. [The perspectives offer no] agreement on important descriptive aspects of the process. . . . What really happened during those nineteen months? From different actors will come the story of entirely different processes (Keck 1984, n.p.).

In my own experience, scholars have challenged the occurrence of events which I observed firsthand.

There are several reasons for the discrepant perceptions of the impact of the popular power movement, starting with the improbability of a socialist revolution in a country as poor and backward as Portugal. It violates our preconceptions that a movement for popular power could have occurred there; because it was over so quickly, the preconceptions may overrule the memories.

But the more fundamental reason for dismissing the movement arises from its program and objectives. Both supporters and opponents of popular power, looking back at the revolution, can find reasons for consigning the events to the same collective oblivion, though the reasons are different in each case. It is surprising to find people on opposite sides reaching such similar positions.

Activists experienced a break with normality and felt a new sense of possibilities which were hard to believe even at the time; but once "normality" was restored, believing in them became even harder. The experience seems so incredible that it is perversely comforting to forget that it happened. It aroused great hopes, and the disappointment was equally great. Even worse, reflection on the lost hope must include acknowledgment that the illusions led to serious political errors.

In the totally different conjuncture after the revolution, activists had to accept the restoration of normality and the limited political possibilities of the new situation. Revolutionary hopes would only get in the way. Others abandoned political activity, but did not want to feel that they had given up. For both, it was more convenient to forget what they had hoped for.

The reasons why opponents of popular power might want to deny the reality of the movement are self-evident—whether they opposed it because they were capitalists whose material interests were threatened, socialists of other persuasions who saw the movement as a competitor for hegemony in the working class, or democrats of the right or left who believed that it was impossibly utopian. They can more easily dismiss the movement if they can argue that it represented no more than a handful of activists who were unrealistic and ideologically motivated (at best) or potentially totalitarian (at worst).

Finally, the defeat of the popular power movement makes it easy to challenge its significance. The history and analysis of a defeated movement are not likely to find a receptive ear. As Zolberg puts it, "moments of madness have had a very bad press in the social sciences" (1972: 205). For one thing, the defeat testifies to the movement's political limits. More importantly, as Keck, author of the report on the Columbia conference, points out, the debate over the Portuguese revolution involves "the appropriation of History. . . . The struggle to define what happened is as much a political struggle as the process itself" (1984, n.p.). And victors write the history books.

But the popular power movement did occur. It generated broad involvement, shook the established order, and aroused profound hopes with its vision of a new society, one of social justice, without exploitation or oppression, in which political participation would be widely shared and would not only guarantee a decent life for all but also empower those who took part.

The Portuguese revolution was unique, and will not be duplicated. But though the revolution's defeat and observers' own differences of values lead many to discount the revolution and the importance of the popular movement within it, it nevertheless stands as a major late twentieth-century example in which ordinary people, workers and neighbors, seized control of their circumstances and demonstrated both the aspiration and the power to rule their own lives.

2

The Fascist Regime

The 1974 coup by the Armed Forces Movement toppled a fascist regime which had held Portugal down for half a century. The old regime was based on an alliance of landowners and industrial capitalists; it invoked such symbols of national unity as Portugal's imperial past and its racial superiority, glorifying and intensifying the domination of its colonies. It created a top-down structure of organizations which, it claimed, ensured class conciliation and harmonized the interests of all those with a stake in the society. But these organizations were dominated by the elite and their real purpose was to keep the population backward and suppress class struggle; the regime developed into a repressive dictatorship.

That dictatorship kept the country economically stagnant, culturally backward, and politically repressed, and it clung to a colonial empire where the people were even worse off and the political system was even more tightly controlled. The regime was maintained by the support of four significant forces—the armed forces, the Catholic church, large landowners, and industrial capitalists—and a social and political structure which relegated most of the population to poverty and ignorance while guaranteeing their quiescence.

The low level of development itself protected the state from active opposition. The poor educational system preserved a high rate of illiteracy. In addition, the highly conservative church held ideological sway in much of the country. An efficient apparatus of repression reinforced ideological hegemony: political organizations were banned, the press was censored, and repression was enforced by the secret police and a dense network of informers.

The result was a stagnant economy dominated by a backward-looking oligarchy whose wealth stood in stark contrast to the poverty of the majority. In the mid-twentieth century, nearly half the economically active population still worked in agriculture, and nearly four-fifths of all farms were smaller than four hectares. Much of industry was technologically primitive. Per capita income in 1950 was only $200, and the levels of life expectancy and infant mortality were among the worst in Europe. While growth accelerated after 1960, it was very uneven, leaving whole regions of the country untouched by the new relative prosperity.

The architect of the regime was Antonio de Oliveira Salazar, who during his forty-year rule imposed autarchic and fiscally conservative policies which guaranteed economic stability and preserved the dominance of the oligarchy but prevented development. In 1926 a military coup had overturned the First Republic, which during its sixteen-year life had brought corrupt and incompetent government, fiscal instability, and political strife. The Republic had become so unpopular that even many of its early supporters welcomed the coup. But the new military leaders were no better able to achieve economic stability, their major goal, than the republican governments before them. So they invited Salazar, an academic economist, to become finance minister in 1928. He accepted, but only on the condition that he be granted absolute veto power over government expenditures. He was thus the dominant figure from the beginning, and he became prime minister in 1932 (the post he retained until 1968).

During the tumultuous republican period, Salazar was attracted to rightwing movements which condemned "demo-liberalism" and bolshevism and proposed to reestablish order on the basis of principles of corporatism, monarchism, Catholicism, antiparliamentarism, and antisemitism (A. O. Marques 1972: 177–79; Martins 1969: 302–9; Wiarda 1977: 70–81). In office, he designed what he called the "new state" on the model of Mussolini's Italy, and embodied it in the constitution of 1933. Invoking corporatist ideology, the constitution established a host of low-level formal organizations of workers, employers, free professionals, and, in the rural sector, landowners, peasants, and farmworkers. The explicit purpose of these organizations was to suppress conflicts among competing interests. They claimed to provide due, if not democratic, representation to all groups, but this structure was a mere façade.

The constitution also provided for a president and a legislature. But the president's sole function was to dismiss the prime minister—which no president ever did. The legislature, a bicameral body consisting of a National Assembly whose members were elected by district and a Corporative Chamber in which the corporatist organizations and institutions such as the army and the church were represented, was a rubber stamp for the government. The National Assembly and the president were nominally elected by popular vote, but until 1945 only the official party could present candidates; thereafter, though the elections allowed token opposition, they remained tightly controlled. Power lay with the prime minister, and Salazar dispensed with even the formal legislative process most of the time to rule by direct decree of the cabinet (Wiarda 1977: 100–2).

Portugal's economy remained stagnant for most of Salazar's rule. The country was entirely dependent on its overseas possessions: for five centuries most of its periods of prosperity were due to booms originating in one colony or another. That dependence created a mentality which shunned economic entrepreneurship in favor of bureaucratic or mercantile careers, so there was no dynamic force promoting growth of the domestic economy.

Stagnation was reinforced by Salazar's policies of fiscal conservatism and autarchy for Portugal and the colonies (which he regarded as a single unit). He insisted on protectionism, a stable currency, and a balanced budget. These policies maintained a steadily positive balance of payments and built up huge gold reserves. Autarchic policies kept foreign capital out, and the state restricted domestic private investment significantly: it had to approve the location of new industrial plants and wage rates in large firms. It was not only the resulting economic stagnation but the policies of protectionism and fiscal conservatism themselves which led many to characterize his economic policy as "medieval."

Stagnation kept the standard of living low. The economy depended on raw materials for foreign exchange: approximately 70 percent of exports in 1950 were agricultural products, fish, and wolframite. The illiteracy rate (30 percent in 1970) was the highest in Europe, East or West, and in the early 1970s, infant mortality and male life expectancy were respectively the second and third worst in Europe (Baklanoff 1978: 111–12; Keefe 1977: 102–5; Murteira 1979: 332).

Most industrial firms were small in scale and technologically backward. In 1972, two-thirds of all firms produced only 12 percent (by value) of industrial output (J.M. Pereira 1974: 17–30; A.R. Santos 1977b: 14–15). But a few firms grew enormously in the postwar period. They had started out as small, privately held companies, but they enjoyed state-granted monopolies over raw materials from the colonies or basic consumer goods. In a pattern which is typical of nations experiencing "late late" industrialization (Kurth 1979: 322–24), they used their monopoly positions to accumulate capital which permitted them to expand into huge conglomerate corporations known as monopoly groups. Through them, a handful of people (reputedly, "forty families") controlled the bulk of the country's industrial wealth.

Seven monopoly groups overwhelmingly dominated the Portuguese economy. They controlled eight of the ten largest firms in the country, five of the seven largest exporters, and more than half of the industrial firms producing more than 500,000 *contos* (in 1974, about $20 million) a year; each possessed important links to the colonies, with interests in the export and processing (in metropolitan Portugal) of raw agricultural and mineral products. In the typical pattern, a monopoly group controlled a bank, an insurance company, a newspaper, and several diversified manufacturing firms. The largest group, CUF (*Companhia União Fabril,* Union Manufacturing Company), was the 173rd largest non-U.S. firm in the world in 1974; its empire was based on chemicals and fertilizers, but it held interests in mining, textiles, petroleum refining, and shipbuilding among its 186 subsidiaries and was responsible for about 20 percent of all Portuguese industry.

These seven groups had virtually complete control of the country's financial system, controlling 80 percent of the volume of commercial banking and 55 percent of the insurance market. Since Portugal had no functioning securities market, bank capital was the major source of industrial investment. The monopoly groups used their control of bank credit to finance their own further expansion, thereby limiting competition, increasing capital concentration, giving expansion an unstable financial basis of pyramids of credit rather than equity investment, and allocating resources very inefficiently (Baklanoff 1978: 104–10; A.R. Santos 1977a: 33; 1977b: 11–14).

By protecting industry against foreign competition, Salazar's economic policies permitted it to remain inefficient and technologically backward, reinforcing economic stagnation. Small capitalists actively supported the regime despite its policies favoring concentration, for repressive control of the labor force kept wages low and protectionism freed them from the necessity to rationalize or adopt advanced technology. Even the monopolists resisted modernization. Despite their huge size and enormous economic power, the monopoly groups were run as family firms. Ideologically the monopolists shared the ''medievalist'' orientation which informed Salazar's autarchic policies. Their interests in Africa gave them a ready source of capital accumulation. They had little need for technical innovation and they were eager to retain the colonies. Like small capitalists, therefore, they supported the existing regime fully.

Capital thus allied itself with the state to control the working class, taming it and obviating any need for economic modernization. Nominally, corporatism created separate organizations—guilds (*grémios*) for owners and unions for workers—which ensured that capital and labor met as equal partners. But owners dominated the guilds, while the organizations which theoretically represented workers and small farmers were controlled by the government. The autonomous trade associations that owners had formed before 1926 were allowed to survive, but the regime destroyed or absorbed unions that had existed under the Republic.

Trade unions (*sindicatos nacionais*) were authorized by the 1933 Labor Statute (the translation "trade union" is hardly exact for these "national syndicates," but I will use it for convenience because the syndical structure was largely retained by the unions after 1974). The statute declared its intention to eliminate class conflict; to that end it made strikes and lockouts illegal, and provided for equal representation of owners and workers in the Corporative Chamber.

Under the Republic, anarchists had dominated workers' organizations; the Socialist Party (founded in 1875) and the Communist Party (founded in 1921) both remained small. Portugal's anarchist-led workers, though without a strong political organization, were combative and strike-prone (C. Oliveira 1974; E. Rodrigues 1981; Schmitter 1975a: 13–14). When the Labor Statute was promulgated in 1933, the anarchist General Confederation of Workers was banned. Rejecting the new regime-sponsored union organizations, anarchists united with Communists to mount a widespread general strike which led to an uprising among the glassworkers of Marinha Grande in 1934. The strike was put down, and was the last civilian attempt to bring the regime down by force. It was also the anarchists' dying gasp, while the Communist Party survived underground to become the major opposition force after World War II.

The unions sponsored by the regime provided workers no significant participation or representation of their interests. Strikes were illegal, and whenever they occurred they were routinely repressed by the police forces. Unions were structured to fragment the working class: they were organized horizontally, by occupation rather than industrial sector, so that in each firm workers in different occupations belonged to different unions. They were also kept small and decentralized: in principle there was to be a separate union for each occupation in each of Portugal's twenty-two districts (though this rule was relaxed for smaller unions, so that multidistrict and even national unions were created). In 1972 there were 325 unions with 1.4 million members and dues-payers (workers were not required to join unions, but many were required to pay dues; Pinto and Moura 1972: 150, 170). In principle these unions were agents of collective bargaining, but they had no bargaining power. Except for some minimal welfare benefits which they provided, they were of virtually no significance to their members. The state had the right to veto the election of unacceptable candidates to union office, making the unions its compliant tools (Lucena 1976, 1: 228–46; Schmitter 1975a: 16–18).

Agriculture was even more backward than industry. In a country where, as recently as 1950, 48 percent of the labor force still worked in the primary sector, the country's landholding patterns were divided between inefficient latifundios and minifundios farmed by peasants who barely eked out their subsistence. In 1968, some 300,000 farms, or 39 percent, occupied less than one hectare of land each, and an additional 39 percent occupied between one and four hectares. As small as they were, they typically consisted of dispersed parcels, and 45 percent of farms were wholly or partially rented. At the same time, the 0.6 percent of farms larger than 100 hectares occupied 45 percent of the agricultural land (Freitas et al. 1976: 78–79).

Geographically, Portugal is divided by the Tagus River. To the north, small farms predominated. Latifundios were concentrated in the arid Alentejo ("beyond the Tagus"), the grain-growing southern province. Neither region was entirely homogeneous—there were some large properties in the north, and many small farmers in the Alentejo, often renters of parcels on the large estates; medium-sized commercial agriculture was common in the middle of the country. But the contrast between north and south was striking. In the north, where the principal crops were corn and grapes, the fertile soil permitted intensive cultivation by individual peasants on small plots. In the south, the large farms were worked by landless day laborers, most of whom found work only during the growing season. Large extensions of land were left uncultivated, held by their owners merely as safe investments or hunting preserves.

The fascist regime deliberately maintained this primitive and inefficient agricultural system because large landholders were among its principal supporters. Landholders actively opposed even minor efforts at agrarian reform. Food production stagnated, making Portugal increasingly dependent on imports for its food—by 1973, while agricultural products (especially wine and cork) still were important exports, fish, meat, and grains constituted 13 percent of its imports (B.H. Fernandes 1975: 15–18, 113–44; Freitas et al. 1976: 46–47; Martins 1968: 330; Moura 1974: Murteira 1979: 333–34).

Farmworkers were denied even the hollow protection of the trade unions. Instead, rural areas were organized into *casas do povo* (houses of the people), a combination of mutual benefit societies and community centers. Similar fishermen's houses (*casas dos pescadores*) were organized in fishing villages. These organizations were authorized by the state and dominated by local elites, large landowners and harbormasters. Moreover, though they were supposed to provide welfare benefits for the entire rural population, they were far from universal: in 1967, *casas do povo* existed in only 30 percent of Portugal's parishes (and some 10 percent of those existed only on paper), and they had a membership of 400,000 out of a rural population of 5 million (Lucena 1976, 1: 247–60; Schmitter 1975a: 18–19; Wiarda 1977: 110–13, 247–48).

Agriculture was even more closely regulated than industry: state agencies established production quotas and kept prices artificially low, stifling any incentive to expand production. Moreover, the regulations created a labyrinthine bureaucracy and a tangle of red tape, leading not only to inefficiency but to corruption and favoritism.

Peasants and farmworkers thus suffered doubly: the regime not only failed to provide the welfare benefits it promised, but maintained an agricultural system in which they could hardly survive economically. Both the owner or renter of a minifundio in the north and the landless farmworker in the south found it increasingly difficult to earn a living. As land on the large properties was either left lying fallow or mechanized, the number of landless farmworkers fell by 47 percent to 444,000 between 1950 and 1970. The number of people working on their own farms declined by 21 percent to 446,000 during the same period (Freitas et al. 1976: 46–47).

While the decline of agriculture pushed peasants and farmworkers off the land, industrial development was slight, forcing many to emigrate to northern Europe or the western hemisphere. Emigration was deliberately sponsored by the regime, both for the emigrants' remittances which bolstered the balance of payments and because new capital investment would otherwise be required to absorb the manpower released from the land (Brettell 1979; Lemos 1978: 15).

If farmworkers and peasants both suffered hardships, they nevertheless reacted very differently. While peasants who farm for subsistence on plots that they themselves control are often politically conservative, wage-earning farmworkers have supported socialist politics in many countries (Linz 1976; Paige 1975; Stinchcombe 1961). In Portugal most northern peasants were politically passive, while farmworkers made the Alentejo the stronghold, first, of the anarchist movement and then, during much of the fascist regime, of the Communist Party. When the revolution came, the northern peasants turned against it while the Alentejan farmworkers not only were among its most fervent supporters but acted on their own to take over farmlands and pushed the government to legislate agrarian reform.

Political Demobilization

To the empty promise of corporatist class conciliation and the economic policies of autarchy and fiscal conservatism, Salazar added some of the trappings of fascist political organizations, among them the National Union and the Portuguese Legion. The National Union was the official political party, and until 1945 the only political organization permitted. But it was not an instrument of rule, nor was Portugal ever a party state. The Legion was a paramilitary organization, a disciplined armed group which recruited volunteers for the Spanish Civil War and occasionally provided the shock troops of repression; in the 1960s, it acted as a pressure group calling for escalation of the colonial war (Martins 1968: 324; Wiarda 1977: 117–21).

These organizations were not instruments of mobilization, for the corporate state relied not on active mobilization but on passive acquiescence to maintain its control. The regime did not even try to use the completely controlled periodic elections to mobilize demonstrations of support.

Instead, it held onto power by a combination of overt repression and enforced apathy. Ignorance contributed: the largely illiterate rural population paid little attention to national affairs. Another major force for apathy was the church, which firmly supported Salazar and which remains a major factor in both belief and social life in the peasant north of Portugal. Salazar's state and the church developed a relation of mutual support. The Portuguese hierarchy is still highly conservative—even in the 1980s, it has hardly felt the modernizing influences of the Second Vatican Council. Throughout the twentieth century, it preached vitriolically against communism: "Just as the Counterreformation took place in a Portugal without protestants, one is tempted to say that anticommunism began to make its effect felt [in the church] before—or almost before—there was an effectively organized Communist Party in the country" (Cerqueira 1973: 482–83; cf. Bruneau 1977). Portugal's holiest shrine was Fatima, where three shepherd children reported seeing a vision of the Virgin Mary in 1917 who told them of evil arising in the East. The message was interpreted as prophesying the Soviet revolution, and the shrine became a religious center of the worldwide struggle against communism. Parish priests spread tales of communist horrors to the villages.

In some areas the church still plays an active social role: priests teach religion, and often secular subjects, in the state schools; parish newspapers, circulated abroad, provide the most continuous link between many emigrants and their home villages. The interpenetration of state and church militated against any organized opposition, for to attack the church was also to attack the state (Brettell 1979: 290–92; Riegelhaupt 1973).

The church's stronghold is the north, where the political passivity typical of smallholding peasants reinforced the indoctrination of the church and the regime. The peasants' demobilization was accentuated by several other circumstances: the uneconomical size of holdings, emigration, and regime policy. Because many landholdings produced less than necessary even for the subsistence of a family, peasants were not vulnerable to market fluctuations which have elsewhere generated rural protest. Emigration, concentrated in the overpopulated north, withdrew people from the labor force, provided an important economic support to the society through remittances, decreased pressure on Portuguese cities, and generated a "heterotopian" consciousness leading migrants and potential migrants to reduce their identification with the home society and minimizing the impulse to challenge its institutions (Brettell 1979; Martins 1971: 85–86).

The most important cause of political quiescence in the rural north was the fascist regime's deliberate policy of demobilization. The political system reinforced peasants' characteristic individualism by permitting (and often in effect requiring) that they use personal connections for private gain while making the definition and achievement of collective goals nearly impossible. The state maintained a dense network of police and informers who not only stifled political opposition but attempted to regulate the most mundane affairs and punished the pettiest of infractions. In villages, licenses were required for such possessions as cigarette lighters, mule carts, and pet dogs; mutual suspicion was cultivated by the belief that government employees who informed on their neighbors received a percentage of the fine. Under the twin leadership of corporatism and the church, peasants were effectively deprived of any sense of opportunity for or potential benefit through political activity (Cutileiro 1971; Riegelhaupt 1979).

Peasants were not the only victims of cultivated apathy; most of the society was actively demobilized. The regime created a political culture of passivity and frustration in which the only permitted enthusiasms were *Fátima, fado e fútebol,* adding to religious devotion and energetically defended loyalties to soccer teams a passion for the melancholy songs of love and despair which are a traditional Portuguese genre.

But more important for the stability of the fascist regime than either the vacuum of political culture or the corporatist claim to meet the needs of the whole society was outright repression. Basic civil rights of freedom of speech and association, though nominally guaranteed by the constitution, were denied. People were reported for making remarks critical of the government, and civil servants accused of doing so could be fired. Prior censorship was exercised over the press, in a particularly harassing form: newspapers were required to submit typeset proofs of articles to the censors, assuring a high degree of self-censorship to avoid wasted expense. Among the items which censors found unsuitable for Portuguese readers were papal pronouncements and Salazar's own interviews with foreign journalists (Soares 1975: 51). Books were not subject to prior censorship, but they could be confiscated after publication. And authors could be harassed for expressing views which had elicited official disapproval. The most celebrated case was that of the "three Marias," three women who wrote *New Portuguese Letters* (Barreno et al. 1975). Their book was banned in 1972 as pornographic, and its authors were jailed. Their lengthy trial ended only after the military coup in 1974. The movement to support them was a manifestation of a highly embryonic feminism in a country where, until a short time before, women who were not high school graduates or heads of families were denied the right to vote.

The principal arm of repression was the secret police, originally called the Vigilance and State Defense Police (PVDE), later the International and State Defense Police (PIDE). In its early years, the PIDE had close contacts with the Gestapo; later, its agents received training in psychological and electrical torture methods from the CIA. It maintained files on a million Portuguese citizens—over 10 percent of the population. Its dense network of agents and informers provided information on activities betraying any hint of opposition. Private companies subsidized the PIDE to pay informers among their workers to ferret out worker discontent which might lead to militancy.

The PIDE was armed with powers of preventive detention (for 180 days, and renewable) without accusation; special courts for political crimes; and summary deportation without trial. The PIDE sent prisoners to the seacoast fortress of Peniche and the notorious Tarrafal concentration camp, the "Camp of Slow Death," in the Cape Verde Islands. There they were routinely tortured: sleep deprivation and the "statue," in which the prisoner was forced to remain standing for days on end, were the most common practices. In later years the PIDE phased out these forms of torture in favor of electric shock and psychological tortures.[1]

The Clandestine Communist Party

While the government hoped to forestall active opposition by controlling the petty details of daily life, its harshest attacks were directed against overt dissent, whether in the form of worker militancy or agitation for political reform. And the clandestine Communist Party (PCP) was the main target.

The Communist Party was the only one of the parties and factions of the Republic to survive the New State's banning of opposition. The fascist regime had been imposed in part by invoking the specter of communism, but the PCP had never been very strong. Founded in 1921, it had its roots in the anarchist movement (unlike most of the communist parties of western Europe, which grew out of socialist parties). When it was banned in 1927, it went underground. The clandestine party suffered schisms and police infiltration, sank to only a handful of members, and was ordered dissolved by the Communist International. But during World War II it began to grow again.

After shedding its early traditions of anarchism, the clandestine party never attempted to bring the regime down by force. Following a popular-front strategy, it attempted to organize all opponents of fascism into political and cultural organizations, most importantly the democratic opposition which contested the periodic sham elections.

The party itself was strongest among workers, both the industrial workers in the Lisbon area and the farmworkers on the latifundios of the Alentejo. Before the advent of the Communist Party, the Alentejo had been a center of the anarchist movement. As wage-earners, farmworkers were predisposed to adopt radical politics, and their leftism was reinforced by their cultural traditions: religious practice had been extremely weak in the Alentejo at least since the early twentieth century (Martins 1971: 81–82).

Both in rural and urban areas in the south, the party led many wildcat strikes and won considerable support among workers. Industrial workers and farmworkers went on wildcat strikes to demand improved wages and conditions. In the early 1960s, farmworkers won the eight-hour day (though not the five-day week) in an important series of strikes in the Alentejo. Legal prohibition, fascist-dominated unions, and penetration by PIDE informers made such activities dangerous and difficult, and their victories were few. Yet a genuine culture of opposition developed in some areas, not only in the Alentejo but in Lisbon's industrial suburbs. Industrial workers who migrated to the Lisbon area from the nearby Alentejo brought their political tradition with them. The high degree of industrial concentration also favored political activity: plants were large, and most of them were in a relatively small area stretching from Lisbon to Setubal, a coastal city thirty miles south which grew with the industrial boom of the 1960s.

The north was less fertile territory, even among industrial workers. Most of these workers came from more conservative home communities. The level of industrial concentration was lower too: factories were smaller, and they were dispersed all along the coast. Many workers lived in villages and maintained small plots of land, and with them the political outlook of their peasant forebears. All these factors made them less receptive to political organization.

At its fifth congress in 1957, in response to the Soviet Communist Party's twentieth congress, the PCP made its gradualism official by adopting a "strategy of transition" which called for antifascist unity to bring down the regime peacefully. The party nominally reversed itself in 1961 (when Alvaro Cunhal became secretary general), criticizing this position as a "rightwing deviation," because it implied that the fascist regime could be transformed from within. Soon the party declared that the regime would be brought down only by a "national uprising" which would require the participation or at least the neutralization of a major segment of the armed forces. But its political strategy remained cautious, and it never attempted to stimulate any uprising. At its sixth congress, held in the Soviet Union in 1965, it declared that Portugal was ripe for a "democratic and national revolution"—short of a socialist revolution, but combatting monopolies and liquidating latifundios and colonialism—which would require collaboration with other democratic and patriotic forces.[2]

The party remained small, never more than a few thousand. It was only the complete lack of other organized forces that allowed it to dominate the opposition. Following Leninist principles, moreover, it preferred to restrict membership and work through other organizations or sympathizers. In response to conditions of repression similar to those for which the Leninist model was designed, the PCP maintained small cells, tight discipline, anonymity among members, and top-down decisionmaking. Many members were full-time functionaries living clandestinely—or in exile. Hundreds of militants were imprisoned and tortured, and many died in the regime's prisons (the Central Committee members who came above ground in 1974 had spent an average of 11.8 years in prison; Schmitter 1975b: 376).[3] This clandestine heritage would seriously affect the outlook of the militants who formulated party strategy during the period of the revolution. Many of them continued to think of political activity as something planned in secret and carried out obediently according to orders from above.

The Revival of Opposition

When World War II ended, the regime's opponents hoped that Allied pressure would force a restoration of democracy; though Portugal had remained formally neutral, Salazar's sympathies for the Axis had been no secret. But Salazar was able to maintain the support of the west with a few cosmetic measures: in 1945 he announced that opposition candidates would be permitted to run in elections; censorship would be lifted for a month, and the opposition would be allowed to campaign freely.

All the forces of opposition—essentially, the Communists and a disorganized and incohesive group of bourgeois liberals—joined in the Democratic Unity Movement to run a common slate in 1945. This election, like the later ones until 1974, was a sham, despite some easing of restrictions on political activity. Campaign workers were repeatedly harassed, and their activities disrupted; despite the nominal lifting of censorship, some candidates' statements were still denied publication. Civil servants lost their jobs for signing nominating petitions for opposition candidates and were punished for attending their rallies. Days before the election, the opposition withdrew and denounced the violation of the promise to provide freedom to campaign. The opposition similarly withdrew its slate from almost all the subsequent elections—the main exception was in 1958; but even when they did not withdraw, the regime always counted the votes.

Opposition forces participated in these elections, often deceived by the slight loosening of restrictions into believing that for once the election would be free and that they would gain some genuine representation or at least have a chance to expose the regime as fraudulent. These campaigns temporarily united the otherwise hopelessly divided opposition—divided not only between Communists and non-Communists but among the many shades of the latter, though none of them had any organizational base. The platform on which they could all agree was a simple one of restoration of democracy; with the "Program for the Democratization of the Republic" (Ferreira and Mota 1969: 169–246), published for the 1961 campaign, they added demands for economic development to meet the needs of the country's poor. But they kept silent on the colonial question long after the wars broke out, both because the regime prohibited discussion of the issue and because the opposition hardly agreed on a colonial policy; some believed that the colonies should be freed, while others hoped they would be granted limited autonomy but remain tied to Portugal.

Since the PCP was the only organized political force, its militants and sympathizers provided the bulk of campaign workers, though the public leaders were generally noncommunists respected for their republican past (in the early years) or for their courage in denouncing the regime and defending victims of repression. Despite the limitations, the brief moments of liberty which the campaign periods offered reminded antifascists that they were not alone and allowed them to show their colors in public.

But the regime maintained redundant controls to assure the outcome. The electorate was highly restricted, and the regime made no effort to expand it or to use elections as occasions for mobilizing support: until 1969, only those who met educational or minimum tax requirements were allowed to vote, with higher requirements for women than for men. Even those registered could be arbitrarily turned away at the polling place for ideological reasons. With these restrictions, and since many of those eligible did not bother to register, only about a quarter of the adult population was on the voter rolls. In one district 50 percent of those on the 1969 electoral roll were state employees, and fewer than 6 percent were manual workers. Even of the small number registered, turnout was very low: only civil servants suffered any penalty for failing to vote, and interest in these controlled elections was slight (Comissão do Livro Negro 1969: 8–9; Schmitter 1977: 94–95).

On top of that, local meetings of the official party kept careful track of the opposition's strength in each area, and the Legion recruited and transported repeaters to vote in several districts. And, in the end, because the regime counted the votes, the counts were widely regarded as fraudulent.

Election campaigns were not the only opposition activity. Groups could hold public meetings as long as they avoided forbidden topics: they could commemorate Human Rights Day, for example, provided that they said nothing about Portugal. Some young people founded bookselling cooperatives, though as cooperatives they were automatically suspect and unacceptable books could be confiscated. Volunteer firefighters' brigades and their firehouses throughout the country were traditional gathering places for the opposition. In a society which forbade any kind of collective action for political pressure, however, all such activities became political: even parents' associations at schools were under watch—often with reason, since people dissatisfied with the regime and hungry for political participation did turn such organizations into opposition nuclei.

The most significant clandestine organizing occurred in workplaces, usually led by the PCP. But, like most election campaigns, it had little impact on employers or the regime.

One campaign aroused more interest and appeared to offer a genuine threat to the regime: the 1958 presidential campaign. The election was largely symbolic because the president was a figurehead. But in 1949 and 1951, opposition candidates took advantage of the limited freedom which the campaign offered and then withdrew at the last minute.

In 1958 the campaign erupted into a totally unexpected explosion of popular enthusiasm and a genuine threat to the survival of fascism. The opposition candidate, General Humberto Delgado, had long been an ardent supporter of Salazar, proud of his participation in the 1926 coup against the Republic. But he became disaffected, began to criticize the regime, and decided to run for president. Campaigning around the country, he attracted huge crowds with his charismatic presence. At first he was supported by moderate oppositionists; the left was suspicious of him for his fascist past. But when the PCP recognized the depth of his appeal it withdrew its own candidate and supported Delgado.

Contrary to custom, Delgado did not withdraw from the election but continued campaigning actively to the end. At a rally in the northern city of Oporto, 200,000 people turned out, about half the city's population. Attempting to prevent a similar demonstration in Lisbon two days later, the police wound up provoking a riot. The response to Delgado was the greatest challenge the regime had experienced. But it declared that the official candidate had won with 76 percent, and, immediately after the election, revised the constitution to eliminate direct election of the president (Raby 1983).

Most of the time the opposition posed little problem for the regime. It expended most of its strength on hopeless election campaigns which did not even bring symbolic concessions, while the forces operating underground had equally little impact. Except perhaps during election campaigns, the opposition never reached most of the population. The majority remained as apathetic as the regime hoped it would be. Nothing which happened suggested that an explosion of popular militancy would shake Portugal once the regime was unseated. If it had been possible to maintain Portugal's splendid isolation without challenge to its colonial empire; the regime might have lasted much longer. But some of these conditions began to change in the 1960s when liberation movements in Africa took up the struggle against colonialism and, partly in response, the regime sought development to strengthen itself economically.

Was It a Fascist Regime?

Is it merely polemical to characterize the regime which governed Portugal for forty-eight years as fascist? Those who reject the term *fascism* prefer the alternatives *corporatism, authoritarianism,* or *administrative state.* They argue that unlike the Italian and German regimes properly called fascist, the

Portuguese regime was not based on mass mobilization. It had been installed by military coup, and it never seriously attempted to mobilize supporters; even the paramilitary and youth organizations which most resembled the movements of other fascist systems did not mobilize a mass membership.

Those who believe the Portuguese regime can best be characterized as corporatist (Salazar himself and, among others, Schmitter [1975a] and Wiarda [1977, 1979]) argue that the Iberian regimes of Franco and Salazar (and some Latin American regimes stemming from the same tradition) are a political form *sui generis,* based on vertically organized, compulsory-membership groups. Wiarda argues that corporatist structures derive from long-standing Iberian traditions with roots going back to Roman law and the common Iberic-Latin value system which views society as an integrated whole and stresses organicism and authority. Portuguese corporatism in particular, he argues, drew from those traditions a genuine desire to achieve social justice, and actually did ameliorate conflict, as its corporatist-Christian roots demanded.

Linz (1964; 1975) calls these regimes authoritarian, allowing limited pluralism and governed by elites not responsible to any publics; he does not regard corporatist structures as particularly significant within them, but differentiates them from fascism and other forms of totalitarianism because they have no explicit ideology and do not depend on mass mobilization. Graham (1975) regards Salazar's regime as a bureaucratic-authoritarian regime, or administrative state, for he believes that the corporatist organizations had little real significance and that the bureaucracy ruled.

These characterizations, whatever their polemical purpose in rejecting the label ''fascist,'' obscure the fundamental characteristics of the regime: the alliance of landowners and capitalists against the working class, the mythology of Portugal's imperial past and its racial superiority, and the political system of dictatorship and repression. The organizations which, in Wiarda's view, made the regime corporatist were modeled after those of Mussolini's Italy, and as to his claim that they were ''organically'' rooted in the traditional organization of Iberian society and represented a genuine effort to achieve social justice, he himself acknowledges that the practice diverged increasingly from the theory (1977: 89).

Lucena aptly characterizes Salazarism as ''a form of fascism without a fascist movement'' (1979: 57). Mass fascist movements have arisen to combat strong organizations of the working class; in Portugal, as Cabral points out (1978), no such movement arose because the working class was so weak that none was necessary. Portuguese scholars of varying political views call the regime fascist (e.g., Martins 1969; A.O. Marques 1972: 177–

94; and the contributors to Pinto 1982), and the term provides the title of a series of official publications known as the "Black Book of Fascism" (e.g., Comissão do Livro Negro 1979). Moreover, the term was current among activists in the popular power movement with which this book is primarily concerned. I follow their example because I believe that the political consequences of Salazar's regime were similar to those of regimes to which the label is indisputably applied, whatever the difference of form: it was structured to guarantee by its repressive nature the interests of the capitalist class (at first, a decadent and nonproductive class; at the regime's end, a class which, facing the contradictions of accumulation, relied on repression to sustain its efforts at development). Whatever term one chooses to call it by, in any case, its character is clear: it evolved from fiscal conservatism and paternalist promotion of apathy and quiescence to a full-fledged repressive dictatorship exploiting both its own citizens and the dominated peoples of its colonies.

3

Colonial War
and the Armed Forces Movement

The challenge that finally toppled Portugal's fascist regime arose in its colonies. Salazar's obstinate determination to hold on to Portugal's colonial possessions forced the people in those countries to fight long and costly wars of liberation. In 1961, war broke out in Angola, and a series of events both there and in Portugal shook the Portuguese regime, sounding a warning of the problems of colonial war and military insubordination which would deepen throughout the next thirteen years and evoking the intransigence which Salazar would maintain as long as he stayed in office.

War in the Colonies

Portugal had formally been a colonial power for more than five centuries, ever since Prince Henry the Navigator sent ships down the African coast to find a sea route to India. But in the sixteenth century Portugal lost all of its Asian empire except Macao, East Timor, and the tiny enclaves of Goa, Damião, and Diu in India, and Brazil declared its independence in the aftermath of the Napoleonic Wars. In Africa Portugal retained Angola, Mozambique, Portuguese Guinea, the Cape Verde Islands, and the small islands of São Tomé and Príncipe off the coast.

Angola and Mozambique represented major sources of revenue. Mozambique's varied agricultural products, Angola's coffee, diamonds, and mineral resources, both colonies' cotton, as well as laborers in the South African mines and shipping to central Africa all brought foreign exchange. The colonies provided a protected market for Portuguese manufactured goods and an outlet for some of Portugal's surplus population.

Official Portuguese myth identified national greatness with the colonial empire—accurately so, since Portugal's greatness had been limited to the time when its American and Asian empire had flourished. But the ideological invocation of the colonial tradition was stepped up under fascism. Salazar always claimed to regard the colonies—twenty-two times as large as continental Portugal—as an integral part of Portuguese territory, on an equal footing with the "metropolis"—Portugal itself. So that school-children might appreciate their imperial heritage, a map hung in classrooms bearing the legend "Portugal is not a small country" and showing the outlines of the colonies superimposed over the whole of Europe.[1]

Portugal took pride in its "civilizing mission" in Africa and denied that it treated blacks as an inferior race. But the myth of civilization was belied not only by the exploitation of the colonies' wealth but by forced labor, illiteracy, and repression even more severe than that prevailing in Portugal itself. Only 1 percent of the colonies' blacks were literate. The church, which ran most schools, allowed the Portuguese government to veto nominations of bishops for the colonies (Hastings 1974: 19). All schooling was in Portuguese, so indigenous languages were slowly lost.

Blacks who became educated and adopted the Portuguese language and culture were assimilated, it was said, on equal terms with whites. Assimilation was a legally recognized status, but it was granted arbitrarily (A.O. Marques 1972: 228–29). Moreover, the same statute which provided for assimilation (and thus "proved" that racism was not a factor in Portuguese treatment of blacks) explicitly distinguished between the vast majority of blacks, who were regarded as *indígenas* (natives), and whites, whether in Portugal or the colonies, who were subject to no literacy tests for full citizenship.

Forced labor was a reality for most Africans. Laborers were drafted not only for public works but also for white-owned plantations. Mozambicans were virtually conscripted to work in South African mines: between sixty-five and one hundred thousand went annually to South Africa, where they constituted one-third of the mineworkers. In return, South Africa guaranteed that 47.5 percent of the seaborne trade to Johannesburg would be routed through the Mozambican port of Lourenço Marques. In addition, Portugal received not only a bounty for each worker, but also the foreign exchange of the workers' wages.

Even nominally independent peasants were subject to coercive labor practices: in the northern regions of both Mozambique and Angola, they were forced to take land out of food production to grow cotton and to sell it to the Portuguese trading monopoly at controlled prices. In Mozambique especially, cotton was grown by women while most men left to work in South Africa and what was then Rhodesia.

Repression was guaranteed by a passbook system, segregation, and a colonial administration which extended to every village. PIDE vigilance came to the colonies to counter the emerging movements for liberation in the 1950s. Any protest was ferociously repressed, as when 50 dockworkers were killed in a 1959 Bissau dock strike, and again when 600 cotton growers, who had assembled peacefully to demand fewer restrictions and higher pay from a Portuguese administrator, were massacred in Mueda, in northern Mozambique, in 1960. These protests remained local, however, and received almost no attention from the outside world.

But as other African countries won their freedom, liberation movements organized in the Portuguese colonies too.[2] The Popular Movement for the Liberation of Angola (MPLA) was founded in 1956 by *mestiços* and "assimilated" blacks, many of whom had studied in Europe. It was centered in the capital, Luanda, and attracted primarily the Mbundu, a central Angolan ethnic group. The Union of the Peoples of Angola (UPA) was founded in 1958 among the Bakongo of northern Angola. In 1962 it gave rise to the National Liberation Front of Angola (FNLA). Ethnic and political differences between these two and other, less important movements were to haunt the drive for Angolan independence throughout the war and into the post-independence civil war of 1975–76.

In Guinea, the African Party for the Independence of Guinea and Cape Verde (PAIGC) was founded in 1956 under the leadership of Amilcar Cabral. In the small colony of Guinea, the PAIGC from the beginning set about organizing rural areas, providing schools and health care, and building an infrastructure for the support of guerrilla war. In 1961, after the outbreak of war in Angola, the PAIGC joined with the MPLA to found the Conference of Nationalist Organizations of the Portuguese Colonies (CONCP). In Mozambique, several liberation movements arose independently. CONCP and statesmen of several African countries encouraged them to merge into the Mozambique Liberation Front (Frelimo) in 1962. Frelimo, led by Eduardo Mondlane, was strongest in the north of Mozambique.

War broke out in Angola at the beginning of 1961, with three independent incidents. The first was an apparently spontaneous outburst by cotton growers in Kasanje in northern Angola in January. Facing declining cotton prices, they protested the system of forced cotton cultivation by refusing to plant. They attacked barges, stores, and Catholic missions, frightening

European settlers. No whites were injured; the insurgents only attacked property and slaughtered cattle. In fierce reprisal, the Portuguese army bombed and strafed villages, and hundreds, perhaps thousands, of Africans were killed.

The second incident grew out of the bizarre hijacking of the *Santa Maria*, a Portuguese luxury cruise ship sailing in the Caribbean. Captain Henrique Galvão, formerly of the Portuguese navy, led a small force of twenty-four men who took over the ship on January 22 and attempted to sail it to Luanda. They hoped to dramatize Portugal's colonial policies and move the new Kennedy administration in the United States to pressure Portugal to change them. While an officer, Galvão had turned against the regime; in 1947, as a colonial administrator, he had condemned forced labor in Angola. Subsequently imprisoned for his opposition activities, he had escaped from jail in Portugal.

As if to underline the quixotic nature of their effort, Galvão and his crew dubbed it "Operation Dulcinea." The U.S. navy intercepted the ship to prevent it from landing in Angola; Galvão ultimately accepted asylum in Brazil. Meanwhile, however, a corps of foreign journalists had gathered in Luanda to meet him. Taking advantage of their presence, a small MPLA force attacked a Luanda prison on February 4 to free African nationalist prisoners and killed several policemen. The policemen's funeral the next day was the beginning of five days of rioting by white policemen and vigilantes who rampaged through the African quarters, killing indiscriminately. The Kasanje killings and previous anticolonial outbursts had gone unnoticed; but the journalists who had come to meet Galvão reported the Luanda attacks in the foreign press.

The third outburst, among the conscript coffee plantation workers of northern Angola, occurred in March, after a coffee plantation manager killed several laborers who demanded back pay. It grew into a major insurrection when UPA fighters based across the border in the (former Belgian) Congo joined it. Again, the reprisals were far fiercer than the provocation. Portuguese troops killed at least 20,000 Angolans. Whole villages were destroyed, even in areas where there had been no uprising. But the involvement of an organized liberation movement meant that the war had begun in earnest. By the end of the year, UPA had liberated and controlled a large area of northern Angola.

Portugal's colonial policies were condemned by the United Nations from 1961 on. Even the United States voted against Portugal at first, though it later reversed itself and supported Portugal for the sake of the Azores airbase. But the Portuguese government, despite some nominal reforms, rejected all outside pressure. The realities of the postwar world were lost on Salazar, who remained convinced that the colonies were part of Portugal and that Africans would come to rejoice in the Portuguese heritage they shared with him. Salazar made clear that despite cosmetic changes in the treatment of the people of the colonies, he would ignore any pressures to free them. If the rest of the world did not acknowledge Portugal's civilizing mission, Portugal would stand "proudly alone" against any demand to liberate the colonies.

But some military officers recognized the worldwide pressures for decolonization, acknowledged the injustice of Portugal's treatment of the African population, and knew that the armed forces were unprepared for war. Among them was the defense minister, General Julio Botelho Moniz. He repeatedly expressed his reservations to Salazar. Following the Kasanje uprising in January, he called for improved working conditions for Africans. After the March uprising, he wrote Salazar of his fear that revolt would spread to all the colonies and to Portugal itself, forcing the armed forces into a "suicide mission." Failing at persuasion, he attempted to overthrow Salazar in a palace coup in April. The plot was discovered, and the minister and several other officers (including Colonel Francisco Costa Gomes, who became president after the revolution) were demoted. Salazar assumed the post of defense minister himself (A. Rodrigues et al. 1974: 183–202).

The Armed Forces and the Regime

Coups and conspiracies were endemic in the armed forces even as the military kept the fascist regime in power. For the officers themselves, this involved no contradiction, because support of the regime and occasional efforts to overthrow it both grew out of their view of their mission as apolitical.

Their support for the regime was paramount most of the time. Along with the church and the industrial and landed oligarchy, the armed forces were among its principal bulwarks. The army had brought the regime to power in the first place. Officers commanded and staffed the paramilitary repressive forces (police, National Republican Guard, and PIDE) and the censorship bureaucracy; they also provided many cabinet officers and the bulk of the colonial administration (Wheeler 1979: 201). The officer corps was traditionally restricted to the sons of the oligarchy, and bound by ties of family interest and tradition to the oligarchical values that lay at the basis of the "new state."

The military espoused a rhetoric that placed it "above politics." Fascist propaganda emphasized the military virtues of discipline, unity, and sacrifice for the nation. As Lourenço remarks, the officer corps enjoyed a symbolic deference that gave it a role comparable to that of a royal family. It regarded itself as a "savior army." Repeatedly in the political crises of the nineteenth and twentieth centuries, only the army (later the armed forces as a whole) was able to muster the authority and the force to restore order. Claiming to be above conflict and to represent the entire nation, the armed forces assumed a preponderant role in every major political transition in the twentieth century: in 1910 and 1926, the founding and toppling of the First Republic; in 1974 and 1975, the beginning and end of the revolution. Military figures commanded almost automatic legitimacy in calmer times as well. All Portuguese presidents under fascism were high-ranking officers. The opposition shared this deference; its only important presidential candidates (Norton de Matos in 1949 and Delgado in 1958) were generals.[3]

Ironically, this tradition of deference and legitimacy gave the officer corps the independence necessary to allow it to organize against the regime. The officers' presumed loyalty would be insulted if they were subject to the same political repression that was exercised against civilians. After the 1926 coup, not all republican officers were dismissed; even among those who welcomed the coup, many hoped that democratic institutions would soon be restored. While the upper echelon of the officer corps was dominated by hardline sympathizers of fascism, a liberal could nevertheless find a safe place in the lower ranks and benefit from some political protection.[4]

Officers mounted many troop mutinies, conspiracies, and coups against the regime. Wheeler lists twenty-one coup attempts or plots between the successful ones in 1926 and 1974, including that of Botelho Moniz in 1961 (all but three were in 1962 or earlier). These plots varied enormously in scope: casualties ranged from "several deflated egos" to three hundred dead and one thousand wounded (Wheeler 1979: 210–15). But most of the coups were little more than barracks plots, poorly planned and adventuristically executed in the hope that most of the armed forces would spontaneously join the plotters.

Salazar's intransigence, already displayed when his defense minister urged better treatment of the colonized African population, flared again when India invaded Goa in December 1961. Ever since its own independence, India had tried to negotiate a peaceful Portuguese withdrawal from Goa. Salazar refused, and many saw in his refusal a further sign of his determination to oppose decolonization in Africa. Finally, India invaded. Though the Portuguese troops faced clearly superior forces, Salazar ordered them to "conquer or die." Governor General Vassalo e Silva exercised the better part of valor and surrendered. In punishment, he and his staff were court-martialed and expelled from the army. Their punishment was far harsher than that meted out a few months earlier to Defense Minister Bothelho Moniz and his fellow conspirators against the regime—most of them had merely been demoted and reassigned. Many felt that the Goa officers were made scapegoats for Salazar's refusal either to countenance the possibility of giving Goa up or to prepare realistically for an invasion.

The treatment of the officers of the Goa garrison and the fear that a long war against colonial liberation movements would provide more occasions for scapegoating stimulated still another coup attempt at the end of the year. Delgado, now in exile, returned clandestinely to Portugal in December. On New Year's Eve a force of his supporters, composed of military officers and radical Catholic civilians, invaded the Beja barracks. The rebels naively hoped that they would spark an uprising which would peacefully topple the regime. But they wanted no bloodshed, so they surrendered when reinforcements were brought in.

All the coup attempts had an apparent political coloration—sometimes of the right, especially in the early years; after World War II, almost always of the left. But all were politically ambiguous. The immediate cause was always a perceived threat to military prerogative (Wheeler 1979). Since officers conspired not for specific political ends but to restore the "honor of the army" and that of the nation (the two were thought of as largely the same), they saw no inconsistency between being above politics and conspiring to overthrow the government. Moreover, they did not see a coup as a political choice but as a necessity imposed on them by the failings of civilian politicians. So they felt no need to formulate or present a clear political definition which would identify them with any particular civilian class or political faction.

What turned professional concerns into challenges to the state itself was the rigidity of the regime. Since it was hardly possible to exert influence for incremental change, civilian and military dissidents alike readily concluded that they could achieve their objectives only by overturning the regime; only the military, however, had the means to try.

The Imperative of Economic Growth

The events of 1961 taught several lessons. The coup attempts showed that the armed forces had some leeway to act against the regime, but not sufficient power to succeed. Guerrilla uprisings in Angola foreshadowed the eventual success of the liberation movements. Those uprisings also aroused Salazar's intransigence, as did the invasion of Goa: he refused to make any concession which might give the African freedom fighters grounds for optimism that they would wear down Portuguese resistance to their freedom.

Salazar had aimed to preserve the corporate state and the colonial empire in splendid isolation. But fighting the war required reversing his long-standing policy of autarchy, in order to seek foreign investment and stimulate economic growth. In the 1960s Portugal opened its doors to foreign capital. It sought the promise of European integration, revenue to finance the increasingly costly colonial war, and political support from those countries seeking to protect their Portuguese investments. Foreign investment grew spectacularly: only 2 million contos during the entire period 1943–60, it reached 20 million between 1961 and 1967. In 1959, foreign capital represented 1 percent of total private investment; in 1966, 25 percent; and in 1969, 40 percent (Baklanoff 1978: 136–38; Bandeira 1976: 29; Keefe 1977: 316; Matos 1973: 100–01; A.R. Santos 1977c: 73).

Characteristic features of the corporate state made Portugal a highly favorable location for new foreign investment in the 1960s. Wages were low and labor militancy was repressed. The inefficient and corrupt customs bureaucracy overlooked questionable accounting practices. Portugal was located close to the more prosperous markets of Western Europe, and its products had privileged access both to the EFTA countries (Portugal had joined in 1959) and the colonies.

But in an autarchic and medieval economy, it was not market forces but state-sponsored development that produced the burgeoning of capitalism. Whereas foreign investors had previously been hamstrung with restrictions, after 1961 they had favorable access to domestic credit, royalty rates, and repatriation of profits. Success in attracting foreign capital also depended on the regime's tight control over society, for multinational firms sought a political environment which prevented labor unrest and kept wages low.

The growth of foreign investment, however, set in motion a complex chain of events which ultimately contributed to the downfall of the regime.

Foreign investment required rationalization of industrial structures to increase efficiency and competitiveness. Both rationalization of production and political ties with the Europe of the Common Market turned out to require domestic political change and to decrease the dependence on the colonies. Both factors created pressure to end the colonial war, even on terms which might be at least relatively favorable to the liberation movements. Paradoxically, then, the economic changes undertaken to strengthen Portugal's ability to fight a colonial war contributed to the country's eventual defeat.

Growth transformed Portugal's economy after 1960 as a vigorous if dependent capitalism developed. Multinational firms established small branch plants in Portugal, many of which employed women as unskilled and low-paid workers, especially in textiles and electronics assembly. Most of the new plants did not produce for the national market, but were integrated into international assembly-and-marketing networks; components would be shipped to Portugal for cheap assembly and the completed products shipped on. Even some firms which did hope to sell to the national market assembled imported components and thus increased Portugal's external dependence.

The economy boomed. Per capita income rose from less than $200 in 1950 to $900 by 1970, and primary sector employment fell to 32 percent. Whereas in 1950 minerals and agricultural products were more than 70 percent of exports, by 1970 manufactured goods constituted 60 percent of the much larger total. Trade with Europe was now greater than trade with the colonies. Real GNP more than doubled between 1963 and 1973, with all the growth located in industry (159%) and services (92%). Tourism and emigrants' remittances sparked a construction boom. Agriculture, however, continued to stagnate (Murteira 1979: 332–33).

Industrial growth drew migrants from the rural areas to the cities. Centuries of colonialism had meant that Portugal had always been dominated by Lisbon, the administrative and political center of an area much larger than the country itself. Beginning in the nineteenth century, the industrialization of the northern coastal area around Oporto led to urban growth there. But the 1960s accentuated what the Portuguese call "macrocephaly." While the population of the whole country remained stable between 1960 and 1970, the Lisbon and Oporto metropolitan regions grew by 17 percent to contain 40 percent of the national population, and the population declined almost everywhere else (Barata 1973: 25). This growth swelled the two cities, creating an acute housing shortage. The cities expanded to overtake many former hamlets, creating densely populated areas without urban infrastructural services such as transportation. Some of the former rural areas lacked even basic sanitary facilities.

Housing for the poor was especially deficient: the major cities contained large run-down neighborhoods several decades old, where families lived in exceedingly tiny houses and apartments, stacked up on hillsides, generally in very poor condition, and often lacking basic sanitary conditions. Neither the private nor the public sector provided sufficient cheap housing for the new migrants.

Shantytowns sprung up on the edges of the cities, where squatters took over empty land. They were not the result of mass invasion; instead, families infiltrated one by one. They built rickety shacks of wood, pasteboard, and sheet metal. These houses of course lacked electricity, running water, and sewers. If the land was privately owned, the shantytown dwellers lived a precarious existence. Under fascism landowners could call on the police forces to expel the squatters, but often they exacted a small rent instead. Since housing construction, like everything else, required a license, squatter settlements were technically illegal, but if owner and tenants reached an agreement the state generally ignored them.

Despite the boom, the growth was insufficient to absorb the whole population. Much of the economically active population was still in agriculture, which offered only declining opportunities. The absolute number of people working in agriculture fell by 400,000 between 1960 and 1970—and that figure is misleadingly low, because 60,000 more women were working in agriculture than had been ten years earlier. Many women stayed home to work the land while men migrated. A hemorrhage of emigration, the only option for most of the unemployable population, swept the country. According to official figures, more than a million people (over 10 percent of the population) emigrated between 1961 and 1972, two-thirds of them after 1965. In addition, an estimated 100,000 draft-eligible men emigrated illegally between 1961 and 1974.[5] Whole villages, especially in the north, were without adult men. Paris became the second largest Portuguese city in the world (Barata 1972: 29; 1973: 37; Brettell 1986; Freitas et al. 1976: 46).

Industrial growth falsified the fascist claim to represent and reconcile the interests of all conflicting classes just as clearly as the economic stagnation which had preceded it. Deterioration in the quality of urban life and the continuing necessity of emigration clearly demonstrated that the new resources generated by industrialization were not being applied to the needs of the population but to those of the capitalist entrepreneurs who sponsored and profited by it.[6] Growth increased their profits and financed colonial war.

Even though foreign investment grew, foreign capital did not come to control the Portuguese economy; much of it was administered by the monopoly groups, which sought it out. Because of the groups' huge size, their requirements for new capital were high. Their stranglehold on bank credit not only meant that they continued to expand at the expense of small and medium capital, but it also permitted them to build complex networks of interlocking companies on highly speculative bases. But the boom which they enjoyed was based largely on the assumption of continued growth. Moreover, inflation and the OPEC oil embargo Portugal suffered in punishment for allowing the United States to use the Azores airbase in the October 1973 war foreshadowed economic problems which would deepen in 1974. These problems, which arose from the monopoly groups' autonomy and the speculative expansion they promoted, would remain to haunt the revolutionary government.

More immediately, capitalist development changed the objective interests of the monopolists, traditional supporters of the regime. Emerging from this group was an echelon of technocratic employees who were culturally oriented to Europe and wanted to rationalize the firms' structure. Capital-intensive investments would require a more highly educated and qualified labor force, which might challenge the repressive regime. As industrial production expanded, moreover, demand for labor grew, giving workers some leverage to demand wage increases and better working conditions.

Closer integration with Europe also forced Portugal to take into account the Common Market countries' distaste for the repressive regime and the colonial war. Though the Common Market granted Portugal a commercial agreement in 1972, its members made clear that they would not admit Portugal as a full member as long as the dictatorship and the colonial war continued (Baklanoff 1976: 201–2; Moura 1974: 244). As Portugal became more dependent on its relations with Europe, moreover, the colonies became less important economically. Thus, industrialization, which was necessary to pay for the war to hold on to the colonies, ultimately made colonialism not only less tenable but also less lucrative.

Caetano's Limited Liberalization

Salazar initiated Portugal's entry into the twentieth century, but he did not witness the consequences. He was incapacitated by a stroke in 1968. His successor, Marcello Caetano, had a reputation as something of a liberal (he had resigned as rector of the University of Lisbon in 1962 to protest police brutality against student demonstrators). Caetano initiated what became known as the "political spring" of 1969, with some changes in economic policy and an increase in political freedom. But his liberalization proved superficial and short-lived; as Caetano himself joked, he "signaled left and turned right."

Caetano attempted to broaden the ruling coalition and allow representation to the new interests produced by economic growth. He included some technocrats (advocates of more rational economic development and European integration) in the official party, the cabinet, and the bureaucracy. In the party he sanctioned a "liberal wing" and included seven of its members on government slates for election to the national legislature in 1969 (several of them were founders of the Popular Democratic Party in 1974, including two future prime ministers, Francisco Sa Carneiro and Francisco Pinto Balsemão). A cabinet reshuffle in 1970 incorporated a small group of technocrats in economic posts. More interested in integration with Europe than in the colonies, they generally favored a negotiated settlement of the war. Liberals in the classical sense, they wanted to relax price controls and protective tariffs to encourage more trade with the rest of Europe (Baklanoff 1978: 112–45; Graham 1975: 29–33).

Caetano's reforms also softened the ban on political activity. People could talk openly in cafés and other public places without fear of serious reprisal. Press censorship was relaxed somewhat, and the democratic opposition was allowed to campaign more freely than usual in the 1969 legislative elections. The above-ground opposition, now calling itself the Democratic Electoral Commissions (CDE), was allowed to hold a congress and adopt a platform which openly called for democratization, civil liberties, and self-determination for the colonies (Ferreira and Mota 1969: 279–82).

Many of Salazar's exiles were allowed to come home, including Dom Antonio Ferreira Gomes, Bishop of Oporto, exiled ten years before for an open letter critical of Salazar, and Mario Soares, leader of the opposition group, Portuguese Socialist Action (precursor of the Socialist Party). In the 1969 election campaign the opposition was not united as it had been in previous elections. Most of it joined the CDE campaign, but Soares and his followers ran separate slates in some districts, charging that the CDE was Communist-dominated. Contrary to custom, the opposition slates did not withdraw but stayed in the campaign to the end; but government control again assured that only official candidates were elected (A.O. Marques 1972: 260–61; Soares 1975: 114–15, 239, 246–58).

Labor relations were also reformed slightly. A June 1969 decree allowed a measure of democracy in the election of trade union executive boards: only officially approved candidates would be allowed to run, but the state would no longer invoke the power to dismiss them once elected, and the elected officials would have the power to negotiate contracts with the respective sectoral employers' organization. Disputes between the union and employers' organization were to be resolved by an arbitration board: the union and the employers' organization were each to name one member, and those two would agree on a third, providing for some neutrality (Lucena 1976: 59–60; Wiarda 1979: 107).

Opposition slates won office in several large industrial and white-collar unions in the Lisbon area and elsewhere, notably among bank workers, store clerks, metalworkers, and textile workers. These unions adopted a somewhat more combative stance in negotiations. Acts of militancy of a sort previously unknown won concessions: in March 1971, for example, 5,000 store clerks held a public demonstration and won a forty-four-hour work week. In 1970 union officials elected on opposition slates formed a coordinating organization, the Intersindical. It represented between 30 and 40 of the country's 325 unions, and even applied for membership in the ILO.

As the trade unions were allowed more freedom to organize, activists in political organizations sought to control or take advantage of them. The Communist Party took the major role: it had led many illegal strikes in the past, and its militants now became the most important force in the Intersindical, dominating most of the slates which won union elections. To the party, the unions became a source of recruitment and a training ground for militants. Some other opposition forces, from the small Catholic left and militants who would later be active in the Socialist Party and the far left, won pockets of strength in textile and metalworkers' unions.

Caetano's ''spring'' proved superficial. Liberalization raised expectations and stimulated demands for further changes, but the regime was not flexible enough to absorb the challenges, and spring gave way to winter. Caetano remained determined to pursue the war and suffer the consequences. The technocrats in the cabinet were ousted in 1971 and 1972. The liberal members of the legislature, finding themselves powerless to do anything but give the government a rubber stamp of approval, resigned in protest in 1971, before their four-year term ended. As the cost of the war mounted, the colonies became a drain on the Portuguese economy, and the free-trade area which had united them with Portugal was abandoned (Graham 1975: 16–17, 40–54; Soares 1975: 278; Wiarda 1977: 258–61).

For the unions, the reversal came even more quickly. The reforms led to few major contract concessions, but new freedoms stimulated spontaneous worker militancy. In 1970 metalworkers went on strike, and the government responded in October with new decrees, restoring its power to suspend elected union officers and providing that the government, not the management- and union-appointed arbitrators, would name the third member of any arbitration board.

With these decrees, the government took away the small freedoms the unions had briefly enjoyed. Boards elected by the opposition were suspended in several unions, and the government occasionally intervened to call off an election in which it feared an opposition victory (Pires n.d.: 38–39). The Intersindical itself was forced underground. The regime was incapable of reforming itself from within; Salazar had just died, and yet his ghost was already returning to haunt his successor.

The suppression of union activism was carried further in 1972 with a decree imposing a two-year wage freeze. But industrialization and the war were bringing rapid inflation. Emigration and universal conscription created a labor shortage. The slight increase in freedom for the trade union movement had given workers a sense of their power, while the war's unpopularity heightened discontent. The hope for reform through the structure of trade unions and collective bargaining had proven vain. But it had raised expectations, and when inflation skyrocketed in 1973, workers in many factories demanded raises despite the freeze.

Employers resisted, and that fall workers responded with an unprecedented strike wave. Illegal strikes spread from factory to factory. In each, an ad hoc workers' commission was formed—often, workers laid down their tools or deserted their assembly lines, held an illegal meeting, voted for a strike on the spot, and elected a commission to represent them. An estimated 60,000 workers went on strike in the six months before April 1974, although most of the strikes were brief. Many strikes were put down by the police forces. Some union leaders, and even some union delegates in individual factories, were jailed, and many more were fired. Nevertheless, many employers conceded a part of the workers' wage demands (Maxwell 1976: 256; A. Rodrigues et al. 1974: 229–31; M.L. Santos et al. 1976, 1: 26–30; A.R. Santos 1977a: 26).

This wave of worker militancy, although much smaller than the one that would follow the coup, was astounding by Portuguese standards. Both in its successes and in its limitations, it already revealed some of the opportunities and problems labor was to face in the revolution: most importantly, it demonstrated the contradiction between institutionalized labor action and locally inspired militancy. During the brief spring, opposition union leaders had tried to reform the existing structure and win concessions through the collective bargaining system established by the state. The inevitable clampdown prevented any institutional gains, while the struggles had little effect on the workers' level of consciousness or organization, because only elected leaders were involved, rather than the working class as a whole.

With the return to repression between 1971 and 1974, the only outlet for worker activity was wildcat strikes, factory by factory. The strikes won some raises—and, as we will see, the strike committees became important channels for the militancy that was to follow the coup in 1974—but no major reforms. The wave of wildcat strikes did involve workers generally, not just their elected leaders. But since the strikes were against individual employers, workers neither attempted nor achieved any wider organization, and thus created no prospect that immediate gains might provide the basis for fundamental changes. It cannot be known, of course, what would have happened if the strike wave had continued: whether the workers' struggle would have reached a higher level or whether the regime would have made any permanent concessions. Instead, the regime fell.

A Divided Opposition

In the early 1960s small groups of militants split off from the Communist Party to create what became known as the far left. The issue that divided the party was not political strategy for Portugal but attitudes toward the Soviet Union. The PCP, in keeping with its Leninist orientation, regarded the Soviet Union as the homeland of socialism and maintained strict ideological fealty to the Soviet Communist Party (and continued to do so even when other Western European parties were striving for independence). Dissidents split off from the party because they sided with China in the Sino-Soviet split; then they questioned the adequacy of the PCP's "revisionist" line, especially in the face of the deepening colonial war. Small groups of militants laid the bases for what would become some of the organizations of the far left in Portugal after 1974. Some of them organized among the draft resisters and deserters in exile in European capitals—and some of those exiles reentered Portugal clandestinely, hoping to organize for an uprising. These small groups, claiming Marxism-Leninism as their ideology and the Chinese Communist Party as their model, all claimed to be (or to be in the process of founding) the "true" Communist Party.

Some leftists turned to armed struggle. Dissidents fed up with PCP inaction founded the Revolutionary Brigades (BR), with no explicit international commitments, specializing in lightning armed actions against military targets. BR activists founded the Proletarian Revolutionary Party (PRP) in 1973. Other groups also carried out armed actions and bank robberies, and the PCP itself, fearing the loss of restive militants, organized an armed wing, Armed Revolutionary Action, which carried out acts of sabotage between 1970 and 1974. The most spectacular act was blowing up a munitions supply ship in Lisbon in 1970 (*Expresso,* January 12, 1974; *O Jornal,* May 16, 1980).

Many who were opposed to the regime rejected both the PCP and the militant far left. This more moderate opposition developed ties to the Socialist International. Led by Mario Soares, they formed Portuguese Socialist Action in 1964 and held the founding congress of the Socialist Party (PS) in 1973, in exile in Germany. Though Soares had created a second opposition slate for the 1969 election to distinguish himself from the Communists, his supporters were part of the CDE in 1973. The PS, in any case, did not organize inside Portugal.

None of these organizations was very large or significant. Even the PCP, though still far larger than any of the others, was weaker in 1974 than it had been a decade before: estimates of membership range from less than a thousand to five thousand (Schmitter 1975b: 376). Its losses to the far-left groups were sufficiently disturbing that Secretary General Alvaro Cunhal published a book in 1971 attacking the defectors' "petty-bourgeois radicalism" (Cunhal 1974). The far-left organizations foreshadowed some tendencies which became important after the April 25 coup. The Marxist-Leninist sects sought revolutionary purity and opposed "revisionism," which in practice meant unmasking the PCP as a traitor to the working class. The PRP experimented with armed struggle. Some progressive Catholics, part of the current which in 1974 converged with some intellectuals to form the Left Socialist Movement (MES), won union office.

All of the far-left groups joined the opposition to the colonial war. Students demonstrated against the draft from 1962 on. The May 1968 events in France and widespread anti-Vietnam protest elsewhere in Europe stimulated heightened student militancy in Portugal, but there it was naturally directed against the war in Africa. Demonstrations organized by far-left groups, especially the Marxist-Leninists, and invariably fiercely repressed by the police, often mobilized large numbers of people who took no active part in any of the groups. In 1969 and 1970 demonstrators closed the universities (Antunes et al. 1975; R. Costa 1979: 199–258; A.O. Marques 1972: 261).

These organizations were all small and clandestine, and none anticipated either in theory or in practice what was to become a major theme of the far left during the revolution: popular power. Though demonstrations were sometimes large, no real organizational base was developed, and no party developed the ideas which might be a guide to organizing and stimulating such a base later. Instead, the far-left groups were astonished—as was everyone else—by the mass movement which arose spontaneously with liberation, and they were strongly influenced and pulled forward by it.

Despite the growth and the diversity of the opposition, despite economic growth which created political and economic contradictions for the regime, despite universal exhaustion with the war and growing active opposition to it, the state's control of civil society was too strong for political opposition to be effective. Recent political and economic changes, and new pressures for change which had found no outlet, remained to condition the post-coup regime, but they were not strong enough to destroy the old one. That would require a coordinated attack by a sufficiently large part of the military.

The Birth of the Armed Forces Movement

Why was the Armed Forces Movement able to bring the government down when others could not? Civilian opposition was clearly too weak to succeed. But many military coups, too, had been attempted in the past (though almost none between 1962 and 1973, presumably because war reinforced the officers' loyalty and kept them too busy to conspire), and all had failed.

What made the difference was the colonial war. Directly and indirectly, the war in Africa created the conditions which made fascism unviable. It stimulated economic and political changes during the 1960s; still more importantly, it turned the young Portuguese officers who fought in it against the regime. In part, they were successful because so many people—officers, soldiers, and civilians—had repudiated the war. But they also planned more carefully and their coup was a bigger operation than previous conspiracies. Disaffection had spread so widely that many junior officers were willing to take part. And although those who were actually involved were still only a small minority of the officer corps, few remained who cared to resist the coup when it came.

By 1974, the war in Africa had dragged on for thirteen years, and seemed to be going on forever. The Portuguese people were increasingly alienated. Nearly every young man was drafted and served in Africa, creating a generation of disillusionment. Combat deaths approached 4,800—proportionally, more than twice the toll of U.S. casualties in Vietnam. The growing resentment did not particularly swell the ranks of active opposition, except among students and those eligible for the draft. But even if most people took no action to express their discontent, they were nevertheless increasingly disaffected and exhausted.

In Angola, fighting was bogged down, restricted largely to the sparsely settled eastern regions of the country. The National Union for the Total Independence of Angola (UNITA), founded in 1966 by Jonas Savimbi, who had left the FNLA in 1964, was based among the Ovimbundu people of central Angola. UNITA and the MPLA directly engaged the Portuguese army most often, but the FNLA had the largest armed forces and controlled major sections of northern Angola. Internecine rivalries and even armed hostilities among the liberation movements continued to hamper the guerrilla effort.

Guerrilla organizations in Mozambique and Guinea had learned a major lesson from Angola: unity and adequate preparation were essential for armed struggle. Mozambique's Frelimo had begun fighting in 1964. Based in Tanzania, it was active in northern Mozambique to which it had easy access. The Portuguese bombed, strafed, and made land forays to wipe out Frelimo's bases, and forced people to resettle into *aldeamentos* (roughly, strategic hamlets) to cut off the guerrilla fighters' support. Villagers who refused resettlement were often regarded as terrorists, and their villages were wiped out.

But in 1969, Frelimo began to penetrate to the center of the country. By 1974 its forces were attacking within one hundred miles of Beira, the second largest city in the colony, striking fear in its white population. Portugal's demoralized troops were more and more wanton in their treatment of blacks. Probably the worst massacre occurred in December 1972 in the village of Wiriyamu, where over three hundred people—men, women, and children—were lined up and shot or brutally tortured. Despite Portuguese denials that it had occurred, the massacre received some worldwide publicity, thanks to the country's increasingly disaffected Roman Catholic clergy (Hastings 1974; Kaplan 1977: 56–60, 196–99).

In Guinea, where the PAIGC began its armed struggle in 1963, Portugal was close to defeat by the 1970s. General Antonio de Spinola, commander of the Portuguese forces in Guinea, had proposed a strategy in 1968 to integrate more decisive military action with psychological warfare and the encouragement of a black bourgeoisie which would support the colonial power. He sponsored Congresses of the People to organize black supporters.

His 1970 invasion of Conakry to destroy PAIGC sanctuaries ended in disaster, but he visited his troops at the front regularly, he was turning himself into a hero among his junior officers, and his own views were evolving to support a peaceful solution to the war which would allow the colonies limited autonomy within a "pluricontinental Portuguese federation." When Spinola returned to Lisbon in 1973 to become vice-chairman of the Joint Chiefs of Staff, however, PAIGC advances stepped up. The PAIGC controlled a large share of the territory, and was recognized as the government by most of the third world and socialist countries in 1973. It appeared that Portugal might be forced to withdraw.

Although Guinea was economically the least significant of the colonies, Caetano regarded it as crucial. In 1972 he told Spinola that he would rather suffer an "honorable military defeat" there than offer the "terrorists" a settlement that liberation movements in the other colonies might take as a sign of weakened resolve (Caetano 1974: 191). Portugal was not defeated in Angola and Mozambique, but only an intolerable escalation would make victory possible.

Most of the Western countries nominally supported self-determination for the colonies, so they gave Portugal military aid with the condition that it not be used in Africa—even though it was clear that all such aid supported the war effort directly or indirectly. NATO aid was substantial. U.S. training in particular enabled the Portuguese military to apply the lessons of Vietnam (forced resettlement in Mozambique, napalm in Angola, civic action to win the hearts and minds of the people in Guinea) while failing to teach the one central lesson: the futility of counterinsurgency against a determined colonized population.

Still, it was clear that Western aid would remain limited and insufficient to assure victory. The war was immensely costly: according to one account, military expenditures reached between 45 and 50 percent of the national budget.[7] Portuguese casualties climbed, even though the Portuguese army depended more and more on African troops. By the end of the war, Portugal claimed that half the soldiers in the field were black (Keefe 1977: 336–38; Minter 1972: 58–66).

The biggest burden fell on the troops in the field and the junior officers who led them. Junior officers were exhausted by a war in which most of them had already served several tours of duty. Still, their discontent might have led them to demand escalation and victory rather than a settlement. Several factors disposed them to choose the latter course. They feared that the armed forces might be made scapegoats for defeat, as they had been in Goa in 1961. The "ultras" who wanted a complete victory were demanding escalation: organization by white settlers in Mozambique and a meeting of veterans in Portugal in June 1973 appeared to many junior officers to be the opening of a scapegoating campaign (Carvalho 1977: 44, 194; A. Rodrigues et al. 1974: 309–10).

By 1974 new recruits to the officer corps were no longer from the same class origin that had made most older officers loyal to fascism. The armed forces, traditionally the preserve of the sons of the oligarchy, had become a less attractive career with the beginning of industrial development. To counter the decline in applications, the Military Academy abolished tuition in 1958, permitting young men from less well-off families to pursue a military career. Thereafter, the typical officer candidate was the son of a petty bourgeois family from the provinces (A. Rodrigues et al. 1974: 345–49). These men became officers at about the time the war began, so they had been fighting it throughout their entire careers. They found themselves fighting in Africa to defend the property of an oligarchy to which they did not belong, while the senior officers who did belong to the oligarchy remained in Portugal in staff positions.

The experience of fighting the liberation movements also affected these officers. In their training courses they studied the works of Mao, Che Guevara, and the African liberation leaders such as Amilcar Cabral of the PAIGC and Eduardo Mondlane of Frelimo (both assassinated by the PIDE). In Africa they were greatly impressed by the effectiveness of guerrilla fighters who enjoyed the support of the population. Especially in Guinea, where defeat was likeliest and where they had the closest view of the liberation movement's activities, they were exhausted and unwilling to continue the fight. Guinea became an early center of the MFA; as officers were rotated back home, they regularly took places in the leading ranks of the new movement.

The officers were also exposed to the politicizing influence of some of their own countrymen. Even though entrance into the military academy had been eased, not enough officer candidates appeared. As the war continued, troop strength increased massively and a military career became even less attractive. Only 72 candidates entered the academy in 1972 compared with 257 in 1961 (Blackburn 1974: 11). In the face of the shortage, military service was made universal and the officer ranks were filled with university students drafted as *milicianos*. Many *milicianos*, politicized in the increasingly radicalized universities of the 1960s, exposed the regular officers to their views.

But their presence had a more important effect. To encourage *milicianos* to reenlist after completing their draft obligation, the government decreed in

July 1973 that they could move into the regular officer corps after a brief additional training course. This decree challenged the regular officers' prerogatives and the value of their professional training. To protest it, some of them began organizing what they called the Captains' Movement—which later became the Armed Forces Movement.

Protecting their status against the pretensions of *milicianos* was at first the Captains' only goal. Organizing against the incorporation of *milicianos* began with petitions of protest circulated in Portugal and the three war zones. Though their documents frequently referred to the "particularly grave situation through which the nation is passing" (e.g., the petition of September 9; A. Rodrigues et al. 1974: 387), the most commonly cited grievance was the loss of prestige by the armed forces or the regular officer corps.

Some MFA men, especially those who were to become its far-left wing, later argued that the movement had political objectives from the beginning but that it used professional rhetoric both as a subterfuge against infiltrators and to appeal to the greatest possible number of officers (Carvalho 1977: 131–32; Almeida 1977: 71–72; see also A. Rodrigues et al. 1974: 313–15, 330–31). A few regular officers were already highly politicized. The PCP had decided in 1965 that its members should infiltrate the armed forces, and many who were at least sympathizers of the PCP later became important figures in the MFA. But they were not among the initial organizers. Vasco Gonçalves and Ernesto Melo Antunes, who would become two of the MFA's leading political figures, apparently did not join until the fall of 1973.

Most officers were drawn in by concern about their professional status, and only after they came up against the regime's refusal to respond did they decide that they had to end the war. That, they knew, required bringing the government down. Their evolution was amazingly rapid: on September 9, 1973, 136 officers at a meeting discussed no proposal more drastic than a strike and a public demonstration. But by November, when one officer called for an immediate coup, many others objected only because they thought the time was not ripe.

Having made that decision, the Captains identified increasingly with the political left. Repudiation of the Chilean coup of September 1973 made them want to dissociate themselves—and by implication, military institutions in general—from fascism. When they decided in December to adopt a program for the government they would install after their coup, they invited Melo Antunes to draft it. Melo Antunes had a reputation as an articulate Marxist, and probably had the most political experience of any officer in the

MFA (in 1969 he had run for parliament on the CDE slate). The program he presented, approved on March 5, 1974, called for democracy and an end to repression; it attacked the monopolies and promised to defend the least privileged sectors. It also recognized the colonies' right to self-determination. Others in the armed forces were also organizing against the government. Ultra-rightist General Kaulza de Arriaga plotted a coup in December, hoping to take power and escalate the war to achieve victory. His allies knew of the Captains' Movement, and they tried unsuccessfully to win its support. Evidently the Captains' rejection of the war was not very clear, even to those who knew about the movement.

Spinola too was organizing for a takeover. In many ways he was a typical senior officer: he had fought with Franco's forces in Spain, he had been a director of the Champalimaud group, one of the three largest monopoly groups, and he was fundamentally quite conservative. Yet after making himself a hero in Guinea, he returned to Portugal in 1973 convinced that a political solution to the war was necessary. He even attempted to negotiate a peaceful transition with Caetano. In February 1974 he published *Portugal and the Future,* in which he proposed to grant the colonies limited autonomy. This moderate gesture was intended as a trial balloon, but it fell like a bombshell, and in March he was dismissed as vice-chairman of the Joint Chiefs of Staff. Immediately after his dismissal, a group of officers loyal to him led an abortive coup at Caldas da Rainha, hoping that their act would inspire the MFA to join them. But the coup was quickly put down.

The MFA did not join the mutineers of Caldas da Rainha; it had decided to bring down the government on its own. But it had not decided to govern. In keeping with both the military's image of itself as apolitical and the conspiratorial tradition which assumed that problems could be resolved by a single blow, the Captains did not expect to take power themselves. Instead, they planned to install a junta of senior officers, more moderate and better known than themselves, whose leadership would give legitimacy to the coup.

Spinola seemed an ideal figurehead. When the MFA asked him to accept the presidency, he rejected parts of the program: he was willing to accept a call for a political rather than a military solution to the war, but he insisted that the reference to self-determination for the colonies be deleted. The differences foreboded political problems to come. But the leaders of the MFA wanted the popular general to be president, because they felt that his political sanction was necessary to give the coup legitimacy. So they gave in to his demands.[8] All was now ready for the coup.

Like earlier military conspiracies, the MFA grew out of officers' professional grievances, and only later adopted political goals. Even if the leaders had clearer politics than their predecessors had had, their program was still vague. Not only that, but they refused to take power in the movement's name. Less than a year later, however, they not only held power but had decided to use it to set Portugal on the road to socialism.

The extent of that apparent transformation raises a question about military governments which has been widely debated, especially with reference to third world countries, since the 1960s: whether they are capable of introducing significant social and economic change (see Jackman 1976; Nordlinger 1977). Some argue that they cannot, or at least that they do not, do so, since by ideology, military officers are almost universally conservative (Abrahamsson 1971; Janowitz 1960: 233–56). The history of coups in most of Latin America since its independence testifies to the officer corps' readiness to intervene in the service of order and the interests of the oligarchy. But since the 1960s, military officers and military governments have often been regarded as a force for economic modernization.

Whether their aims are radical or conservative, coups have generally occurred in societies where civilian governments cannot control widespread disorder and especially ethnic conflict. A coup unseats incompetent civilian politicians (in the view of the military leaders) and suspends democracy to restore order. Huntington argues that officers who take power will act to strengthen the middle class. They therefore favor social change in backward societies where the middle class is weak and support the status quo in more developed societies where it is already strong.[9]

This argument would lead one to expect any military government in Portugal to be highly conservative: Portugal is culturally homogeneous and its economy, though dependent, is far more developed than the economies of most countries which have experienced military rule. But the MFA's coup differs from most coups in other respects as well: it was inspired not by domestic disorder, economic decline, or any other problem of domestic civil society, but rather by the officers' refusal to pursue the colonial war. Moreover, it was made not against an ineffective democratic government but against an authoritarian government and with the explicit intention of restoring democracy.

The MFA's claim to defend the least privileged sectors and its later espousal of socialism appear to exemplify progressive military rule favoring radical redistribution. I will argue, however, that the decisive accomplishments of the Portuguese revolution did indeed serve the class interests of the officers who promoted it and of the civilian class of which they were part. The officer corps was no longer tied to the oligarchy. By origin and current position, its members were identified with the modernizing nonmonopoly bourgeoisie, both its technocratic and its capitalist segments.

The lasting accomplishments of the Portuguese revolution were to establish liberal democracy and strengthen the state sector within a framework which remained capitalist. These transformations served the class interests of the military and the civilian nonmonopoly bourgeoisie at the expense of the landowning and monopolistic oligarchy. A segment of the MFA adopted more radical democratic and socialist objectives in response to the demands of a mass movement of the working class, but they did not attain those objectives: the major gains of the working class were reversed.

At the beginning, however, no class contradiction was evident. The MFA assumed that it could establish a democracy, meet the needs of the least favored sectors of the population, and relinquish responsibility—all at once, by a successful coup. That optimism was shared by much of the population, as the mass response to the coup showed.

4

The Revolution of the Carnations

The April 25 coup was almost entirely peaceful. Major Otelo Saraiva de Carvalho, the MFA's chief strategist, had laid careful plans. When "Grândola" was played on the radio shortly after midnight, troops moved. They first occupied the main points of access to Lisbon, then the radio and television stations, then the military ministries. Units elsewhere in the country also took their assigned targets. A tank column from the Santarem Cavalry School occupied Commerce Square on the Tagus River to control the ministries of defense, army, and navy, and faced off a cavalry unit ready to defend the government. When the defenders' commander ordered a junior officer to fire, he refused and surrendered instead.

By then it was daybreak and the MFA had read a communiqué over the radio announcing the "liberation of the country from the regime that has dominated it for so long," a clear signal that the coup was made in repudiation of fascism (A. Rodrigues et al. 1974: 35). Crowds of people immediately swept into the streets to celebrate—despite the appeals in the same radio announcements to keep calm and stay at home.

After facing off the hostile unit and capturing the ministries, the tank contingent in Commerce Square next saw a frigate in the harbor aim its artillery toward the square. Prime Minister Caetano had ordered it to bombard; but its junior officers disobeyed and ordered the guns pointed toward the sky. The cavalrymen turned with relief to their next task, to capture the National Republican Guard garrison in Carmo Plaza, where Caetano had taken refuge.

The garrison was only a few hundred meters away, but up a very steep hill. The tanks had to be pushed—and civilians who were streaming from their homes to welcome liberation joined in pushing, in a symbolic anticipation of the collaboration that was to develop between the MFA and the popular movement. At the garrison the Guard offered no resistance, but refused to surrender until Caetano gave the order. He in turn was delaying. He sent a message to Spinola that he would surrender peacefully, but only to Spinola in person; Spinola, he was confident, was a responsible man who would maintain order.

Meanwhile, what would turn out to be one of the major operations of the coup was about to begin: coup planners had deliberately delayed the assault on the PIDE headquarters, hoping that if the coup was going smoothly the secret police officers would recognize that the cause was lost and surrender. But a crowd had already gathered outside the PIDE building. Shots were fired from inside, and one civilian was killed—the only fatality of the coup. Soon a detachment of naval fusiliers arrived to besiege the headquarters. The PIDE held out until the next morning, but finally surrendered.

Spinola, in contact with the conspirators, demanded that they bow to his conditions for accepting the presidency. When they agreed, he went to Carmo to meet Caetano. Late in the afternoon he proceeded to the Pontinha Engineering Regiment, where the MFA had its command post. Face to face, they discovered that there were still differences to resolve. Spinola still argued heatedly with the authors of the coup for several hours until they finally agreed to delete from the program the call for self-determination for the colonies. It was after midnight when Spinola read the program to the nation (A. Rodrigues et al. 1974: 36–43; Insight Team 1975: 91–97).

The MFA program made sweeping promises, and immediately put many of them into effect: freedom of speech was declared and censorship abolished; all political prisoners were freed; political parties and trade unions began to organize right away. Even if the program waffled on the colonial question and did not explain how the new government would fight the monopolies and serve the "least privileged sectors," even if the Captains themselves were unsure of their political intentions, the coup offered democracy—the system from which Portugal had been protected for so many years. Those who had long hoped for democracy could welcome the immediate changes and overlook the vagueness and the contradictions.

People responded immediately. They marched through the streets, gathered in crowds, and embraced the soldiers. People wore red carnations and handed them out to others, creating an instant, joyous symbol of liberation. They seized the unaccustomed opportunity to demonstrate and organize with a zeal which could not have been predicted. The outpouring demonstrated how strong was the desire for change, and created a basis of political support which made possible the sweeping changes to come. The MFA made the coup, but the people of Portugal made the revolution.

Revolution and Everyday Life

The masses of people who poured into the streets on April 25 set the tone for what Philippe Schmitter has called a "civic orgy" of both political activity and ordinary social relations. What made it possible was the dismantling of the repressive apparatus. Informers no longer reported private conversations to the PIDE, and meetings could be held without being broken up by police wielding clubs. Well-known political figures and thousands of draft resisters and deserters returned from exile as heroes. Huge crowds turned out to greet Communist Party leader Alvaro Cunhal and Socialist Party leader Mario Soares when they arrived. Those who came back from exile or emerged from underground especially welcomed the opportunity to *sair à rua*—to go out into the streets and breathe the air of daylight.

But there was something more than an end to overt repression. Even for ordinary citizens, a weight was lifted: people began to abandon the self-imposed privacy in which their lives had been enclosed, to shake off the habits of avoidance they had cultivated for years. Any civic involvement, any effort to change things, had so evidently been futile; now it might not be. No longer did people have to be suspicious; they could engage each other socially without fear of entrapment.

The atmosphere was euphoric. Neighbors gathered freely on street corners just to talk, and strangers happily struck up conversations, discussing everything from politics to soccer. Talking freely and long, people who were accustomed to keeping silent either out of fear or because they seemed stuck in ordinary events suddenly discovered that events were not so ordinary. Some burst spontaneously into political songs in public—the International, the Communist Party hymn—and small groups of young people marched down the street chanting slogans. Even before serious political organizing began, these public acts were important. They proved—to oneself as much as to others—that freedom really *had* come.[1]

In that heady atmosphere, it seemed that everything was possible. It was not just political changes which were felt, but an opening up of one's whole life. The entire society seemed to have made a dramatic break with the past.

That new consciousness enabled an apparently apathetic and politically unprepared people to attempt a revolution in the next few months.

In a process called *saneamento* (literally, "purification"), miniature coups imitated the military coup everywhere: in newspapers, schools, universities, local governments, trade unions, and even some factories, workers or citizens demanded the removal of the former editors, principals, council members, officers, and bosses who they claimed had supported the fascist regime. Overturning the regime obviously required more than ousting the heads of state. Because fascism had penetrated all these institutions, they too had to be overturned if democracy was to prevail. No institution was exempt—and most of the ousters stuck.

The moment called for a complete reappraisal of culture and social life. Books by Marx and Lenin, suddenly available, topped the best-seller lists. For the first time, pornographic films were shown in movie theaters. Thorough reforms of institutions were proposed: school curricula were revised, and newspapers abounded with articles such as "The Task of Linguistics in the New Portugal." Newspapers carried real news as well as visions of the future: not only were they not censored, but events were happening which were worth reading about. The tone of the papers and the evening news changed dramatically. Censoring themselves, reporters had fluently parroted the government line or, occasionally, criticized it in veiled language. Now they clothed their reports in leftist language and openly joined in celebrating the new freedoms.

Demonstrations took place almost daily; but the biggest occurred on May Day, a week after the coup. Illegal May Day demonstrations had been planned clandestinely, as they were every year, but to affirm the new political freedoms, International Workers' Day was declared a holiday. A million people joined the joyous celebration in Lisbon, and more marched in demonstrations around the country. To some who were still wary, May Day made it clear that their new political freedom was real. The workers at TAP, the national airline, first met to formulate demands on May 3. "Why didn't we meet before then? Because of May Day," a worker explained to me. "On May Day it became obvious what the sentiment of the people was: May Day left no doubt."

More than fifty political parties either emerged from underground or were founded within a few months. Most of them were paper organizations at best, but even their tenuous existence was a sign of the popular explosion. They all seemed to have their grafitti artists, whose handiwork ranged from hastily scrawled slogans to elaborate murals (see *As paredes em liberdade* 1974, and *As paredes na revolução* 1978, for examples).

Only a few parties were destined to grow. It became clear immediately that the Communist Party was by far the best organized. Long-time clandestine militants now proudly declared their affiliation, and many discovered to their surprise that friends and workmates were also members. The PCP declared (and repeatedly demonstrated) its full support for the MFA. It acted with moderation because it was genuinely concerned to consolidate the democratic process, and it hoped to prove its democratic faith to the officers. Recognizing their need for civilian collaborators, many officers were receptive. At the same time the Communist Party was eager to insure a place for itself in the process, and it propelled its members and sympathizers into key organizational positions, especially in the unions and local governments where former officials were removed by *saneamento*.

The Socialist Party quickly began establishing an organization, hoping to catch up with the Communists. Among the newly formed parties, two would become most important. The Popular Democratic Party (PPD), which espoused social democracy on the Western European model, was formed by several veterans of Caetano's short-lived "liberal wing." Further to the right, the Democratic Social Center (CDS) was founded by people with even closer links to the old regime but who now claimed to be democrats. The new parties chose names which symbolically echoed the repudiation of fascism and the general desire for radical changes. Virtually all hoped to sound progressive, even the Party of Progress and the Labor Party, which took extreme rightwing positions.

The CDE, as the legal opposition to fascism had called itself in recent years, announced its transformation into the Portuguese Democratic Movement (MDP). It claimed not to be a party but a nonpartisan civic organization welcoming the affiliation of all individuals and organizations which supported democracy. The PCP, the PS, and the PPD joined it; but just as the PCP had dominated the democratic opposition under fascism, its militants and sympathizers were the most active in the new MDP. The PS and the PPD were never more than nominal members, and they had withdrawn by the fall of 1974.

The euphoric atmosphere and the apparently universal desire to change things masked ambiguities and contradictions among civilian politicians and within the armed forces themselves. The most immediate issue was the colonial question: how to end the colonial war and how to deal with the colonies' demand for independence. But looming large behind the colonial question was the issue of the Portuguese economy. The MFA program's progressive language implied hostility to the monopoly groups and service to the poor. But while the word *socialism* was on many lips, it meant different things to different people, and the program did not spell out any economic policy for the new government. The MFA's leftism consisted more in a repudiation of the old regime than the expression of a clearly defined position. The new rulers, moreover, did not want to frighten away investors. They repeatedly gave assurances that the MFA's program did not authorize fundamental structural reforms but only short-term measures; final decisions would have to wait for the new constitution and a democratically elected government.

Moreover, the MFA had delivered power to senior officers who could not be assumed to share whatever radical intentions it had. Spinola, the new president, and the other six members of the Junta of National Salvation were all senior officers. A few of them were more progressive than Spinola— General Costa Gomes had taken part in the 1961 coup against Salazar, and the two navy officers were thought to be on the left. But Spinola was the dominant figure, and the others deferred to him, at least for a while. The MFA itself was still led by its twenty-member Coordinating Commission, but it claimed no formal governing authority.

An elaborate governing structure was established, though it was meant to be temporary, to last only until the forthcoming Constituent Assembly elections. A Council of State was created, consisting of the seven junta members, seven MFA representatives, and seven more members (including some civilians) named by Spinola. Spinola thus enjoyed a comfortable majority. In principle, the Council of State was the final authority, but it never exercised power. Despite these formal structures, real power lay with the military, but it was ambiguously and uncomfortably divided between the junta and the MFA Coordinating Commission, even though the latter had no official role.

The MFA program called on the junta to name a civilian provisional government, and this was duly announced on May 15. Led by Prime Minister Adelino Palma Carlos and nominally a coalition of the MDP, the PCP, the PPD, and the PS, the government included Cunhal and PPD Secretary General Francisco Sa Carneiro as ministers without portfolio and Soares as foreign minister. Avelino Gonçalves, a Communist and bank workers' union leader, was minister of labor.

In the absence of a parliament, the government—the prime minister and the cabinet—had the power to decree laws. But in practice its main functions were administrative. The military lay down the policies which the government enacted into law, and these policies reflected the outcome of struggles carried on elsewhere. Whenever the government fell—and there were to be six provisional governments in the course of the next eighteen months—it was because of disputes that were fought out and resolved outside of it.

Workers Respond to Freedom

People acted on their newfound freedom in their workplaces as enthusiastically as they did in the streets. They demanded raises and long-denied workers' rights and took over the fascist trade unions. The PCP began a drive to consolidate its position in the unions. It attempted to lay hold of the existing union structure rather than transform it: it accepted the system of horizontal unionism, a separate union for each occupation in a plant.

Saneamento came to union executive boards still controlled by officers who had collaborated with the old regime (the great majority): they were immediately unseated and replaced by new officers chosen from members who had been active in opposition. The *saneamento* was carried out by political activists; workers who were not already active in the unions had little to do with the reorganization process. The new boards represented a broad array of political forces, but Communists were usually in the majority, taking a strong position in most unions. New unions were quickly created by workers who had been prohibited from organizing even fascist unions— most importantly, public employees and the farmworkers of the Alentejo.

The Intersindical emerged from underground and declared itself Portugal's new trade union federation. It was the official sponsor of the May Day rallies. To avoid the appearance of Communist domination, the Intersindical invited Socialist leader Soares as well as Communist leader Cunhal to address the Lisbon rally, even though the PS had no significant strength in the working class or in the unions.

The PCP's support of the MFA and the new government was most clearly shown in its leadership of labor. It hoped to use its strong union base to prevent work stoppages and excessive wage demands that would interfere with production or put a strain on the economy, and thereby avoid antagonizing the right. It was because of the PCP's presumed influence over workers that it had received and accepted the labor portfolio in the cabinet.

But workers did not accept the call for moderation. They were determined to use their newfound freedom to raise demands. In the first days after the coup, in factory after factory, workers held an assembly to write up a *caderno reivindicativo,* a list of grievances to present to management. The immediate demands in these *cadernos reivindicativos* were for wage increases and for *saneamento* of overbearingly authoritarian supervisors and PIDE informers.

Many owners, unaccustomed to hearing workers' demands or negotiating with their representatives, turned them down outright. They responded with a tremendous strike wave. Strikes broke out so suddenly and widely because workers realized that normal restraints were released: the PIDE was totally dismantled, its most prominent collaborators had been expelled from the firms, and the lower-level collaborators who had spied on their colleagues and reported militant activities were doing their best to remain undiscovered. In this new atmosphere, workers felt that they could ask for—if not always get—anything. Literally hundreds of labor conflicts expressing the pent-up demands of many years broke out in a few weeks. Strikes were still formally illegal, but workers took the MFA's declarations of freedom seriously. In the Lisbon area alone, over 200 firms were struck in May, and the new government, reluctant to put the strikes down by force, kept out of the disputes (Neves 1978: 191–202; A. Rodrigues et al. 1976: 57–68; M.L. Santos et al. 1976).

The overwhelming majority of demands were economic, for higher wages or fringe benefits such as meal subsidies and paid vacations. But some went further. A study of the strikes in the Lisbon area showed that the second most common demand was for *saneamento* of managers. Workers regarded their bosses as part and parcel of the fascist regime, and the task of destroying the regime included getting rid of them. Other demands concerned working conditions or worker control.[2] Such demands represented a first step toward claiming a voice in the way firms were run—a modest step, but nevertheless one in which Portuguese workers claimed far greater rights than they had exercised under fascism, or than workers normally exercise under capitalism.

Because the trade unions echoed the PCP's calls for moderation, and because their horizontal structure meant that no one union represented all the workers in a plant, they did not lead the strike wave. Workers sought new, independent channels for their militancy. They found them in the workers' commissions. An ad hoc workers' commission was generally elected by the same workers' assembly that drew up the *caderno reivindicativo*.

Many of the workers' commissions formed to conduct the illegal strikes in the last months before the coup had survived or were resurrected. Other firms had never had one. In the Cergal brewery, one activist told me, "the first meeting was called more or less secretly. We didn't hold it in the factory because we still didn't have confidence. Three other workers and I asked the director of a club in Sintra to lend us his hall. We made posters. We thought that if fifty workers showed up we would be satisfied. We were astonished when, at the announced time, everyone showed up—not only the workers but the managers too.''

In some firms, a new commission was initially elected with the support of management: management had either supported the formation of a commission before April 25 (as in Lisnave, the large shipyard, and CUF, the giant chemical company) or sponsored the creation of one shortly thereafter, hoping to curry workers' favor and at the same time manipulate the election of commission members (as occurred in the ITT manufacturing subsidiary Standard Electric). These commissions did not press demands with the vigor workers soon insisted upon and did not last very long; most of them were challenged within a few months and were unseated in new elections.

New worker leaders began to emerge. Many of them, disillusioned by the PCP's call for restraint, were attracted to the newly formed far-left parties. Workers' commissions quickly became their major base. In the strike movement, workers resisted top-down leadership and pressed their own demands, becoming aware, in the process, of their collective power. The new commission leaders encouraged that consciousness in order to accelerate the revolutionary dynamic they sensed was in progress. In pushing for more, they rejected the PCP's strategy of union organization, moderation of demands, and unconditional support of the government.

The PCP went so far as to call a demonstration opposing strikes on June 1. But by that time the strike wave had passed its peak. The new provisional government had responded to the workers' main demands three days earlier with a package of economic measures. Most important was a minimum wage of 3,300 escudos (about $130) per month, higher than the prevailing wage for about 40 percent of the workers covered (the decree did not cover farmworkers or domestic workers). Their most immediate demands satisfied by this decree (or by management capitulation in many of the firms where wages were already higher), strikers returned to work.

But the commissions remained active. Even in firms where they had won large wage settlements relatively easily, there were other wage-related issues to be discussed, and they won further gains either formally or informally over the next several months. Disputes arose over hours of work, especially night-shift work. In many factories, workers won a reduction in the forty-eight hour week—still quite common—and in some the night shift was eliminated or reduced. (In Sorefame, which manufactured railroad cars, the night shift was reduced to forty hours and the day shift to forty-five, with a promise of a further reduction to forty-two the next year; in the Lisnave shipyard, the night shift was eliminated.)

Workers in many firms demanded fixed salaries instead of piece rates. A common demand was that the firm supplement disability insurance, which paid only 60 percent of salary to workers who lost time due to accident or illness. Many workers' commissions demanded other benefits, such as day care, food service, and locker rooms. Some of these demands were for new benefits, others for improvements. Often the issue was not so much the benefit in itself but the way in which it was provided; a workers' commission often established a special committee to oversee a lunchroom or some other service on an ongoing basis.

Many commissions struggled to reduce wage inequality, either among manual workers or between them and white collar and technical employees. They frequently succeeded. Raises were generally highest for the lowest paid workers, and many new contracts reduced the number of job categories or positions on the salary scale. White-collar workers had normally been favored with longer vacations, sick pay, and bonuses; in many firms, blue-collar workers won equal fringe benefits.

These battles were not fought only against management; sometimes they set workers against each other. The members of workers' commissions were usually the most politically conscious workers, and while they did not advocate absolute wage equality, they were strongly in favor of reducing differentials. Some commissions demanded that the wages of blue-collar workers be raised while those of the generally better-paid white-collar employees be essentially frozen. The white-collar workers, many of whom identified with management anyway, were of course alienated by this proposal. Such disputes often left bitter divisions between white-collar and manual workers which prevented united action later.

A common target of demands for equalization was the gap between men and women. Most women were segregated into lower-paying jobs, and even when they held the same jobs as men they were almost invariably paid less. Male workers objected to equalizing women's salaries. In Lusalite, a fiberboard factory west of Lisbon, many women did substantially the same jobs as men, but at lower pay. The workers' commission demanded equal wages for equal work. Some men objected, but the proposal eventually carried among the workers and management acceded. In the Cergal brewery, most of the workers were men, but the lowest paid were cleaning women. The workers' commission proposed raising their salaries to the level of the lowest paid male workers. The men, however, rejected this, and the workers' commission had to give in; it demanded a higher raise for the cleaning women than for other workers, but their pay remained lower. The traditional attitudes of workers themselves, who often suc-cumbed to management's long-standing efforts to divide them, were as big an obstacle to equalization as was management refusal to raise the lowest wages.

Workers also demanded major changes in the work process. They were free to object to unsafe conditions which they had always tolerated, and the commissions negotiated improvements. Even more commonly, they com-plained about the harsh discipline imposed by supervisors. The authoritari-anism of the fascist state had been matched—and reinforced—by authori-tarian factory discipline, and workers immediately demanded that it be eased. Their commissions attempted to combat rigid discipline either by moderating the practices or changing the personnel. When a dispute arose between a worker and a supervisor, a workers' commission member would be called in informally to mediate.

In many factories, managers learned to live with the commissions. Some commission members were released from their regular work to handle commission affairs full time, with pay. Commission members made the rounds of a plant all day long to hear grievances and attempted to resolve them on the spot. While the initial strike wave had grown so fast because so many managers obstinately refused to negotiate, many of them soon realized that to continue to operate, they would have to deal with the workers' new assertiveness.

Though the strike wave receded, some strikes continued, often with political as well as economic objectives. Postal workers went on strike for four days in June. Like other public employees, postal workers had had no union before April 25, and PCP militants led the drive to form one. Here too the Communist unionists were most concerned to contain the workers' militancy and avoid a political challenge, while other activists wanted to take advantage of the fluid situation to win as much as possible. Workers called assemblies in the post offices and, against the wishes of the union, demanded *saneamento* and a large salary increase. Early in May several high postal officials were removed, but the government rejected the salary demands. A wildcat strike began in two large Lisbon post offices on June 17 and quickly spread throughout the country. The PCP opposed the mail strike as it opposed most others; the PS, somewhat opportunistically, publicly supported it, hoping to accumulate political capital among workers at the expense of the PCP.

This time the government intervened decisively, mobilizing troops to replace the striking postal workers. Two *milicianos* who refused to scab were jailed for several months in punishment (Neves et al. 1978: 199–200; A. Rodrigues et al. 1976: 58–59). The mail strike was a pivotal test of the government's claim to defend workers' interests. To keep the mail moving, the government decided to repress the workers.

Another strike with important political consequences became a precedent for later action: on June 21 workers of the Lisbon Water Company, sympathetic to the PCP, occupied their premises to demand not higher pay but nationalization of the company and the *saneamento* of some officers of the company accused of fascism. They were the first workers to demand that their firm be made public property. The provisional government acceded, though it refused to call the takeover a nationalization (Neves et al. 1978: 216–18; A. Rodrigues et al. 1976: 58).

Events in two foreign-owned firms provided a different kind of precedent, as the first examples of worker control. The new minimum wage was beyond the economic resources of some marginal firms, and the new militancy alienated many managers, especially in branches of multinational firms. Having located in Portugal specifically to take advantage of the low wages they thought would be guaranteed by repressive control of the labor force, many of them now threatened to lay off large numbers of workers or even to close entirely.

Sogantal was a French-owned factory with forty-eight workers, all women, who sewed precut pieces (sent from the firm's French factory) into jogging suits. Shortly after April 25, the workers' *caderno reivindicativo* demanded a wage increase from 1,600 to 2,850 escudos. On May 30 management announced its refusal, even though the wage demanded was lower than the new national minimum wage. In response, the workers began a slowdown strike and on June 12 the owners announced that they were closing the factory. The workers refused to leave, continued production with the materials in stock, and sold the suits to anyone who would buy.

Applied Magnetics, which was U.S.-owned, made computer components that were sent to its plant in Puerto Rico for final assembly. Most of its 750 workers, too, were women. Immediately after April 25, management was conciliatory, and granted them a forty-hour week and a month's vacation. But soon the company reneged. On July 12 it announced that 116 workers would be laid off, and demanded that the rest of the workers give up their gains; they were told to work forty-four hours a week, and their vacations were reduced to eighteen days. The workers voted to reject both the layoffs and the givebacks. After a few weeks of negotiation management announced on August 3 that it was shutting down, and the workers occupied the factory (*Combate*, June 21, 1974 and September 13, 1974; *Radical America* 1975).

Since these firms both belonged to multinationals, they were dependent on the parent firms for raw materials and markets, and neither survived under worker control. But both takeovers were widely publicized. Workers did organize production without bosses for a while, proving that they could operate on their own. It is significant that both were firms with a labor force exclusively or largely female. Women's work was concentrated in exactly those industries paying very low wages which could not afford, or could afford to refuse, to pay the new minimum wage; many other factories closed during this period, and some continued to pay sub-minimum wages. But in Sogantal and Applied Magnetics, women led the way in showing Portuguese workers that worker control was at least a conceivable alternative to unemployment.

Owners of firms experienced unheard-of challenges: strikes, demands for raises, workers' commissions which exercised de facto power, and even worker takeovers. Their government, moreover, was a coalition of a social democratic party, a socialist party, and a communist party. Capitalists hardly dared imagine what its economic policies would be. In fact the government insisted that it would not intervene decisively in the economy— certainly not to take over private firms. In the face of the worldwide economic downturn which had begun in 1973, it hoped to maintain the confidence of its capitalist class. But capitalists' experiences with their own workers left them insecure. To them, what was going on already appeared to be a revolution.

Workers did not believe they were making revolution—they were merely raising legitimate and normal grievances. But their experiences in the early months after the coup already exhibited the latent tension between centralism and popular power as models of revolutionary practice. The PCP's consolidation of its position in the trade unions and the nationalization of the Water Company followed the centralist model of revolution, based on strengthening first the working-class organizations, and second, state power over the economy. The more embryonic practice of popular power could be discerned in the strike wave, independent of existing organizations. It could also be seen in the workers' commissions, alert to mismanagement and to violation of workers' interests, and in the two firms where workers took control of production. The conflict between the two models was clearest in the unions, claiming to represent the workers' institutionalized power while at the same time discouraging the militancy of workers trying to redress their most pressing grievances.

The Beginning of the Neighborhood Movement

Following the coup, people organized in urban neighborhoods too, where they founded neighborhood commissions (as I translate *comissões de moradores,* literally, "dwellers' commissions"). Like the workers' commissions, the neighborhood commissions initially attempted to deal primarily with immediate necessities. Their main task was to improve housing conditions. The poor and working class, and even many moderately well-off people, suffered from the overcrowding, disrepair, and absolute lack of housing which became acute with the rapid urban growth accompanying the boom of the 1960s and early 1970s.

Despite the shortage of adequate housing, there was a fairly large stock of housing removed from the market. Landlords left apartments and whole buildings empty in the older areas of the cities, hoping a developer would purchase the site; new buildings built for speculation were not sold or rented; public housing projects often remained empty for long periods after completion because the corrupt and inefficient bureaucracy failed to fill them. One public project at Monsanto on the western outskirts of Lisbon, of two- and three-room apartments, stood empty for two years after it was finished. Its apartments were intended for single persons or elderly couples evicted from shantytowns. But according to an architect working at the Ministry of Public Works, the Lisbon police who evicted them refused to send them to the housing authorities, claiming that they did not need public housing. Elderly people could always live with their grown children, the police assumed, so if they were living in shantytowns it must be because they chose to.

Empty housing projects became a target for takeovers. The Monsanto project was the scene of the first occupation, on April 29, when residents of a nearby shantytown invaded and stayed. Within two weeks, several other finished or nearly finished public housing projects were occupied—1500 to 2000 units in Lisbon, and more in other cities (Downs 1983: 162). A small Maoist organization, the Reorganizing Movement for the Proletarian Party (MRPP), organized some of these occupations. While the junta responded on May 11 by prohibiting further occupations, it implicitly accepted those that had occurred (which had in any case exhausted virtually all the empty government-built housing).

Tenants of public housing projects also mobilized. The municipal projects of Oporto were begun in 1956 as part of a major urban renewal plan. Slums were cleared and families were removed to the new projects, located in a remote part of town inadequately served by public transportation. Tenants were subject to rigid rules and evicted if any violations were detected. The projects had a history of struggle, even under fascism: twice in 1973 groups of neighbors gathered to protest evictions, and they succeeded in preventing one.

It was here that the first neighborhood commissions in Oporto were formed. In one project, nicknamed "Tarrafal" after the Cape Verde prison, residents met on April 30 to demand easing of the rules. During the spring and summer, commissions were organized in other projects, and a coordinating body with representatives of all the projects was set up. When these commissions demanded that the projects' rules be revoked, the authorities gave no formal response, but the rules were suspended de facto (A.A. Costa 1979: 29–31, 42–44; Downs 1983).

Shantytown residents formed their own neighborhood commissions. The Quinta das Fonsecas, near the University City in the north of Lisbon, was a shantytown whose 250 families paid a small rent to the landowner. They held an assembly on May 11 to demand electricity, water, and decent housing. To underline their demands, the entire assembly marched to the president's palace, some eight kilometers away, to deliver their *caderno reivindicativo*. Shortly afterward, they went on rent strike, demanding that the landlord allow them to install pipes and build public fountains. Other shantytowns organized commissions in the spring and summer.

The first neighborhood commissions were created in the poorest neighborhoods: the municipal projects of Oporto and the shantytowns of Lisbon and Setubal, which spawned both the first occupations of government housing projects and the first demands for government action. In Setubal, Portugal's second largest industrial center, commissions were formed in most poor neighborhoods by June, and nearly all neighborhoods had them by March of 1975. Most of the first neighborhood commissions sprang up spontaneously and had no ties to political organizations.

The immediate demands of these poorest neighborhoods were to satisfy obvious needs: physical improvements such as leveling the ground and installing public fountains tapping the city water supply, or even running water and electricity in the houses. Later the commissions also called for new housing. While demanding government assistance, they also attempted to mobilize their own resources. Many commissions attempted to create or pressure the government to provide other services such as utilities, daycare centers, public transportation, garbage collection, and schools.

The MFA also provided an impetus to neighborhood organization. Though it still had no formal power, it had authority and the respect of the public. Officers were the main representatives of the government in localities, and individuals would ask officers or soldiers at nearby bases for some form of assistance. These initial contacts converged with the intentions of many MFA officers to build ties with the civilian population.

Military units began sending delegations to commission meetings to offer various kinds of assistance and often political exhortation as well. The officers, preferring to deal with organized groups rather than with individual requests one by one, called on the residents to get organized. Some commissions owed their origin to those early contacts, and in some cases a neighborhood group and a nearby regiment established an ongoing relationship. The meetings also contributed to the officers' politicization, as they saw firsthand the living conditions in the slums and shantytowns. Regiments able to supply equipment or other material services to neighborhoods were particularly likely to be sought out. These contacts later became formalized in the MFA's "cultural dynamization" campaign.

The government created a housing program for poor neighborhoods in the Mobile Local Support Service (SAAL), a project of the Ministry of Public Works (*Equipamento Social e Ambiente*), designed to assist slumdwellers' self-help projects. SAAL was created primarily to fix up roads and install running water and sewer systems, and secondarily to rehabilitate houses. It was announced in June, but it did not get under way until the fall. At first it seemed merely a symbolic gesture, and many criticized it as an effort to coopt neighborhood commissions and prevent further occupations. But in 1975 it would become an important base for neighborhood commissions' efforts to solve the housing problem by building entirely new housing.

Although neighborhood commissions had no obvious immediate purpose in wealthier areas, some were formed in the spring of 1974—more from excitement at the opportunity than because of urgent needs. Some people who were active in these commissions described how they searched for a role: they surveyed the population to determine priorities and addressed a document to the local government. "I remember we called it a *caderno reivindicativo*," recalled a man from the well-off Lisbon suburb of Oeiras some years later, grinning in slight embarrassment at the militant phrase. These commissions often immediately produced an elaborate structure of subcommissions to deal with problems of schools, health, transportation, recreation, daycare, and other concerns, only to see that structure die aborning for lack of interest.

Between May and July, at the same time that commissions were being established in neighborhoods, a process of *saneamento* was going on in local governments, in both rural and urban areas, especially those with some leftist traditions and some organizational structure inherited from the CDE. The old governing councils of *freguesias* and *concelhos* were declared out of office, and public meetings were called to choose new officers.[3] Usually there were multiple nominations for each office, and then a vote by paper ballot or show of hands.

As they did in the unions, the Communists relied on their superior organization to take the lead in these councils. Although noncommunist antifascists were often invited to join the slates, Communists or explicit allies usually occupied key positions. They were the only ones who had a network, and they took advantage of it. The newly founded MDP became a reliable Communist ally and most of the new local governments were elected under is official auspices.

The PCP's strategy of supporting the revolution at the same time that it built its own strength in institutions meant that its members took positions in local governments, as they did in trade unions, without trying to transform their structures. Local governments were given no new powers, and because the central government was still dominant they were highly restricted in what they could accomplish. The only local governments which had much effect were the ones that sympathized with the base-level neighborhood commissions and used the pressure generated by the commissions to reinforce their demands on the central government.

Organizing the Rural Areas

In rural areas the response to April 25 was varied. In the Alentejo the farmworkers' tradition of struggle provided a base for rapid organization. They mobilized rapidly to take over local governments and to create unions. In the northern villages, where the peasants had no political tradition to draw on and no employers to organize against, the response was slower.

In the Alentejo, farmworkers organized unions in May and June. Farmworkers had had no legal union in the past and were not covered by the newly decreed national minimum wage. But the PCP had a long history of organizing in the Alentejo and its networks were able to move quickly: small meetings were held in most villages, and then bigger meetings and rallies in the major towns to sign up workers.

Because the PCP was the only organization which had done political work among the farmworkers in the past, no significant far-left opposition arose as it did in the factories. PCP institution-building did not conflict with spontaneous activity in the Alentejo, in any case, because the party supported the farmworkers' demands and built organizations to serve their needs rather than calling on the farmworkers to restrain themselves. Though here too the unions attempted to preserve an image of nonpartisanship, Communist leadership was even more monolithic than it was in the industrial unions.

The new unions immediately demanded not only higher wages and shorter hours but also collective contracts from the landowners. The first contract was signed for the *concelho* of Beja on June 10, valid for the rest of the summer. The workers won significant wage increases: to 160 escudos (slightly over $6) a day for men (slightly more for skilled men such as tractor drivers) and 120 escudos for women. This represented an increase of about 80 percent for men and 120 percent for women, even though the traditional male wage advantage was maintained. Hours were reduced from forty-eight a week to forty-five, and employers agreed to pay for holidays and vacations and provide transportation to work. (Traditionally, most farmworkers, who owned no land and lived in villages, had had to walk long distances to the outlying farms.)

But the contract also contained some important gains which went beyond wages and hours. Especially important to the chronically underemployed farmworkers of the Alentejo, each landowner guaranteed work to all men and to women heads of families who had been regular workers on the property in the past. Even more important was the fact that workers had a contract. It was binding on all the landowners of the *concelho,* who were accustomed to dealing with workers individually, firing them at will for any offense, and hiring them by the day and laying them off indefinitely at the end of the growing season.

Organization and contract negotiation quickly spread: workers in other *concelhos* in the district of Beja won a similar contract the following month. In Evora landowners were more resistant. Giving in at first, they signed a district-wide contract in August, with terms similar to those in Beja. But the contract expired at the end of the month, and when the union tried to negotiate a contract for the next growing year, beginning in September, landowners refused to pay the wages they had agreed to in the first contract: they offered fifty escudos a day less than the union demanded. They also laid off workers to whom they had guaranteed work in the previous contract, and threatened not to sow for the following year and even to plow up land already planted rather than hire workers as they had promised.

As a great deal of land was then lying fallow, the union accused the growers of sabotaging the economy. Workers in some areas of the district struck to enforce the contract, and a district-wide strike of farmworkers was threatened. The impasse was resolved only when the minister of labor went to Evora to pressure the landowners, and the contract that was finally signed awarded workers forty escudos of the fifty-escudo differential. Contracts in other districts followed in short order.

These contracts were a major victory for the farmworkers, but they were hard to enforce. Growers fired workers even where the contract guaranteed them work, and refused to pay them for holidays and overtime. In response, the unions hardened their own position. In negotiations for new year-long contracts, they sought a guarantee that owners would sow all their lands to provide maximum employment (Barros 1979: 53–58; B. H. Fernandes 1975: 58–85; B. H. Fernandes 1978: 40–46; *Expresso,* September 7 and September 21, 1974).

In the rural north, where the church was the major cultural institution, organization did not come so easily. The fear of Communism, which the church spread so actively, was most easily aroused where the danger was least, since the north had seen little activity by Communists or any other political forces. The marginal organized political opposition to the fascist regime which had existed was concentrated among members of the middle class and in the larger towns; the CDE had been practically its only vehicle.

Because there had been so little active opposition, repression had not been very harsh. Conscious disaffection from the regime was therefore slight, and so was the sense of liberation at its downfall. The quiet northern villages seldom saw daily newspapers and in 1974 many of them were virtually depleted of men (traditionally far more attentive to politics than women) because they had emigrated to find work. From the start, the conservative clergy raised doubts about the new regime and preyed on the long-standing fear of communism.

Still, *saneamentos* occurred in the north as well. The MDP, taking advantage of the CDE's rudimentary organization, played an especially active role in the north in the *saneamentos* of *concelho* governments. As in the urban areas, it provided an appearance of political neutrality while establishing a leadership sympathetic to the Communists in many local governments.

In many northern villages *freguesia* councils were not unseated, in some cases because there were no opposition forces eager to root them out, and in others, because *freguesia* council members had not been active collaborators with fascism. Local governments were so unimportant that the old regime had not always insisted on controlling them tightly, and many council members had not been regime sympathizers but civic-minded citizens. The *casas do povo* were more likely to be targets. They were more important than the *freguesia* councils because as providers of social insurance they had large budgets.

Many northerners, habitually cautious and deferential, were wary about using their new freedom. One day a few months after April 25, the *freguesia* council of the tiny village of Soajo, on the northern border, learned from the Ministry of Public Works that the long-awaited repair of its village hall would be delayed even longer. Four men—one of them a member of the *freguesia* council, another an emigrant home on vacation—resolved to go immediately to Viana do Castelo, the district capital, to seek action. An engineer in the ministry told them that the money was already budgeted for the repairs and that they could speed the project by agreeing to hire workers and supervise it themselves. They had been quiet, even timid, in the engineer's office; as they left, they shouted and slapped each other on the back. They had taken a political matter into their own hands, for perhaps the first time in their lives, and won a minor victory.

In the summer the Communist Student Union sponsored a campaign to "bring April 25 to the north." University students went to northern villages for a few weeks to conduct literacy classes and public health education. The students' stay was brief, and they could claim very little success, in part because their Communist sponsorship aroused considerable hostility in some villages.

Again the Colonial Question

During the first months after the coup, the MFA moved steadily to the left, pushed by continuing conflict with Spinola over Portugal's colonial policy. Spinola and the conservative senior officers placed in power by the MFA not only failed to recognize the depth of the younger officers' repudiation of the war, but hoped to end the conflict without granting the colonies full independence—as Spinola had shown when he insisted that the MFA's program not refer to self-determination. The Captains were determined simply to end the war, and they knew that this would only happen with independence. The discovery that they would have to fight with Spinola kept them united and pushed them to assert their power, and, soon, to force Spinola's resignation.

The program announced by the provisional government in May already threatened that the war would continue: while it repeated the "political rather than military solution" formula, it explicitly promised to continue "defensive operations to safeguard lives and property" (*Revolução das Flores* 1974: 305). On many occasions Spinola publicly promoted his project of a "pluricontinental Portuguese federation," allowing the colonies only limited autonomy. Black Africans who hoped to take office in his neocolonial system created new self-styled "liberation movements" in all the colonies to compete with the movements that had waged the independence struggle. At the same time, white settlers threatened to declare unilateral independence, Rhodesian-style, in both Angola and Mozambique, and racial clashes broke out in the capitals of both colonies.

The leaders of the genuine liberation movements would accept nothing short of independence (Guinea-Bissau had already declared itself free the previous year), and Portuguese soldiers and NCOs in the colonies went into virtual mutiny, refusing to fight, especially in Guinea. The MFA made clear that the war had to end, and that the colonies would therefore have to be freed.

But Spinola, occupying the limelight, clung to his project of a neocolonial federation. At the same time he made no secret of his dismay at the spread of what he saw as anarchy among Portuguese workers. He found several means to undercut the MFA. He publicly announced his federalist plan and demanded protection for white settlers and blacks who had been recognized as assimilated or had served in the colonial administration or the Portuguese army. He gave speeches condemning the "disorder" that was overwhelming Portugal as strikes and purges spread. More broadly, he demanded that the MFA dissolve itself or else that it be extended to the whole armed forces (which would have amounted to the same thing). Then, on May 20, without consulting the MFA, Spinola and the junta allowed Caetano and Americo Thomaz, the deposed president, to leave house arrest for exile in Brazil. This decision not only meant that the deposed fascist leaders would not stand trial; it made clear to the MFA that it would have to fight the junta which it had placed in power.

The MFA was reluctant to expose these differences publicly. Many civilians, especially on the far left, saw signs that the new regime intended to perpetuate colonialism in a new form. Frequent demonstrations throughout the summer called for an immediate end to the war—in one, police killed a demonstrator. When the newspaper of the Maoist MRPP published an editorial calling on soldiers to refuse to fight, its editor was jailed and the paper was closed down. Fines imposed on other papers and censorship of television news seemed to call into question the junta's commitment to freedom of the press.

Attempting to circumvent the MFA, Spinola encouraged Prime Minister

Palma Carlos to call for an immediate plebiscite on Spinola's presidency in July and a two-year postponement of elections for a constituent assembly. If the plan had worked, Spinola would undoubtedly have won the plebiscite and been able to order the MFA "back to the barracks." Sabers were rattled, not for the last time. The MFA knew that it had more support in the armed forces than Spinola. Making veiled threats of a new military coup, it forced a different solution: Palma Carlos would be fired and the MFA would name a new prime minister and cabinet committed to full decolonization.

The MFA Coordinating Commission chose its head, Vasco Gonçalves, to be prime minister. Gonçalves was the only colonel among the "Captains." Unbeknownst to many in the MFA, he was also apparently a long-time Communist Party sympathizer and possibly a party militant, and as prime minister he followed party policies closely. He took office on July 18, with the second provisional government. And on July 27 Spinola was forced to recognize publicly the colonies' right to self-determination.

With Spinola's announcement the colonial question was for all practical purposes resolved: there would be no further attempts to stall or place obstacles in the way of full decolonization. Portugal recognized the independence of Guinea-Bissau in September, and a transitional government was established in Mozambique which would hand power over to Frelimo. The Angolan question was more complicated, but the only dispute concerned which of the liberation movements would be favored by the independence settlement: the MPLA or the FNLA and UNITA (the latter two of which later allied with South Africa in the Angolan civil war).

The victory in the "Palma Carlos crisis" allowed the MFA to assert its dominance of the revolutionary process and reinforced the sense of unity within the Coordinating Commission (a sense which would prove deceptive the next year). The MFA also reorganized the operational structure of the armed forces, creating the Continental Operational Command (COPCON), a special domestic military intervention force. Units led by MFA officers were integrated into the COPCON under the command of Otelo Saraiva de Carvalho, the military strategist of April 25, in effect circumventing the military chain of command. The COPCON often acted as a police force, intervening in civilian disputes. Though the MFA had originally agreed to shun individual publicity, Otelo (he was invariably referred to by his first name) was in the public eye more and more. When the MFA split among moderates, Communist sympathizers, and the far left the next year, he became the leading figure of the far leftists.

During the struggle with Spinola over decolonization the MFA had recognized that it needed to secure a civilian base of popular support. The popular upsurge in response to freedom after April 25 had galvanized the officers of the MFA. In the months since their takeover, the MFA had begun to develop an alliance with the left political parties, especially the PCP and the MDP. Strikes, *saneamentos,* and housing occupations frightened the conservative senior officers, but the MFA recognized that civilian mobilization offered a potential resource.

Still the new provisional government had to keep order, as well as to allay conservative fears. In his inaugural address on July 18, Prime Minister Gonçalves reiterated that the MFA program did not authorize radical changes; decisive measures would have to wait for an elected government. A strike law, intended to forestall another strike wave, was decreed on August 16. The law legalized strikes for the first time but set up a series of restrictions: bargaining procedures had to be exhausted before a strike could be called; factory occupations and strikes for political motives were prohibited; lockouts were permitted against illegal strikes. The PCP criticized the law weakly but announced it would abide by it, while the far-left parties criticized it roundly (Gonçalves 1976: 18; Neves 1978: 221–22). The prohibition against political strikes was hotly contested and soon became a dead letter when two strikes broke out to enforce *saneamentos.* One, in the daily *Jornal do Comércio,* stimulated a one-day sympathy strike by all of Lisbon's newspapers.

The other strike took place in the Lisnave shipyard, one of the largest and most modern workplaces in Portugal. The workers, who were young, skilled, well-paid, and highly politicized, rejected the moderation of the PCP. Far leftists, especially from the small Marxist-Leninist groups, were strong in the workers' *saneamento* committee and demanded ousters; management refused to comply. A heavily attended workers' assembly decided to hold a march through Lisbon to the Ministry of Labor on September 12 to demand *saneamento.* The PCP's Lisnave cell denounced the demonstration, while the government banned it and sent troops to several points along the march. Despite this opposition some 4,000 workers marched, over 60 percent of the shipyard's workforce. And instead of interfering, the troops held lively conversations with the men at the front of the march. This was the first occasion, but not the last, on which troops refused to follow orders to intervene against civilians (Neves 1978: 231–33; Patriarca 1978).

Another labor dispute simmered at the national airline, TAP. TAP was another traditional center of militancy, where in 1973 police had violently broken up a workers' assembly. But earlier struggles had also revealed differences among the workers: the mechanics were traditionally militant and ready to fight, while the very highly paid pilots often refused to go along. Immediately after April 25, workers demanded the *saneamento* of the TAP administration and rehiring of workers who had been fired the year before. The junta complied, announcing on May 7 that the management of TAP would be handed over to an administrative commission of a president, three members named by the junta, and three members named by the workers.

Workers next demanded salary increases, but the new administrative commission refused to grant them. In July the commission suspended contract negotiations, claiming that the company's deficit was too big to allow raises. It threatened massive layoffs and demanded productivity increases. The workers rejected the implication that they were to blame for the deficit, and demanded that the commission be dismissed. Deciding that it could not deal with the workers, the commission resigned on July 15, but the junta ordered it to remain and negotiate. Finally, at the end of August, workers went on strike. To keep the planes flying, the government placed the workers under military discipline and threatened any striker with immediate dismissal. The pilots withdrew from the strike, and the mechanics recognized defeat and called it off. But the problem remained, and TAP continued to be buffeted by brief strikes for several months.

In the anticolonial demonstrations, the mail and TAP strikes, the Lisnave demonstration, and the strike law itself, the new government had to face not only the divisions separating Spinola and his allies from the MFA but the contradictions of a government which tries to carry out reforms while seeking to maintain the confidence of its own capitalist class and the international capitalist system. Even a progressive government is obliged to maintain order. But maintaining order may require demobilizing the most enthusiastic supporters and undercut the government's program.

The March of the "Silent Majority"

During all these months, the right was silent against the revolutionary onslaught. Capitalists who resented worker unrest, hard-line defenders of the colonial empire, and ordinary people shocked at the apparent turmoil cowered at the rush of events—until September 28. They had suffered defeat after defeat since April both in the popular mobilizations and within the government. Spinola repeatedly spoke in public about his growing fear of chaos. In his July 27 speech acknowledging self-determination for the colonies, he had called on the country's so-called silent majority to defend its liberty, and he repeated the call on September 10 when he recognized the independence of Guinea-Bissau. This was the signal for which the right had been waiting. Calls went out for the "silent majority" to come to Lisbon to demonstrate its support of Spinola on September 28. A well-financed publicity campaign immediately produced posters appealing to the "silent majority" and sent leaflets to the conservative northern districts.

As the day approached, rumors spread that the demonstration would be the occasion for a rightwing countercoup. Leftwing parties, unions, and workers' commissions called on their members to mobilize against the threat. Soldiers and civilians mounted barricades the night before the demonstration, stopped cars on the roads leading into Lisbon, and inspected them for weapons. Thousands of people were in the streets and on the alert, in Lisbon and elsewhere that night and the next day. Their presence in the streets was a new factor which led the government to ban the demonstration.

Accusing Spinola of having given at least tacit support to a demonstration intended as the prelude to a coup, the MFA forced him and three other junta members out of office. As president they chose General Francisco Costa Gomes, chairman of the Joint Chiefs of Staff and one of the progressive junta members. Spinola's allies in the cabinet were also removed, and a new provisional government, the third, was announced. The three rightwing parties which had covertly organized the demonstration—the Party of Progress, the Liberal Party, and the Labor Party—were banned. The MFA won the showdown; though still without formal power, it was clearly in charge. Its defense against the coup attempt enhanced its popularity, while the old oligarchy, which had supported fascism and had apparently been involved in a countercoup, was thoroughly repudiated. In reaction to the threat from the right, the MFA was ready to move further left.

The trade unions, the workers' commissions, the larger left political parties (the PCP and the PS), and especially the MDP played major roles in the mobilization against the "silent majority." Many people who sympathized with no particular party also wanted to act against the threat from the right, and they joined the barricades under the direction of the PCP, the MDP, or the unions.

This civilian mobilization was the culmination of the political activity of the previous months. Organization had begun in factory, field, and neighborhood to raise specific grievances: demands for higher wages, better housing, and job security. But in every case, initial successes had opened the prospect of more, and the "more" increasingly meant not just quantitative increases in benefits but qualitative changes. The popular movement overwhelmed the MFA's intentions. It would not be content with representative democracy, but demanded political institutions based on the active participation of all citizens. It also proved its political power: it contributed directly to ousting the president, preserving the leftward course of the revolution, and ratifying the MFA's determination to mobilize progressive civilian allies. The popular movement would develop an increasingly articulate political program in the future and mobilize even more forcefully to demand that that program be implemented.

The MFA would determine the course of the revolution. But the popular movement greatly influenced the officers' political thinking, and they realized that by encouraging the movement they could strengthen themselves politically and implement their proposed changes. In the late fall of 1974 the MFA and civilian leftists saw a chance to make rapid strides toward socialism.

5

Laying the Groundwork

Addressing the nation after the cancellation of the September 28 "silent majority" demonstration, Prime Minister Gonçalves called for a symbolic show of national unity behind the MFA for the next weekend. Saturday, October 5, would be a holiday commemorating the founding of the First Republic. But the day after would be a day of work: Gonçalves called on the people to spend Sunday at their jobs, voluntarily, to bolster the economy. He addressed his call for sacrifice to the whole people: the revolution was not just for the working class or any particular group, he implied, and he asked everyone to work for the good of the nation as a whole.

That Sunday, many people did go to work. They were paid for the day; but unions encouraged their members to donate the extra pay to the national treasury or to charities. Theater and opera companies gave free performances in the evening. Brigades of children and teenagers patrolled the city with mops and scrub brushes, scraping five months' accumulation of grafitti and posters from walls and statues.

The September 28 events changed the balance of political forces in Portugal. The civilian left became stronger, its standing with the MFA and the public improved by the mobilization of thousands to the barricades to fight off the threat of reaction. The PCP showed by its all-out mobilization that it would not just offer its passive support to the new regime but would actively promote the progressives in the MFA. But the policies it called for were still limited. The PCP was not ready to place itself in the forefront, or even to define the situation as a revolution.

The right was further discredited. Many leading businessmen were arrested, accused of participating in a conspiracy to bring down the fledgling democracy. The removal from the junta of Spinola and his allies, who were closely identified with the monopoly groups, left the monopolists without a voice in the councils of power.

97

Above all, the showdown on September 28 confirmed the predominance of the MFA, even though it still lacked formal power. Its growing radicalization was also evident. In the battle over decolonization the Captains had begun to seek an alliance with the popular movement, and they spoke publicly of socialism. Nevertheless, their politics were still not well defined, and they repeated that they would take only short-term measures, install a pluralist democracy, and leave major decisions to the elected civilian government. The shift in the balance of forces after September 28 was important, therefore, not because those who now held power had a revolutionary program, but because the obstacles to developing one had been removed (see J.M. Pereira 1976: 210).

Workers' Commissions Organize

After September 28, workers awaited the MFA's next moves quietly and with relative confidence. They continued to see a unique opportunity in the new political climate, even though the MFA had not yet opted for a radical program. There was little political protest or labor strife during this period. But if appearances were calm, preparations were being made for the more spectacular advances which would follow the next year.

The workers' commissions which had led the strike wave of the previous May now worked to consolidate their power and expanded the range of their demands. Usually without further strikes or overt militancy, many commissions won significant concessions not only on bread-and-butter issues but on questions of authority and work routine.

Workers' actions are often classified as economic or political, the former raising "quantitative" demands for better wages, hours, and working conditions, and the latter raising "qualitative" demands which fundamentally challenge the authority of capital. Theorists of post-industrial society generally regard economic action and quantitative demands as appropriate to a "mature" system of industrial relations, in which labor does not fundamentally question its place in the system. Theorists of a new working class, on the other hand, argue that advanced capitalism stimulates political action and qualitative demands because it requires workers with high levels of intellectual and technical training, the kind of workers who demand autonomy and intrinsic satisfaction in the work process itself.

In some respects events in Portugal's workplaces in 1974 and 1975 appear to represent a progression from quantitative to qualitative demands. But the two cannot be separated; and neither workers nor capitalists perceived any real distinction. Capitalists regarded both economic demands and challenges to their authority as revolutionary, because both flouted prerogatives which they had taken for granted under the old regime. For the workers, moving from economic to political demands did not mean consciously moving on to a new kind of struggle. They saw it as a logical progression: early successes encouraged them to demand more, and if the first efforts failed, the new political situation encouraged them to respond with audacity rather than submission.

The inseparability of "quantitative" and a "qualitative" demands is illustrated by the salary question, normally a "quantitative" issue pure and simple. In a sense all the subsequent workers' commission activities derived from the initial struggles for higher wages. A commission member later recalled the beginning of the strike in his textile factory in May: "The next day [after the strike began] we presented a *caderno reivindicativo*, and it was no longer just a question of salaries. If the salary demands had been accepted at the beginning, the rest might have been different." But for other commissions, it is likely that the opposite was the case: capitulation, rather than resistance to their demands, spurred them to raise more grievances.

Throughout the summer and fall of 1974, workers and their commissions continued to demand improvements in conditions, to defend workers in disputes, and to exert pressure over matters on which workers had previously bowed to management authority. Some commissions demanded access to company books and other information about management activities. Gradually and imperceptibly, the demand for informal power and for limits to managerial prerogatives turned into a demand for formal power and the exercise of management itself. In an atmosphere where it was possible for the first time to protest or even discuss such issues, many conditions once taken for granted became matters for challenge.

At year's end a new issue of wage equality arose. Employers often paid a "thirteenth month" bonus equal to each worker's regular salary rather than an equal amount for all, or they singled out some workers for bonuses. A number of workers' commissions challenged this practice. The National Steel Company, for example, normally paid generous Christmas bonuses to its middle management, but not to its workers. At the urging of the commission, a general meeting of workers voted in December to demand that these bonuses be withheld. The veiled threat of disruption which accompanied their demand brought the intervention of the Ministry of Labor, and the would-be bonus recipients were pressured to agree to donate the bonuses to a company social fund.

As the informal powers of workers' commissions expanded, they were formally recognized in some factories. At Sorefame, the railroad car factory, the workers' commission and management established a joint disciplinary commission, with equal representation, to determine penalties, such as fines or suspensions, for violations of work rules. In some firms, workers chose their own supervisors: foremen (normally promoted from the ranks of workers in any case) were elected by members of a section.

Workers' commissions took different positions on the appropriateness of sharing power. The commission at the Cergal brewery, where workers chose their foremen, did not seek to name higher supervisors. "Our position," a commission member told me, "was that heads of departments and higher levels acted as an instrument of management and capital, and we said that the workers shouldn't elect the people who are going to be controlling and repressing them." But (in an exceptional case) workers' representatives at Mague, a maker of heavy equipment and one of the largest manufacturing firms in Portugal, attended directors' meetings, though they had no vote.

The right to choose managers, however, inevitably implied the right to dismiss them, and many workers' commissions demanded *saneamentos*. While some superiors were expelled from workplaces immediately after April 25, most expulsions took longer. In general, people were removed for one of two reasons: they had informed to the PIDE or had been unduly harsh as supervisors. In both cases, workers' commissions attempted to provide at least formal procedural guarantees, holding public hearings and giving the accused person the right of reply. They gathered evidence and deliberated the cases for months, often well into 1975.

An official Commission to Dissolve the PIDE was set up to go through the secret police's files and identify its informers and collaborators. Workers' commissions contacted the Commission to identify informers from their workplaces and used the information as the grounds for *saneamento*. In some workplaces people were removed for membership in other fascist organizations. In Lisnave, where the demand for *saneamento* was the major cause of the strike in September, the workers' commission also tried to bring charges against former members of the Portuguese Legion.

Supervisors, generally first-line foremen, who had been exceptionally abusive were also brought up for dismissal. In such cases, the workers' commission or a special *saneamento* committee gathered testimony from workers about the person's offenses and held a public hearing. Punishment was determined by a vote either of the commission or of a general assembly of workers. Some supervisors were fired outright; some lost their supervisory positions but kept working for the company; others were removed but were still paid.

The number of people actually dismissed without pay was small, rarely as many as ten in a firm, even in the larger firms where formal processes of investigation and *saneamento* were most common. The process was important less for the removal of undesirable personnel than as a symbol of the workers' strength in their struggle against management. The demand to oust managers, after all, clearly transgressed the customary boundary between legitimate grievance and management prerogative.

Saneamento was just the last straw for capitalists. Even those who were not thrown out found themselves deprived of their power in every imaginable way. They were used to the speculative investment boom of the 1960s and to a cheap, docile labor force. The boom had permitted many capitalists to profit from irregular dealings: under- and overinvoicing of imports and exports, private purchases with company funds, real estate held for speculation. Now all that was threatened. The PIDE, which had guaranteed the docility of the labor force, had been disbanded, and authoritarian middle managers had been expelled or were cowed by worker militancy. Some of the shadier financial practices were endangered by workers' commissions' demands to see company books.

The economic prospects for capitalists, moreover, were bleak. The worldwide economic crisis spurred by the oil price hike of 1973 was compounded in Portugal by political uncertainty and worker militancy. The power of capital was being attacked rhetorically—and some capitalists were imprisoned, accused of conspiring against the new regime. Many responded by curtailing investments, which only exacerbated the incipient economic crisis. Some refused to pay newly won wage settlements and threatened massive layoffs or even plant closings, especially in the smaller firms, where forced wage increases hurt owners most. Most of these firms, moreover, were owned and managed by a single individual, a few partners, or a family accustomed to paternalistic relations with workers. They were also small enough to be readily converted into liquid assets.

With unemployment already increasing, the MFA recognized the need to maintain business confidence and prevent a capital strike. It gave repeated assurances that it would not adopt economic policies threatening capitalists' interests. But a law promulgated in November could only heighten their insecurities: it prohibited ''economic sabotage'' and gave the government the power to intervene—in effect, to take over management, though not ownership—in firms which were withdrawing capital or not using it productively.

The law was clearly intended to shore up the economy, not to transform it. In fact, it was adopted to stave off the imminent failure of the Portuguese Intercontinental Bank; though chartered as a commercial bank, its risky investments had made the bank a flagrant example of the high-flying speculation of the boom years (U.S. Department of Commerce 1975: 6). Yet it is symptomatic of the tenor of the times that the government chose to combat the economic crisis not by providing loans, guarantees, or other forms of support to owners but rather by implicitly accusing them of sabotage and taking control of the firms.

The workers' commissions also reflected the temper of the times: instead of offering concessions to help management resolve financial difficulties, they demanded concessions themselves. Alert to mismanagement and suspicious of fraud by their managers and owners, the commissions began to practice what they called "vigilance against economic sabotage." Workers, especially those in strategic positions such as accounting departments, kept track of shipments of orders and other movements of goods, and took note of sales of assets, declining levels of stocks, and any other sign that the owner might be preparing to close the business down.

If an owner complained of low profit levels and planned to lay workers off, the commission demanded that the company open its books. If the commission thought that a closing or layoffs were unjustified, it demanded that the company reinvest profits to save jobs. Sometimes workers occupied the factory to force the owner to continue to operate, and took over the operation if the owner refused. Workers in several firms claimed that a revealing document was found in the garbage just in time for them to prevent owners from decapitalizing or closing down the plant; or, if it was too late, then the document justified occupying. While this story was told commonly enough to be regarded as a sort of Moses myth, it illustrates the workers' moral condemnation of capitalists, who were seen not as victims of an economic crisis but as its deliberate and conspiratorial perpetrators.

There were other cases where, without threatening layoffs or closing, an owner nevertheless resisted granting a commission any power, or even consulting with it. Such recalcitrance of course only heightened the workers' insistence. In some firms hostility between owners and workers became so great that the owners could no longer run the plant—or they simply gave up in frustration. This happened infrequently in 1974, but in 1975 owners abandoned far more frequently.

Faced with owner abandonment and the unemployment of a firm's entire workforce, the commissions took over management completely—the only way to keep the factory open. Workers' commissions often clothed their actions of vigilance and even takeover with a patriotic rhetoric, claiming that they were defending the national economy, and hence the revolution, against sabotage. But their members' jobs were far more important to them than the health of the economy, although the two were closely linked. The cases of Sogantal and Applied Magnetics, the two factories taken over in the summer of 1974 by their women workers, were important as models of worker control which other workers might imitate, but they were also harbingers of the danger that other firms, too, might close down and cast their workers into unemployment.

The commissions not only made demands; they also organized activities for the workers. Commissions published newsletters and sponsored literacy classes and political discussion groups. Along with the neighborhood commissions, they also became active outside their immediate bailiwicks. The commissions which had well-defined political sympathies mobilized their members to take part in demonstrations, such as the rallies in support of the Intersindical in the trade union dispute and the far left's march in opposition to NATO, both discussed below.

Workers did not win every battle, nor did everything run smoothly. They did not always win their wage demands or prevent layoffs. There were also divisions within the workers' commissions themselves, divisions which were reflected in what was often a long process of adopting a formal constitution and in battles for election to the commission. Many battles for control of commissions were fought among workers of different party sympathies or of different job and status levels within the firm. Different forms of election had political consequences. Sometimes an entire slate was elected on a factory-wide basis, producing a united commission but often leaving minorities, such as white-collar workers, unrepresented. Sometimes each work section elected its own representative; this procedure often produced a commission which included members of conflicting political tendencies who proved unable to work together.

Workers' commissions were not all alike; commission activity varied in different kinds of firms, and also depended on the political sympathies of activists. In the small, poorly capitalized, and technologically backward plants—most of them on the north coast, but many also in the Lisbon area—workers' commissions were most likely to act only when economic necessity or owner recalcitrance made shutdown likely.

The most militant commissions arose in the large new plants, most of them in heavy industry and almost all in the Lisbon-Setubal area, with large numbers of younger male workers who were veterans of the colonial war. Workers in these plants were especially likely to be attracted by the militancy of the far-left parties. Their commissions pursued *saneamentos* and wage equalization most vigorously. They were very likely to become involved in political organization outside the plant. These commissions often rejected formal power within the firm, not wishing to compromise themselves by shouldering capitalists' responsibilities.

The PCP was initially most powerful in large but older factories, also in Lisbon's industrial suburbs, where its organization went back many years. There, the commissions, like the Communist-dominated trade unions, were more concerned with consolidating their own power and creating a well-structured organization than with confrontation. Far more than the commissions led by far leftists, they worked to secure formal management recognition of their right to share in decisionmaking. In 1975, as we shall see, PCP-dominated workers' commissions led the struggles for nationalization, and where it occurred the commissions played an active role in carrying it out.

The difference between commissions dominated by the PCP and the far left is clearly illustrated at Lisnave, where the older and smaller docks on the Lisbon side of the river were predominantly Communist, while the newer, larger docks on the south bank, with a much younger labor force, were the breeding ground of much far-left activity. Workers on the south bank organized the September 12 demonstration described in the last chapter and carried it out despite official prohibition, while workers on the Lisbon side voted not to support it.

Despite political divisions, the first year of the Portuguese revolution was a very exciting time for workers, who were constantly discovering new resources within themselves and new powers over the employers who had dominated them for so long. Many workers became active, even those who were not elected to the commissions: one commission member said of the workers in his factory, "everything they did, they did with enthusiasm and dedication. They picked up on the smallest detail as if it were very important. And they didn't let anything escape." Commission members themselves were busy all day, every day, constantly confronting new problems. One explained it to me this way: "In a short time we lived centuries and centuries full of everything; people's lives changed completely. We would be at the factory, then the workers' commission, then the general assembly of all the workers. At night we would go on to the popular assembly, which was the organization of all the workers' and neighborhood commissions of the area. It was a time of tremendous excitement. We traded a situation of anonymity, a dull everyday life, for one that was completely open and tremendously effervescent."

An amazingly rapid escalation of political consciousness was occurring.

New possibilities for action appeared almost daily, and initiatives often succeeded. Opportunities seized had a cumulative effect, for each new experiment or demand by one group of workers, whether for recognition of a workers' commission, for shorter hours, to see the company's books, to alter investment policies, or to take over the factory, became an example to workers elsewhere: either to be imitated directly, or to spur them on to even more audacious creativity. They did not consciously move from economism to revolution, but their partial efforts raised their consciousness and prepared them for the revolutionary struggle which was soon to come.

The Far Left and the Popular Power Movement

Popular mobilization escalated not only in workplaces but in neighborhoods, schools, and barracks. With an increasingly radical anticapitalist rhetoric, workers called for a clearer definition of the revolution and began urging the state to take over private firms to solve the unemployment problem. These demands were asserted in frequent demonstrations. The commissions, especially the workers' commissions, were at the center of the heterogeneous forces which were by now known as the popular power movement.

The movement remained outside of Communist control. The PCP was initially suspicious of the movement's spontaneous collective action, and its demands far exceeded the limits the PCP attempted to impose on popular militancy. The popular power movement was not controlled by any other party either, although several parties on the far left identified with it. The far-left parties called for immediate revolution. They rejected bourgeois democracy and did not share the center parties' faith in elections; but they also explicitly rejected the tactical moderation of the Communist Party, which called for supporting the MFA and consolidating the democratic process.

For the far left, the popular power movement was the expression of its own ideology and vision. The movement seemed to represent the class consciousness which, the far left was certain, was latent in the hearts of all members of the working and exploited classes. Its militancy demonstrated empirically what the far-left parties theorized: the triumph of the working class over capitalist domination at the point of production—and the movement's victories seemed to prove that it would soon be possible to take the next step and overthrow capitalist control of the state.

All the far-left parties were very small. While most of them had roots in organizations that had arisen under fascism, they all recruited new militants from activists who promoted struggles which the PCP failed to support. These parties had two main orientations, one Maoist and one favoring popular power. A number of small Maoist groups founded three competing electoral fronts to contest the 1975 elections (the most important was the Popular Democratic Union [UDP], founded in December 1974) and late in 1975 they converged in the Portuguese Communist Party (Reconstructed) (PCP[R]), the ''true'' Communist party. Adamantly opposed to the moderate line of the PCP, these organizations argued that the revolution would be made through a vanguard organized as a Leninist party. Given their avowed Leninism, they did not see the popular movement as a fundamentally important new form of organization, but rather as an expression of the class consciousness of the workers who, once awakened to the revisionism of the PCP, would join the true communists to make a revolution.

The popular power orientation included the MES, the PRP, and some smaller parties, though there were nuances of differences among them. They argued that the experiences of popular power in workplaces, neighborhoods, and latifundios would be the basis for a transition to a new socialist society, one which would be governed not by a representative system but by a direct democracy in which all could participate directly in making the decisions by which they were governed (F.P. Marques 1977: 143–58; Vieira and Oliveira 1976: 19–33).

Of these parties, the MES exercised important ideological leadership, even though it vacillated, at times advocating tactical collaboration with the Communist Party. At its first congress in December 1974, a division arose between the party's founders, who advocated continuing to concentrate on building base organizations, and a competing tendency which argued that the most important task of the left was to work with the PCP to prevent the resurgence of fascism. The second line won at the congress, and some of the founders left the party. But within a few months the MES had drawn away from the PCP and returned to its advocacy of popular power.

The PRP became especially influential within the far left of the MFA. It alternated between popular power and insurrectionalism, calling on the popular organizations to arm themselves to fight the coming reactionary onslaught, and apparently believing that such an insurrection was in fact a viable option in which the popular movement had some chance of victory.

On some issues, the far left was united, and though it remained dispersed in small parties, it developed a surprising capacity to mobilize. On February 7, 1975, far-left workers' commissions called a demonstration to oppose layoffs and the presence in Lisbon harbor of NATO ships preparing for maneuvers. Even though it was prohibited and the PCP vigorously opposed it, the demonstration attracted 50,000 people. Troops from the First Light Artillery Regiment, known as the "Red Regiment," assigned to protect the Ministry of Labor, openly disobeyed orders and raised their fists to show their solidarity with the demonstrators.

The entire far left rejected the PCP's centralist model of society. When the PCP began to call for nationalization of major industries early in 1975, far leftists were articulating demands for local control and self-management to prevent what they saw as the danger of bureaucratic state capitalism inherent in the PCP's proposals. The far left also tried to unite the base organizations which supported it. The February 7 demonstration was called by the Interempresas, a new body which made the first attempt to coordinate workers' commissions in the Lisbon area. Most of the participating commissions were influenced by the Marxism-Leninism of the UDP and the parties that later converged in the PCP(R)—or, without a clear ideological line, gravitated toward the same position, which seemed to offer the best alternative to the PCP. But despite the demonstration's signal success, the Interempresas did not survive, because most militants' activity was dissipated in the organization of the competing far-left parties.

None of the competing parties achieved hegemony within the far left, and many activists identified with popular power as a tendency rather than with any party. Nuances of doctrine and twists of strategy prevented the parties from uniting. The emphasis of some of them on the spontaneous activity of base organizations precluded attempts to control those organizations or use them as a recruiting ground for party membership. The differences among the parties, moreover, were less important to some activists than their common differences from the PCP.

Three more small Maoist organizations—the MRPP, the Portuguese Communist Party (Marxist-Leninist) (PCP[ML]), and the Worker-Peasant Alliance (AOC, not an independent party but a creature of the PCP[ML])—also claimed a place on the far left. The MRPP, founded in 1970, cultivated the most militant image. It organized some of the first housing occupations in April and May 1974 and sponsored many rallies to demand an immediate end to the colonial war. The group did not hesitate to criticize the MFA, arguing that the delay in negotiating with the liberation movements proved that the MFA hoped to continue to dominate the colonies. In the fall and winter it began an aggressive campaign against the CDS, which it claimed was working to restore fascism, and disrupted CDS meetings with militant demonstrations. These Maoist groups eventually rejected the revolution. They were so hostile to the PCP—arguing that its "social fascism" (the

MRPP's term) was the main obstacle to revolution—that they ultimately identified with the right.

Policy Debates in the MFA

Initially, the MFA's political objectives were limited to the restoration of democratic freedoms and the election of a Constituent Assembly. Its vague economic proposals, coupled with its self-imposed limits, meant that the MFA hoped only to hold the economy together with short-term measures. Even the Economic Sabotage Law, which would later be used to justify state intervention in many firms, had been adopted only to forestall a major bankruptcy.

Then, barely six months after the coup, many in the MFA wanted to embark on a transition to socialism. It had become clear that the MFA did have the power to undertake more than short-term economic measures. The bourgeoisie had lost some decisive battles (especially after the abortive demonstration on September 28) and had shown that it was disoriented and unable to fight back. The working class had demonstrated in massive mobilizations that it was strong and favored a more radical course. As the popular movement grew in strength and consciousness, leftists in the MFA began to rely on it to guarantee their own ability to move toward socialism. The movement was thus both a stimulus and a resource for these progressive officers. The process was dialectical, as popular mobilization exerted political pressure on leftist military leaders and affected their consciousness at the same time that their growing influence encouraged the popular movement.

But once the MFA had defeated Spinola and consolidated its own power, differences within it came to the fore. A moderate faction emerged, led by Melo Antunes, who had written the MFA program. Melo Antunes, whom Spinola had wrongly judged to be the MFA's most dangerous radical, thought that the changes already made should be consolidated in a fashion that would preserve the support of the whole population. He also opposed too close an identification with the PCP.

The MFA still lacked any formal power, but the battle over economic policy was nevertheless fought out in the MFA Assembly (formally the MFA Delegates' Assembly), with 200 members from the various branches of the armed forces. The assembly assigned Melo Antunes to write a comprehensive economic plan; initially promised for December, it was delayed from week to week while the debate raged on. Lacking economic expertise, the officers debated the issue as one of relations between classes: Melo Antunes argued that moving too fast would destroy the confidence of the middle classes, which had to be preserved if the revolution was to succeed. Prime Minister Gonçalves, speaking for the progressive wing, argued that the revolution depended on the workers, and that their support would be maintained only with a more vigorous anticapitalist policy (R. Correia et al. n.d. [a]: 72–105; A. Rodrigues et al. 1976: 132–36).

Specifically, Melo Antunes thought that the state should take over only 51 percent ownership of the banks and not expropriate all large farmlands immediately. The progressives demanded outright nationalization of the banks and an immediate agrarian reform. This division should not be exaggerated, for the MFA as a whole had moved quite a long way. Progressives and moderates alike had decided that the state should assert significant control over the country's economic resources; their disagreement was over tactics, and over the pace of change.

But they were also divided over the role of the MFA itself: moderates thought that the military should have only minimal powers and be subordinate to the democratic electoral system, while progressives wanted to "institutionalize" the MFA, ensuring that it would exercise a permanent hegemonic role and have constitutionally recognized powers of decision. MFA leaders who had promised an early return to the barracks now equivocated, believing that they should use the MFA's power to determine the country's political course.

Many in the progressive faction pointed to the Peruvian military government under Velasco Alvarado as a model. Various possibilities were proposed: that the MFA should run as a party in the coming election, that it should claim a share of the seats in the Constituent Assembly for itself, and that it should have the power to veto legislation. The question had clear implications for the nature of the entire future political system, for institutionalization would severely limit the power of any elected legislature.

The split between the factions was accentuated by other issues, among them trade union organization. A law was proposed to enforce trade union unity by recognizing the Intersindical as the national trade union federation and prohibiting the formation of competing federations. The law would prevent domestic- or foreign-sponsored divisionist intervention, ensuring the unity of the labor movement in support of the revolution. But it would also clearly cement PCP leadership of labor. Not surprisingly, the PCP vigorously supported the law. The PS and the parties to its right, which themselves hoped to win some influence in organized labor, called for "trade-union pluralism," believing that they could best challenge Communist domination of the trade unions by forming competing unions and a competing federation. MFA moderates supported their position.

The future structure of trade unions was not an abstract issue, but involved a direct contest for power, one for which each side was prepared to fight. Both sides worked hard to mobilize popular support, calling big public demonstrations in January, in order to pressure the MFA to support their positions. Unions which supported the Intersindical passed resolutions approving the proposed law in well-attended membership meetings. The MFA ultimately came out for unity, reflecting the growing influence of the PCP within its ranks. But the mutual provocations among the political parties had taken their toll. Tensions between the PCP and its coalition partners had been evident from the beginning, but they had never been so high as in the trade-union dispute. The PS threatened to abandon the coalition over the issue. For the first time it openly accused the PCP of being antidemocratic and the MFA of being too Communist-influenced.

The moderates within the MFA won some victories too, however: on the same day that approval of the trade union law was announced, the Constituent Assembly election was set for April 12, despite some Communists' calls for an indefinite postponement. And in February the MFA approved Melo Antunes' moderate economic plan.

The Communist Campaign for Nationalization

The Intersindical's attempts to contain worker militancy during and after the May strike wave reflected the PCP's consistent effort to project an image of moderation and responsibility. It hoped to persuade the MFA and the public that it was committed to democratization and would not demand a radical economic program. That position was ratified at the party's extraordinary one-day congress on October 20, the first congress of any party. The congress reaffirmed the party program's call for agrarian reform and nationalization of basic industries, but it explicitly rejected them for the immediate future, calling nationalizations "unrealistic" (Cunhal 1976: 119; Schmitter 1975b: 386).

The congress was brief and its decisions unanimous; as in all the PCP's activities, the agenda was carefully controlled. One decision was to remove any reference to the "dictatorship of the proletariat" from the party program. Denying that it was revising its ideology, the party said that it was making the change because the word "dictatorship" meant something different to a people who had suffered fifty years of fascism than it had meant to Marx.[1]

Several factors contributed to this consistent moderation. Nearly all the party's leaders had been in exile for years, and even on returning, some argued, they were out of touch with the ferment in the country. They also exhibited a characteristic suspicion of initiatives which arose from the base, escaped from the party's control, and threatened to get in the way of its own plans. They maintained that suspicion even during the party's later radicalization. Moreover, the party wanted to demonstrate its reliability to the MFA, the real powerholders, and take advantage of its close relation with them to build its own institutional strength. Finally, it was well aware that all of NATO was watching its ascendancy with fear.

Nor was the PCP's moderation purely tactical. It was consistent with the analysis the party had made for the last decade: socialism was premature in Portugal, which was at a stage requiring a democratic and national revolution. Moreover, the PCP was genuinely afraid of a resurgent fascism, and feared that the petty bourgeoisie and the peasants, vital allies in support of democracy, would be alienated if socializing measures were undertaken too soon.

But by the winter of 1975 the PCP, like the MFA, recognized that it had underestimated its opportunities and decided to push for immediate moves toward socialism. This change of line had several causes. Most important was the emergence of the progressive wing of the MFA. The MFA eventually adopted the moderate economic program, but only after a debate that made clear that many officers wanted to move faster.

There were also signs that the party was losing support, and it was expected to do badly in the coming election. The Communists were even losing some ground in the unions: in December and January its slates lost elections to predominantly PS slates in several white-collar unions, including some of the largest in the country. Losses among white-collar workers were not so surprising. But the strike wave and the radicalization of workers' commissions in industry showed that many of its most active factory militants were rejecting the PCP line. Many others, swept up in the workplace and neighborhood movements, took part in activities condemned by the party line, even though they still belonged to the party or sympathized with it. The anti-NATO demonstration of February 7 seemed to show how much initiative the party was losing to the far left (even though just two weeks before, the demonstration in favor of trade union unity had been one of the largest yet).

The PCP recognized that its greatest strengths lay in its ability to mobilize and in its alliance with the progressives in the MFA. Taking a more radical position might restore the support of the most militant workers, thus compensating for its weakness in the population as a whole, and at the same time reinforce its support where it counted most, in the military.

As 1974 ended, therefore, the PCP began a campaign to demand wholesale nationalization of banks, sectors of basic industry, and the huge monopoly groups. Nationalization was the logical outcome of the PCP's analysis of the nature of Portuguese capitalism, enunciated a decade before. In 1964 Alvaro Cunhal, party leader, had published the book *Rumo à Vitória (Road to Victory)*, the theoretical statement which provided the party's strategic guidelines. In it he called for a struggle against the monopolies, which he considered an essential part of the democratic and national revolution.

Cunhal argued that monopolization hurt not only workers but small and medium capitalists as well, making them natural potential allies in the struggle to end fascism. At the same time, capital was so concentrated in the monopolies that its power might be destroyed with a few rapid blows. Monopolization therefore created objective conditions making the economy ripe for takeover by the state in the interest of the working class and of the (putative) antimonopoly bloc as a whole (1979: 31–43).

The idea that monopoly capital brought a new stage of capitalism was not original (indeed, the theory was far more highly developed in other European Communist parties than it was in the PCP). But in Portugal, the concentration of capital in the hands of seven highly visible monopoly groups made the analysis seem especially relevant. The monopoly groups were not only an obvious focus for criticism of the capitalist system in general; they had also been integrally linked to the fascist regime, so it seemed natural that the complete destruction of fascism required breaking their power.

Signs of the PCP's new line first emerged in December 1974, when Cunhal and other party leaders began speaking more frequently about the need for nationalization. With the new year, the calls for nationalization became a major theme of Communist rallies. Although their slogan was "nationalization under worker control," the PCP and its military allies envisioned state takeover. The tone of the campaign was illustrated by Central Committee member José Magro in a speech to bank workers: he said that the political conditions for nationalization of the banks were not yet present, but that mass pressure might create them.

Mass pressure did indeed follow the party's lead—and its direction. The campaign was carried out by ostensibly nonpartisan working-class organizations: beginning in January, many workers' commissions passed resolutions calling for nationalization of their firms and formed study committees to make concrete proposals. Industry-wide commissions met to discuss the ways in which the separate firms could be integrated into a single entity. In January, assemblies of bank and insurance workers called for nationalization of their respective sectors. In February, a PCP-led Unitary National Workers' Conference called for the nationalization of the steel industry, and representatives at the conference called for nationalization of their own sectors (Lima et al. 1977: 879, 892–93).

In February, the contents of the Melo Antunes plan became known, revealing that some industries were not candidates for nationalization. Workers' commissions in some of those firms stepped up the struggle; many workers occupied their factories to back up their demands for nationalization. Occupations (illegal under the strike law passed the previous August) were not strikes: workers continued to produce, but in some cases blockaded the doors to keep management out. A major struggle occurred in the Sociedade Central de Cervejas brewery, where workers not only refused to let managers in but took over the company's books and claimed to find evidence of economic sabotage.

The PCP also began to recognize the strategic importance of the workers' commissions. Unions were traditionally more concerned with bread-and-butter issues, but the commissions sought a share of power in the firms. Furthermore, the horizontal structure of the unions made them less effective for workplace-based mobilization than the commissions. The PCP succeeded in recapturing the commissions from the far left in the most important industrial plants (and many of the smaller ones as well). Its success was due partly to its strong latent support among industrial workers, and partly because many of the early commission leaders, having joined one or another far-left party, became less active in the commissions. But most important was the party's new militancy. It supported many workplace struggles, including some it would have discouraged the year before. The nationalization campaign also won back many workers who had been impatient with the party's moderation. Even in some plants where the far left had struck its deepest roots, such as Lisnave, the PCP gained control.

The PCP's reversal of its prior moderation did not imply changing its attitude toward spontaneous militancy, however. Its theory gave the PCP a complete blueprint for socialist revolution; in which nationalization of the economy played a key role. Base militancy, in contrast, was superfluous, because the economy would be run in the interest of the working class. The party still did not recognize the creative power of worker initiative, even though it had been amply demonstrated in the preceding months.

Moving Toward Elections

While the far left attempted to mobilize the base and the Communists urged those in power to begin the transition to socialism, the more moderate parties concentrated on the coming elections, which they saw as their most promising opportunity. At different times, both rightists and leftists attempted to suspend or postpone the elections, but the MFA insisted on their realization as a "point of honor." Of the dozens of political parties which had formed immediately after the April 25 coup, only three, besides the Communists, actually won many voters: the Socialists (PS) and the Popular Democrats (PPD), both members of the coalition government, and the CDS.

The Socialist Party, created in exile, relied on the coming elections to build a base in Portugal. It was said that the MFA's use of the word *socialism* to identify its goal gave the Socialist Party an advantage. But as a matter of principle the party was ideologically heterogeneous, proud of the internal pluralism which offered a home to a variety of positions. It included old republicans and many supporters of democracy whose politics were otherwise undefined, as well as those who supported a socialism built from the base and opposed the party's alignment with the social-democratic parties of the Socialist International.

At its congress in December, moreover, the PS ratified a program which, on paper, was the most radical of any party. It called for agrarian reform and nationalization of credit and many basic industries; unlike the PCP's program, it did not suggest that those measures might have to wait. But in the election to the national committee, a leftist slate (which did not challenge Soares' leadership) lost to the moderate slate supported by Soares. The leftists' leader, Manuel Serra, soon abandoned the party to form the schismatic Popular Socialist Front (FSP).

The Popular Democratic Party claimed to be social-democratic, but did not define its position more clearly. Although it was clearly to the right of the PS, it nominally supported the government's policies until it resigned from the governing coalition in July 1975.

The CDS, like the PPD, was founded immediately after April 25. Its leaders were careful to avoid involvement in conspiratorial activities against the new government, but their ties to the old regime made many far leftists attack the party, claiming that its program amounted to a restoration of fascism. Its meetings were often disrupted, most spectacularly when militants of the Maoist MRPP besieged its congress in Oporto in February, forcing distinguished foreign visitors to be evacuated by helicopter. The CDS joined the European Christian Democratic Union shortly after its founding, and intended to run in the 1975 election in coalition with the Christian Democratic Party.

The MDP was a reliable ally of the PCP as its predecessor the CDE had been in the past. After the PS and the PPD dropped their nominal adherence to the MDP, accusing Communists and Communist allies of dominating it, it declared itself a party and prepared to run candidates for the Constituent Assembly.

The Beginning of Land Reform

The contracts that the new farmworkers' unions in the Alentejo had won in the summer of 1974 had expired at the end of the harvest in August. The farmworkers and their unions, seeking guarantees of employment for the new growing season, demanded that landowners agree in the new contract to hire enough workers to cultivate their lands fully.

The farmworkers, who were dependent on the latifundios, much of whose land lay idle, had long suffered from chronic unemployment. If all the land were farmed, they believed, there would be work for everyone. If not, unemployment threatened to be worse than usual in 1975, as many landowners, fearing that the new regime would expropriate them, did not plan to sow for the 1975 harvest. Moreover, with unemployment rising in the cities, many urban workers—especially construction workers—returned to seek work in the villages from which they had migrated only recently.

Negotiations for a new contract began in September, but despite pressure from the Ministry of Labor in support of the farmworkers, the growers refused to negotiate seriously. The defeat of the ''silent majority'' demonstration, however, changed the political climate. At least some landowners recognized that they now had little choice but to accede to the workers' demands. At the end of October the landowners' association of the district of Beja signed a contract with the district union. It not only offered a small raise over the previous contract but set up a commission in each *concelho* to evaluate the productive potential of uncultivated lands and establish quotas of farmworkers to be hired to work them. By the end of the year the Ministry of Labor imposed the same conditions on the landowners of the districts of Evora and Portalegre. The unions played a direct role in hiring, a role previously unknown among Portuguese unions. Some accused the unions, closely tied to the Communist Party, of using their power to provide jobs to favor the party's supporters.

The unions' assertion of the right to impose hiring quotas was unheard-of in Portugal, especially in a sector where unions had not even existed six months before. It deprived the landowners of what they regarded as a basic property right. As Barros points out (1979: 60–61), the latifundio system depended on seasonal unemployment because it required a large available workforce willing to work during the peak growing season but unable to demand wages at other times. The end of seasonal labor would make the latifundio unviable.

Some landowners disregarded the contract and refused to hire the workers allocated to them by the commissions (Bermeo 1986: 49–50). Landowners, like urban capitalists, were accused of sabotage. It was alleged that they were not only refusing to farm but were selling off their livestock and machinery, and in November the government decreed a law making it compulsory for owners to rent unfarmed lands.

Farmworkers used a more direct tactic against some of those who refused: workers occupied and farmed the lands themselves. A few occupations occurred at the end of 1974, and more in the winter of 1975. The occupiers claimed the slender legal cover of the two decrees of the previous November, the Economic Sabotage Law and the compulsory renting law. Since they generally had little or no cash and could barely afford to sow, they had a very difficult time at the beginning. Some of them undoubtedly assumed that once they began working the land, the owners would accept their presence and pay their wages. When they did not, workers often went without wages until the harvest.

The occupations were led by *seareiros* (tenant farmers) or tractor owners, small farmers who had managed to amass enough capital to buy a tractor and rent their services to other farmers. *Seareiros* and tractor owners, unlike farmworkers, were in effect small businessmen. Tenant farmers stood to lose their capital entirely if they were unable to rent the land for this year, as did tractor owners if others' failure to sow deprived them of work.

Occupations were thus not inspired by the principle that the land should belong to those who work it but simply by the desire for work; the cooperative movement which developed in 1975 was largely an after-effect. Nor, at this stage, did they have the encouragement of the unions or of the major political parties, even of the PCP, which in October had explicitly rejected agrarian reform for the immediate future. Nevertheless, the occupations grew naturally out of the unions' previous gains. The hiring commissions were not consciously intended as a challenge to the owners' right to property but merely to guarantee jobs to workers; a landowner who refused to accept the judgment of a hiring commission was violating the contract, and occupying was merely a further form of pressure.

But the occupations that occurred influenced the farmworkers' unions. In the winter of 1975, as popular demands for an acceleration of the revolutionary process welled up in urban areas, the rural unions began to demand agrarian reform. After a series of rallies and small meetings sponsored by the district unions, a conference of southern farmworkers met on February 9 to demand "an agrarian reform which will liquidate the latifundios and give the land to those who work it" (Baptista 1978: 12; A. Rodrigues et al. 1976: 186–87). Cunhal's speeches opening and closing the conference made clear that the PCP had changed its policy and now was pushing for radicalization of the revolution in the countryside as well.

While the conference was widely seen as demanding immediate land reform, however, its language was still somewhat cautious. Since farmworkers were more interested in employment than in structural change, the resolutions included demands for interim measures to prevent undercultivation, including continued placement of workers and compulsory rental of unfarmed lands (O PCP 1975: 149–56). And the demand for land reform did not produce a wider occupation movement.

The Contradictions of the Revolution

The nature of the Portuguese revolution remained ambiguous throughout the winter of 1975. On the one hand, the MFA attempted to assure the moderate political parties of its commitment to pluralism. But it could hardly impose a transition to socialism while respecting the sovereignty of a future parliament. The MFA undertook what it described as "negotiations" for a political pact with the parties which intended to run for the Constituent Assembly, insisting that they endorse major provisions of the new constitution in advance (with the unstated threat that any party not agreeing to the conditions would not be allowed to run).

But the negotiations were less between the MFA and the parties than between the progressive and moderate factions in the MFA. While they agreed on greater government control of the economy and on some form of institutionalization of the MFA, they disagreed on the form each was to take, and correspondingly on what restrictions to place on the Constituent Assembly. At the beginning of March, the two wings agreed to impose only very vague conditions: that the parties endorse the principle of socialism and a "progressive" interpretation of the Melo Antunes plan—which was not so difficult since the most progressive proposals had been ruled out of it. The armed forces would be constitutionally independent of the parliament and the government it named, subject to the direct and sole jurisdiction of the president (who, it was widely assumed, would be a senior officer).

The MFA also wanted to democratize the armed forces themselves, calling elections for branch councils in the army, navy, and air force. Again, however, there was a contradiction between democracy and its substantive goals, for while the MFA liked to think of itself as embracing the entire armed forces, it did not. Many officers who accepted the coup at first were disaffected as the MFA moved left; others, even among those of the same age and experience of colonial war as the Captains, remained sympathetic to the values that they had been trained to serve.

When elections to the branch councils in the army were held in the first week of March, these conservative officers defeated some of the leading MFA men. The Artillery, the Cavalry, and the Commandos, it turned out, were centers of conservatism; the Artillery failed to elect either Otelo or Melo Antunes. The conservatives saw Spinola as their most likely leader. The deposed president, who had remained in eclipse since his ouster, reappeared in the winter. He met with his allies. He gave a speech at a military college reunion. Evidently he still enjoyed the support of many officers. Rumors spread that they were planning a coup. The branch elections, the negotiations with the parties, and the reemergence of Spinola created an atmosphere of high tension during the first days of March.

Just as the MFA did not represent the whole of the armed forces, neither did the popular movement represent the whole population. Capitalists were threatened both by workers' usurpation of their economic power and by political disruptions which aimed to destroy the conservative parties. Many who did not share the economic interests which the conservative parties represented nevertheless opposed the attacks on them and believed that pluralist democracy required tolerance of all political forces. Finally, whole sections of the country had not been touched by the revolution at all. There, the new programs presented the specter of communism, a reaction exacerbated by the provocations of some far-left parties, for which the PCP was often blamed.

The popular movement faced a contradiction: many of those to whom it hoped to appeal opposed the revolution's leftward course. Advocates of popular power were persuaded that many of these people stood to gain from the revolution; they would have to be won over to recognize the benefits the revolution offered if capitalist opponents were to be neutralized. Disdaining the procedural restrictions of bourgeois democracy, the popular movement believed that the way to incorporate the potential supporters was continued mobilization. But if heightened mobilization might bring more participants into the revolutionary process, it could also create hostility and unite those who opposed the revolution out of class interest, commitment to pluralism, or anticommunism. Noisy demands for nationalizations and the attacks on the conservative parties added to the mounting tension at the end of the winter.

Supporters of the movement did not believe that they were destroying capitalism—at least not yet. They still acted on capitalist assumptions. Farmworkers assumed that property would remain property; they were only struggling for employment. Even the Agricultural Workers' Conference apparently did not envision immediate agrarian reform (though landowners feared it did). Nor did workers' commissions challenge the right of property in itself, demanding only that capitalists contribute to the national welfare— if they did not, the workers would do it for them.

These workers were addressing immediate and pressing problems. Even as the movement acted with more daring and usurped more of the rights of ownership, activists viewed each new step merely as a logical outgrowth of the preceding steps. If socialism came, they assumed, it would come from state action, through an electoral process—or at least one sanctioned by legitimate authority. They did not yet envision building socialism themselves from the base up.

Workers' consciousness had certainly developed: forms of protest which would have been dismissed a few months before as unrealistic by early 1975 seemed natural and logical. The possibility of sweeping changes in the entire social system gradually appeared on the horizon. The development remained gradual, and it is impossible to point to a moment of sudden change. But the challenges to capitalist authority which the popular movement had successfully raised were the preconditions for what would, very soon, become a full-scale attempt from within the state apparatus to build socialism.

6

Housing and Neighborhood Commissions

As with the workers' commissions, neighborhood organization spread and developed in the months after September 28.[1] Neighborhood commissions organized quietly and with little public notice. The idea and practice of local self-government were far more important in the neighborhood commissions than in the workers' commissions. These commissions sought widespread participation and attempted to democratize the provision of public services. They developed an ideology of popular power, self-consciously modeled after their own political practice, which they wanted to see generalized to society as a whole.

There were several reasons why neighborhood commissions adopted a more explicitly political conception of their role than did the workers' commissions. First, while each workers' commission dealt primarily with its firm's management, the neighborhood commissions had no obvious target for their demands except the political authorities, and their own territorial base made an appeal to the territorially constituted authorities seem natural. Some commissions organized to take advantage of SAAL, the neighborhood self-help project, which as a government program naturally connected them to the bureaucracy. Second, in March 1975, the government announced that it would nationalize basic sectors of the economy; this dramatic shift appeared to resolve the extra-workplace demands of organized workers, although they would still have to push to get nationalization implemented effectively. Third, out of both necessity and opportunity, the neighborhood commissions cooperated more closely with the armed forces than did the workers' commissions, at a time when the armed forces had almost completely supplanted the police forces.

The relationship of the neighborhood commissions to the political authorities was close but ambiguous. The provisional government claimed to serve the poor, and did encourage poor neighborhoods to organize to

improve their condition. Far from satisfying neighborhood activists, however, that encouragement heightened their consciousness and militancy and
made them step up their pressure. Actual assistance from the state was so
limited that they saw the state as a target of conflict and felt that they had to
force it to do more.

Although all the neighborhood commissions adopted a political focus for
their actions, there were major differences among them. Poor neighborhoods and moderately well-off ones had very different needs. Commissions
also had different political orientations, which were in part determined by
each neighborhood's needs and in part by external ideological factors. Needs
and political orientation together determined how each commission acted.

The SAAL Process

SAAL, the housing program for the shantytowns, eventually became a
major focus for neighborhood organization. Announced in July 1974, it only
began to take shape in the fall. Its principal designer was Nuno Portas,
secretary of state for housing in the first three provisional governments (until
March 1975). In Portas' conception, SAAL was to help slumdwellers fix up
their homes and neighborhoods, sending small teams of technical assistants
to help poor communities survey their needs and find solutions. The goals
were limited: SAAL brigades were to help shantytowns to lay down basic
infrastructure (roads, water and sewers, and electricity) and perhaps to
rehabilitate existing buildings or lay the foundations for "evolving houses"
like those built in many South American shantytowns over periods of several
years. But the residents themselves or local governments were responsible
for most of the financing, and SAAL was not intended to build new housing.

SAAL was organized in a much more democratic way than any previous
public works project: it called on residents to contribute labor and even to
participate in decisionmaking. It was intended to serve communities which,
even though they were poor, were organized and capable of at least some
self-help, so that even with limited resources it could make a real difference
in the level of living of some of Portugal's poorest people.

In retrospect it is hard to appreciate the audacity of this innovation: a mere
two months after the fall of a regime based on repression and demobilization—and before the people had fully demonstrated their capacity for
autonomous organization—a new program was announced which assumed
not only that it should be responsive to its beneficiaries but that the state

should actively encourage them to organize. SAAL was generally called "the SAAL process" rather than, for example, "the SAAL program," attesting to its dynamic, open-ended nature. People influenced its evolving design in a process of conflictual interaction with the state apparatus.

Moreover, SAAL was designed to circumvent the bureaucratic requirements that hampered most public projects. For Portas, it was particularly important that the program begin immediately—even without bureaucratic clearance and with many problems unresolved—rather than be strangled by red tape and delay (Portas 1978: 14–15; 1979b: 93–94). The lack of careful planning and financial support later drew criticism from the beneficiaries, but it permitted the project a quick takeoff in a favorable political climate and probably enabled it to accomplish much more than it otherwise would have.

Since a request for help from SAAL had to come from a neighborhood commission which was already organized and able to take responsibility for the project, the first brigades went to the shantytowns where commissions already existed. Not surprisingly, commissions were quickly organized in other shantytowns to take advantage of SAAL. By the end of October 1974, brigades had begun working in twenty-two neighborhoods in Lisbon. By the end of the year, forty-five operations had begun around the country, serving commissions with a membership of nearly 21,000 families.

The SAAL brigades included architects, drafters, social workers, some clerical workers, and students. To avoid delay in starting the project, professionals and technicians were hired on contracts rather than as civil servants in protected jobs. This provisional status denied them job security but gave them freedom to take some risks, and it probably meant that they were more daring than most civil servants. The brigade members became an important goad in later confrontations between the commissions and the central administration of SAAL.

The first step for each brigade was to meet with the neighborhood commission and discuss needs. In many shantytowns, a minor project, such as installing water, was chosen first. Shantytowns lacked piped water and sewers; most of them did not even have outdoor fountains. Water had to be carried from the edge of the shantytown or even farther away (normally a woman's task). Both the city government and, if the land was privately owned, its owner had to approve before water could be installed. Permission had rarely been granted—or even sought—before April 25 because the regime, although unable to control squatter settlements, did not want to encourage them.

In several neighborhoods, the first project of the commission and the SAAL brigade was to dig the ditches and lay the pipes which supplied water to one or more centrally located fountains. In the shantytown of Alto do Damaia, just outside of Lisbon, the commission called on residents to provide the labor, and the brigade provided the materials. Working every night, they took just a week to complete the pipelines and install the fountain. In other neighborhoods, roads were laid out. These projects provided tangible signs of success and broadened the commissions' support. For shantytown residents who had never believed that efforts to improve themselves would do any good, even a small victory inspired hope.

At first, neighborhood commissions and the SAAL brigades planned only small projects, accepting the limits built into the program. But they all soon decided to demand more than minor improvements. They would use SAAL to extract a major financial commitment from the government. With the help of the SAAL brigades they began planning small housing projects to replace their shacks.

Many commissions were in effect licensed by local governments to control further settlement in the shantytowns. The city governments were supposed to wipe out shantytowns when they sprang up, but in the past they had generally acted only when squatters occupied public land which was already destined for some other purpose or private land whose owner insisted that the police evict them. Now some cities delegated the commissions to forbid the construction of new shacks. The commissions exercised that authority vigorously: they did not want interlopers entering the shantytown once a project had been designed to house exactly the number of families already there, and after the current residents had already invested time, energy, and some money in the project.

Some commissions also decided to limit improvements on existing shacks because they wanted all their residents to retain an interest in the completion of their new houses. The commission of Quinta das Fonsecas in Lisbon installed electrical connections, but decided not to pipe water into the houses; for the same reason, the commission of Alto do Damaia refused to wire the shanties, though it did install streetlights. All commissions prohibited permanent brick construction. (When the SAAL process slowed down in 1976 and later, commissions no longer exercised these powers, because neither the cities nor the residents, whose optimism about the completion of the new houses was fading, recognized their authority any longer.)

It was evident to the commissions that to build new houses they would need far more money than the amount allocated, and that they would only get it by exerting political pressure. SAAL commissions from several shantytowns therefore came together to present common demands. SAAL commissions in Oporto met on December 2, 1974, and called a demonstration for January

25 to coincide with Portas' visit to Oporto to meet with commission delegates.

Shortly thereafter, commissions in Lisbon also came together, forming a Coordinating Commission (*Intercomissões*) of Poor and Run-down Neighborhoods on January 4, 1975. The Coordinating Commission eventually represented thirty-eight Lisbon neighborhoods, all of which were planning new housing projects under SAAL's auspices. Relations between the commissions and SAAL were less hostile than in Oporto; in Lisbon, SAAL commissions and the SAAL workers together confronted city hall and the housing bureaucracy.

In February the shantytowns of Setubal and the Lisbon suburbs formed their own coordinating commissions. The various coordinating commissions throughout the country drew up similar sets of demands. A *caderno reivindicativo* drawn up by the Lisbon group was approved by an assembly on February 15 and then discussed in meetings in each neighborhood. Most urgently, residents demanded that the government support new housing on their terms: construction in the same area where they already lived, and the right to decide what kinds of houses were to be built. They demanded that the government expropriate suitable land and provide grants and interest-free loans for construction, sufficient to assure that no family would have to pay more than 10 percent of its income. They demanded a subsidy of 60,000 to 90,000 escudos (equivalent then to $2,400 to $3,600) for each dwelling unit and loans for the balance at 3 percent interest.

Finally, they rejected "self-help construction" (*autoconstrução*), insisting that housing should be built not by voluntary labor but by regularly employed construction workers (*Livro Branco do SAAL* 1976: 116–19). The rejection of self-help construction became a principal polemical point for the SAAL commissions, and one which violated the initial spirit of SAAL. Shantytown residents argued that self-help construction would lead to inequalities among participating families, only some of whom could provide labor, and take jobs away from construction workers, especially vulnerable to unemployment in the current stagnant economy. One political manifesto said that self-help construction would condemn shantytown dwellers to "self-management of their own poverty" (*Livro Branco do SAAL* 1976: 149). But they were also motivated by the sense that they might win: their early successes encouraged them to demand the maximum from the government.

Conservatives criticized SAAL for giving decisions over housing construction to residents of individual neighborhoods, thus removing them from the domain of public policy. But that criticism was specious, since the decisions were normally left to the private marketplace, which had proven itself woefully inadequate in housing the poor population, especially in recent decades.

Some on the left dismissed SAAL as a mere mechanism of cooptation to buy off the poorest neighborhoods with a few small physical improvements and halt the occupation movement. Portas' office had issued a statement on July 5, 1974, reminding shantytown residents that housing occupations had been banned since May 10 and urging them to work with the new brigades to improve their living conditions (even though those brigades did not begin to work until more than two months later). Still, it seems unlikely that forestalling occupations was SAAL's main purpose. The first wave of occupations lasted barely two weeks and ended when all the available public housing was occupied, and the later wave of occupations, discussed below, did not begin until 1975, well after SAAL was under way. But the benefits SAAL was to provide were so limited that it did appear designed to coopt as much as to serve the poor.

A reformist initiative such as SAAL inevitably found itself bound up in a contradiction. In creating SAAL, Portas envisioned a process of "conflictual cooperation" (1979a: 120; 1979b: 103–4): he recognized that if the commissions were incorporated into the process, their interests and those of the government would inevitably come into conflict, but he hoped that they would be able to reach agreement and work together.

The officials who designed SAAL genuinely wanted to improve the housing conditions of the poor. They kept the program small not because they wished to limit it but because they saw no possibility of anything greater. At the same time, however, they promoted the program, defending it against resistance from the bureaucracy. They created the mechanisms by which residents would join in planning the projects—which later permitted the commissions to force SAAL beyond its initial intentions (though some of SAAL's designers were later clearly hostile to the politicization of the program by the neighborhood commissions).

But the commissions, often failing to acknowledge the planners' good intentions, adopted a stance of confrontation—as when they rejected self-help construction. They recognized that the government was not fully committed to meeting their needs and would do so only under pressure. They were right: militancy won them some victories, and the most militant SAAL commissions got the farthest with their projects. But their militancy also contributed to the growing political tension which ultimately derailed the revolution.

In fact, the problem lay not in the intentions of the planners but in the ambiguous nature of the government's overall program. SAAL exemplified both the promise and the limits of programs undertaken by a reformist government which has limited resources and is not completely won over to a revolution.

The Struggle of Subtenants in Oporto

Another struggle of the poorest and worst housed was the struggle against subleases in Oporto, where landlords rented apartments to entrepreneurs who in turn sublet individual rooms to poor families. Density in these "beehive houses" was enormous and, per square meter, so was the rent. Subtenants had no legal rights, and could be evicted at the landlord's will. Evictions were frequent because the run-down buildings were prime candidates for demolition.

Although relatively few families were involved, the struggle against subtenancy was important because they won new legislation to protect them. The first protest among the subtenants of a beehive house occurred on September 13, 1974. Faced with eviction, they distributed leaflets throughout the city calling on other tenants to help them resist. The demonstrators who gathered not only prevented the eviction but won a rent decrease. Subtenants continued to organize and frequently showed up *en masse* to prevent evictions. On November 30 demonstrators invaded a closed meeting of the city administrative commission, after which the commission president promised to consider their demands.[2] His promise was kept, minimally: a Decree/Law on January 7 suspended evictions from apartments in Oporto and neighboring areas. The promised law to regulate subleases, however, did not appear for many more months.

Housing Occupations

Most of the active neighborhood commissions formed in 1974 were in the poorest neighborhoods. In 1975 they spread to most residential areas of the major cities. Although the new commissions often floundered in activities that never got off the ground, many of them found a major role in the occupation of empty houses and apartments.

The largest cities contained many privately owned buildings which stood empty. Some were mansions whose wealthy owners had fled the country. Others were old, rent-controlled apartment buildings, whose landlords, unable to increase their profit margins, allowed them to deteriorate, hoping to drive out the tenants, demolish them, and build new highrises. Many of the abandoned buildings had reverted to the government for tax delinquency or other reasons and were administered by the city. Still others were new buildings which remained empty because the construction boom of the previous decade had produced a surplus of expensive apartments.

Neighborhood groups began to protest that these apartments should be turned over to families without decent housing. In response, the government issued Decree/Law 445/74 on September 12, which prohibited demolitions and provided that apartments had to be rented within 120 days. Apartments which remained empty were to be registered with the *freguesia* council (the local government), which had authority to inspect them and rent out those it deemed habitable.

New *freguesia* councils had been named after the *saneamento* of the old councils shortly after April 25. Most of the new members had been active in the moderate, legal antifascist opposition, and while they regarded themselves as progressive, they were inclined to favor traditional legality and decorum. More important, newly vested with political authority, they sought to maintain stability, and regarded any conflict as a challenge to their office. Consequently, they were reluctant to use even their limited powers. Almost no empty apartments were registered in compliance with the September decree, and the councils did nothing to enforce registration. So they were unlikely to risk offending private property by taking over the empty apartments. The neighborhood commissions, fearing further inaction, prepared to act.

The 120-day period for renting apartments expired, after a postponement, on February 18. On the next night neighborhood commissions occupied dozens of empty buildings which they had identified ahead of time. Homeless families entered and spent the night, accompanied by commission activists who remained to resist any eviction attempt. In many of these buildings, the police and the troops of the COPCON entered to evict them forcibly.

Neighborhood commissions began to take on occupations as a regular activity. In many commissions, a housing subcommittee was formed to organize occupations; in others, the occupations became the main activity of the whole commission. They compiled lists of empty housing—single apartments or whole buildings—from information supplied by members, and received requests from people claiming to be in need.

At first, joining occupations took some courage, as no one knew whether the forces of order would respond violently. But when they did not, occupations became routine. An invasion would be planned for a given night, and widely publicized in the hope that a large crowd would join in. Commission members, other activists, and the family or families to be housed would gather at the building. "If we could get in, fine; if not, either a neighbor would let us climb down from a veranda or a staircase and break a window, or else we forced the door open and went in," an activist of the commission of Prazeres, an old neighborhood of central Lisbon, told me.

Despite the questionable legality of the occupations, the neighborhood commissions were often supported (as were farmworkers in land occupations) by the troops of the COPCON, the special command which the MFA had created the previous summer to circumvent the old military hierarchy. Though it forcibly dislodged some occupiers when the occupations of private housing began in February, the COPCON came to support the occupations enthusiastically. Regiments frequently sent a representative to certify an occupation and prevent the landlord from attempting to recapture the property.

After the first occupations in February, however, few efforts were made to evict. The COPCON's support provided an enormous stimulus to the occupations and to the popular movement in general: the armed forces, traditionally the arm of repression and defender of capital, joined in and encouraged the attack on private property. The occupations would not have succeeded without at least their passive acquiescence, for they could have evicted all the occupiers if they had chosen to. But their active support reinforced the occupiers' determination to overturn bourgeois legality and the conviction that they could solve the problems of the poor by direct action.

The government did not share their position: although failing to rent apartments was illegal, so was occupying private property. Nor did the entire MFA; COPCON officers became the bulwark of the MFA's far-left faction as a result of their contact with civilian movements. Some in the popular movement ignored the fact that they had not won over the entire armed forces—a serious misperception, and one that would cost them dearly. But with power divided, no other authority opposed the COPCON by trying to prevent occupations.

In at least one case, a landlord learned vividly that the armed forces were "on the side of the people." A *miliciano* told me: "One night at eleven o'clock a family arrived at the base. It was during the heavy rains, and their shack had been inundated. They had no house. We would have let them stay overnight at the base, but somebody thought to get in touch with the nearby neighborhood commissions to see if there was an empty house. I went and interrupted a meeting to tell them it was an urgent case, and they had a list of apartments. We chose one and went immediately. Of course we made a lot of noise, it was night, and someone phoned the landlord. He phoned the base, and complained that people in uniform were breaking into his house. The duty officer asked him, 'How long has it been since you lived there?' For him it was like a cowboy movie: he called our unit to complain and ask for protection, when it was the unit that was occupying!''

Upon entry the occupiers would determine whether the apartment was indeed empty. In Prazeres, "if the house was furnished, we stayed out; we invited a military unit of the COPCON, normally the Military Police, to send an officer in a jeep to take an inventory. Everything was then stored in a warehouse to be returned to the owner if we could find him." People hostile to occupations told many stories of apartments occupied while their residents were on vacation or for some other reason were not present to protect their homes. Occupiers, in contrast, insisted that they scrupulously observed the rights of any tenants already in an apartment; they admitted that they occasionally made a mistake and entered an apartment which was not genuinely empty, but claimed that they always recognized their error and left.

This new wave of occupations occurred mainly in the older neighborhoods of Lisbon, the suburbs across the river, and Setubal. It continued intensely until April, more gradually thereafter. Most of the apartments involved were in old buildings, some of them so run-down as to be unacceptable to anyone not living in a shack. (Some commissions raised funds to help occupiers fix them up.) While there were many new buildings which were by law equally subject to compulsory rental, realism kept occupiers out of them, because they recognized that the force of a landlord's opposition was likely to be much greater in the case of a new building. In any case, occupiers, who planned to sign a lease and pay rent for the apartment, could not afford the rents in new highrises. Moreover, since the law provided that buildings had to be "habitable" to be eligible for compulsory rental, developers often refused to install minor fixtures such as light switches and claimed that the buildings were not finished.

Once occupations took off, families living in shanties or temporary quarters came to the commissions to ask for an apartment. The commission tried to assign houses to the most needy. In some commissions a subcommittee made these decisions. Others, however, recognized that the assignment of housing was bound to cause controversy and decided that to prevent disputes and accusations of favoritism, only a vote of a general assembly of the neighborhood commission could decide.

Once settled in an apartment, the family made strenuous efforts to sign a lease. Occupiers assumed they would pay rent, and felt that they were merely enforcing their right under the law to live in an apartment that a landlord had refused to rent. One activist explained, "We tried to avoid run-ins with the landlord, we tried to enter into dialogue and say that we really wanted to rent the house and were ready to pay. Or else we tried to find out what was the rent allowed by law, the same as the last time it was rented [in the older neighborhoods of Lisbon, rents were controlled]. The rent was then deposited in the name of the landlord in the *Caixa Geral de Depósitos* [a public savings bank] until the case would be resolved in court." In Lapa, another central-Lisbon *freguesia*, according to a commission activist, "the housing committee drew up a lease. Usually the landlords refused to sign the lease, and the [occupiers] signed the lease with the *freguesia* council."

While commission activists eagerly defied bourgeois legality, occupying families tried to maintain its forms meticulously. They wanted to show, in the event of a court case, that they had met their obligations under the law and had the right to keep the apartment. Some tenants made improvements on their run-down dwellings, installing new plumbing and electrical connections and rebuilding walls. They deducted the costs from the rent and saved all receipts to prove that they had acted in good faith.

A complicated dialectic arose between neighborhood commissions and *freguesia* councils. Those most active in the commissions were young people who were militants or sympathizers of the far-left parties, especially the UDP, the PRP, and the League for Revolutionary Unity and Action (LUAR). Their ideology made them eager to challenge private property and take advantage of the revolutionary opportunity to act on the slogan "As long as there are people without houses, there should be no houses without people."

Most *freguesia* council members, on the other hand, were opposed in principle to the commissions' taking the law into their own hands, and many of them identified with the PS and the PCP, which opposed occupations. But some *freguesia* councils recognized the occupations as a fact of life and were drawn against their will into cooperating with the process which the popular movement had begun: commissions acted; councils stalled, and then acquiesced. If the landlord refused to sign a lease, the council recognized the family as legal tenant, as the law authorized, and gave the family a certificate of tenancy which was required to connect utilities. (If the council refused to give the certificate, a COPCON representative sometimes gave one, which was usually recognized by the utility companies.) Some councils went even further, organizing a housing census to locate abandoned houses and allowing neighborhood commissions to sponsor occupations. Councils also attempted, to a limited degree, to prevent occupations of dwellings that were ineligible either because they were legitimately occupied or because they were too run-down to be habitable.

Even where relations between a *freguesia* council and a neighborhood commission were relatively cooperative, political differences remained. The council members did not want to take over unrented houses. The neighborhood commissions claimed that the revolutionary situation required revolutionary legality, flaunting the laws which enforced bourgeois domination. They denounced the councils rhetorically as arms of the bourgeois government with which they abjured all cooperation. Yet, to protect the rights of occupying families, they sought to have the occupations legalized. In practice, the two sides cooperated, more than either was comfortable admitting.

Neighborhood Commission Organization

All commissions were founded in roughly the same way. A small group would form an interim commission and post announcements of a public meeting around the neighborhood. All residents of the area—in Lisbon, usually a *freguesia*, but sometimes a smaller neighborhood or shantytown— were invited. At the first meeting, a few people, often the initiators, would be chosen to serve as the commission's elected members. In some cases they were elected by block or some other small division of the *freguesia;* more often, a general slate was elected in the meeting. Often the commission chosen at the first meeting was still only temporary, assigned to propose a set of by-laws for later ratification. Only then would the commission be officially elected.

Each commission claimed to be a base-level organization governed by direct democracy, in which everyone who lived in the area had the right (and duty) to participate. All residents were eligible to vote in general assemblies. The by-laws invariably specified that the commission was a "unitary" organization, open to everyone and not connected to any political party.

The term *neighborhood commission* technically meant the commission's elected members, but it was more commonly used to refer to the commission as a whole and all its activities. And many commissions' by-laws specified that the most important decisions could only be taken by a general assembly where all residents of the commission's area were eligible to attend and to vote. During the active period, meetings were frequent: a general assembly might meet every week; the elected members of the commission might also meet weekly, on another night; and subcommittee meetings were held on other nights. All these meetings were generally open to the public. In the *freguesia* of Prazeres, the housing committee always had the biggest attendance: "People who had gotten houses through the neighborhood commission felt they had to fight to keep their house, so as not to have to go back to a shack. They felt that they had to go to the meetings, because that was the guarantee for the house. They brought their children and everyone."

The commissions adopted the model of direct democracy to which the neighborhood movement aspired. Constituents had the right to recall elected commission members at any time. Voting in general assemblies was by a show of hands. Some commissions chose families to be housed in open meetings, specifically to avoid any charge of favoritism.

While the commissions' main focus was housing, they also made other efforts to improve the quality of life of their neighborhoods. Often the first step was to take a survey of needs, which became the basis for a *caderno reivindicativo*, usually addressed to the *freguesia* council. Some commissions demanded local control of public institutions, such as clinics and schools, or of church-sponsored charities, which in the past had been controlled from the top. In some cases they succeeded in replacing those in charge with people chosen by the surrounding community.

Many commissions established community services such as clinics and day care centers. Professional day care had hardly existed before April 25, despite the high proportion of two-earner couples in the cities. The effort to provide it became the popular movement's main response to women's issues. Sometimes buildings were occupied for these facilities, or for headquarters of parties and other organizations.

Cultural activities, especially amateur theater, also flourished: Brecht, banned under fascism, was the most popular playwright for the many amateur companies (most of them short-lived) which sprung up. Commissions also established public laundries and drugstores, protested the lack of streetlights or public transportation, offered recreational activities for children (such as taking them to the beach and to museums, often on COPCON-provided buses), and organized consumer vigilance to see that local stores were obeying price control regulations. All these activities remained secondary to providing housing (by construction or occupation), however, and by themselves they were rarely enough to keep a commission going. Neighborhood commissions were relatively inactive in areas which had no shantytowns and few empty houses to occupy.

Some neighborhoods already had sports clubs. But they rarely linked up to the neighborhood commissions, because their sponsorship of soccer teams created rivalries, and because soccer, to many political activists, had a faint (or not so faint) odor of fascism.

To many, neighborhood commissions opened the possibility of political participation for the first time. The expansion of participation was greatest among the working class, according to the systematic study of neighborhood commissions in Setubal by Downs and colleagues (Downs 1980; Downs et al. 1978). As mentioned, almost all the first neighborhood commissions were formed in the poorest areas, shantytowns and municipal projects. The exceptions were commissions formed in mixed (and even elite) neighborhoods soon after April 25 under the stimulus of the MDP and the new city governments. But most of those commissions were not very active until later, because they had few urgent needs to meet. Though commissions later covered most of the area of the major cities, they were still more common in working-class neighborhoods. Downs classifies Setubal's neighborhoods as elite, interclass, and popular according to the occupations of the residents. Nearly all the popular neighborhoods (20 out of 24), just over half of the interclass neighborhoods (10 out of 16), and only two of the five elite neighborhoods formed commissions.

Within neighborhoods, too, participation was heavily skewed toward the working class. Even in the interclass and elite neighborhoods, elected members of commissions and active participants were predominantly manual workers, especially in modern and heavy industry, which employed the greatest proportion of Setubal's labor force. In Lisbon, workers were not always so prominent. According to a housing committee activist from Lapa, a predominantly middle-class area, ''some people weren't so visible: in a meeting, they didn't dare speak to the *Senhor Doutor* or the *Senhor Engenheiro* [engineer], and they couldn't stay until two in the morning because they had to get up at six to go to work.''

The commissions affected neighborhood culture in ways that went beyond programmed activities. Working together created neighborliness and solidarity. In Lapa, one member told me: ''Where I live it's all highrises. People can live there twenty years and maybe only know the people across the hall; but now everyone got to know each other. It was an unblocking for Portuguese society. Just an example: people used to be afraid to let their children go out alone to the store. Now anyone in the building will send kids out. I know all four thousand people in my neighborhood! We say good morning, good afternoon, and with some we really became friends.''

The change was greatest in high-density neighborhoods. Shantytown residents enjoyed a neighborliness before. But it was impressive, in interviewing neighborhood commission activists—even several years later—to hear them tell how the life of their neighborhoods improved just because people got to know each other and worked together.

The MFA and "Cultural Dynamization"

The progressives in the MFA maintained close contacts with the neighborhood commissions. These contacts had important effects on both sides, encouraging the commissions and educating the officers about the problems of the poorest neighborhoods. Soon after the coup, officers began making informal contacts and encouraging residents to form commissions. But the relationship was strengthened on September 28 when soldiers and civilians joined to mount the barricades against the counterrevolutionary demonstration, and officers in many regiments seized the opportunity to cement the ties.

The MFA expanded its unique program of political education and community development, calling it the "cultural dynamization campaign." Many units established "dynamization offices" to maintain contacts with nearby commissions, and the Fifth Division of the General Staff was assigned to coordinate them. In January 1975, the first campaigns, organized from Lisbon, began in Tras-os-Montes and Minho, the two northern-most provinces—and the two poorest. The Fifth Division began publishing the *MFA Bulletin* which openly discussed the need for the armed forces to provide education to the politically backward areas of the country.

The cultural dynamization campaign visited northern villages with movies, "clarification sessions," and attempts at community development. In March the *MFA Bulletin* reported that 2,000 sessions had already been held. But cultural dynamization won little support from northern peasants: the officers preached revolution with a radical rhetoric which attacked local traditions and especially the church (the *Bulletin* itself criticized their rhetorical excesses). Priests counterattacked with equal venom in their sermons. The campaign did succeed in opening some roads and starting community development in some areas, but in general the reaction to its attempts to bring revolution to the conservative north ranged from incomprehension to hostility (but the most detailed account is sympathetic: Correia et al n.d.[b]; see also S. Ferreira 1975).

Units in Lisbon and the south stimulated local organization more success-fully, in direct contact with their surrounding areas. Units which had offered material assistance or supported occupations had already developed a good relationship with the neighborhoods and the population was in any case far less conservative and more willing to listen to their message.

One regiment which supported the neighborhood commissions actively was the Pontinha Engineering Regiment, located in the center of a heavily industrialized area of northwest Lisbon and its neighboring suburbs, which included many shantytowns with SAAL brigades. The regiment was from the beginning a center of leftist officers: army engineers had studied at the civilian Technical Institute, and they were less identified with the military hierarchy than most officers. Many officers at Pontinha had supported the MFA before April 25, and the command center of the coup had been located there. The Pontinha regiment's services were in demand among the neigh-borhood commissions because it could offer them heavy equipment and labor to dig ditches, level roads, and make other improvements in the shantytowns.

The armed forces also came to exercise major police functions: the regular police, cowed by accusations of fascism and fears of *saneamento,* were reluctant to intervene in civilian disputes, and the people often turned to the MFA to resolve them. Units were enlisted to solve family problems, to prevent employers from abusing their workers, to help control noisy nightclubs, and to control drug traffic.

Since military units acted as forces of order, they could define what was legal—occupations, for example. But their power was not only coercive: they had moral authority too. While they supported the occupation of empty houses even against landlords' protests, they also occasionally tried to persuade property owners to help the poor voluntarily. A small shantytown near Pontinha, for example, was on the side of a steep hill and accessible only by a staircase. The residents wanted to build a road, but the only possible site crossed private land. The commission and officers from Pontinha approached the owner and urged him to offer a strip of land for the road. He acceded, making coercion unnecessary, but he may have regarded the loss of his property as a de facto expropriation.

In encouraging and supporting the poor neighborhoods' efforts to organ-ize, many in the military identified with the demands of the poor and developed a new sense of their own mission. With the end of the colonial war, which had given the armed forces their major purpose for more than a decade, supporting the civilian movements and especially the neighborhood commissions' extralegal activities became the units' main activity and even the justification for their existence. Without at first using the term, they came to identify with popular power.

Many officers were also radicalized by their own enlisted men, who demanded that they be included in the MFA and that the armed forces become more democratic. Disciplinary regulations were in effect revoked in some units of the army and navy. (The air force, more conservative, generally retained traditional discipline.) Separate officers' mess was abolished, and Unit Delegate Assemblies of officers, sergeants, and soldiers were given authority on their bases (Domingos et al., 1977: 39–67; A. Rodrigues et al., 1976: 188–91).

Some leftist officers, rejecting the demands of conservative officers and their civilian allies that the Armed Forces Movement give up its political influence in favor of civilian democracy, responded by backing civilian popular power. This position was embraced by Prime Minister Gonçalves in a speech to a dynamization session in the small village of Sabugo on February 20:

> [I] said in Oporto on October 5 of last year that once the new organizations of the State were instituted the MFA would return to the barracks and the Armed Forces, having been democratized, would defend democracy whatever the cost. . . . The historic experience of the past months shows that the MFA has more to do than that; that the Armed Forces must be a driving force and a guarantor of the Portuguese revolution (Gonçalves 1976: 160).

Parties and Political Orientation

Although neighborhood commissions all claimed to be nonpartisan, and all the parties paid lip service to their "unitariness," it was inevitable in an atmosphere as politically charged as that of 1975 in Portugal that parties and tendencies should seek to dominate particular commissions. Some of them became the scenes of partisan battles—violating the unitary spirit by which the commissions claimed to be guided.

The claim of neighborhood commissions (and workers' commissions) to reject party affiliation was clearly self-serving to some extent: they could more easily claim the justice of their cause. Denouncing poor working conditions, exploitation, run-down housing, or other capitalist abuses would evoke sympathy, whereas any admission of partisan affiliation challenged the public to take sides—and with the plethora of political tendencies to choose from, only a small minority was likely to be on the commission's side in any dispute.

But the claim of nonpartisanship was often valid. If it was in the interest of the commissions to emphasize their independence, their opponents could benefit from accusing them of ties to parties. And in many commissions, nonpartisanship was rigorously maintained, to avoid a likely source of conflict in a situation where people had to work together to succeed. So the commissions wanted to prevent either the appearance or the reality of party control.

Even if the commissions avoided identification with particular parties, however, activists participated out of political conviction, and they attempted to inspire the commissions with their views and to influence them to take actions consistent with their political objectives. So either explicitly or implicitly, commissions adopted particular political lines.

The orientation of the far left predominated in many of the most active and militant neighborhood commissions, far more than in workers' commissions or the agrarian reform cooperatives. The neighborhood commissions were ready to engage in tactics of mass mobilization and direct action and, naturally, to enter into direct conflict with the state. They not only adopted militant tactics to resolve the problems of the neighborhood; they also supported far-left positions on larger political questions. Most of them later gravitated to popular power and called for a radical restructuring of state institutions to correspond to the forms of political organization they themselves had developed locally.

There were several reasons for the predominance of the far left in the neighborhood commissions. One was neglect by the PCP, which paid little attention to the commissions. They were smaller, more decentralized, more militant, and apparently harder to control than workers' commissions—they defiantly confronted the government which the PCP supported and regarded as correctly revolutionary. The far left was not especially important in the neighborhood commissions at the beginning either, for most were founded without ties to parties. Far-left ideology (like the PCP's ideology) regarded workplaces as more important than neighborhoods. But when the PCP won over many of the workers' commissions in the winter of 1975, the far left saw a new opportunity in the neighborhood commissions.

The class composition of the far left and of the neighborhood commissions themselves offered the far left greater opportunity for influence than in industrial workplaces. The history of clandestine industrial struggle had made industrial workers sympathetic to the PCP. Most neighborhood commissions were socially more heterogeneous. They also had more members with no prior political activity and more who had participated in political activities not led by the PCP. The class composition of far-left parties themselves made their work in neighborhood commissions more natural: students and intellectuals played a proportionately much greater role in the far-left parties than in the PCP. Unlikely to be industrial workers, they were not natural constituents of workers' commissions; but, like everyone else, they lived somewhere, so they were available to take an active part in the neighborhood commissions.

But the problems the commissions faced were in the end more responsible for the militancy than was the presence of far leftists. In the SAAL commissions, as Downs (1980: 429–31) has argued, the militant positions of the far left came to predominate because once they defined the problem and started looking for solutions, objective necessity required inter-neighborhood organization and confrontation with the government to win greater financial and technical support, and their militant posture made the orientation of the far left more congenial than that of the more moderate left parties. These commissions were all in shantytowns and slums, and their membership, like their constituencies, was distinctly poor and working class.

Despite their militant posture, the SAAL commissions did not often suffer divisions or opposition by members who did not sympathize with the far left, because all who were active embraced the common project of building new houses (as did most who were not active, even though they may have been skeptical that it would succeed). The SAAL commissions could thus legitimately claim to represent virtually all their constituents and faced relatively few problems of party conflict, and most of them avoided identification with any particular party. Neither creating a housing project nor protesting government inaction implied any partisan commitment. Some commission leaders were clearly identified with one or another party, but they took pains to keep that identification from interfering with the shared objectives of the commission and its constituents.

The commissions most active in occupations claimed to represent areas much larger than any shantytown, and their neighborhoods usually included a broad spectrum of classes. The far left predominated in these commissions, too, because the occupation movement attracted people ideologically disposed to defy the laws of private property. These were mainly people who already held far-left views, although some who had far more moderate political beliefs on most issues nevertheless came to sympathize with the occupations and took active part or at least cooperated passively. But the commissions never represented more than a minority of the residents, and many were opposed by residents who rejected their political orientation. In some cases a commission split into two or more commissions representing smaller areas which were more socially homogeneous, and therefore less subject to partisan divisions; a few commissions split because different areas, of different social statuses, wanted to pursue different kinds of activities (though in such cases partisan conflict was usually also a factor.) Other commissions did not split, but their leaders were challenged by other residents who opposed the partisan line or activity of the group in control. There were also cases where two distinct groups each claimed to be the neighborhood commission for an area.

Some commissions adopted a more moderate stance. Downs' study of all the neighborhood commissions in Setubal shows that this position was characteristic of commissions which had been founded when the city Administrative Commission encouraged them as a vehicle to decentralize its government activity. They were intended to act as intermediaries and collaborate with the Administrative Commission. These commissions avoided militancy and confrontation in favor of negotiation and more traditional forms of influence. Most of them were dominated by the PCP, as was the city government. Most were in neighborhoods with housing stock in fairly good condition and with moderate rents. Three shantytown commissions adopted the same moderate orientation. They had all split off from commissions which had been formed to represent larger areas but had fallen apart in factionalism.

Nearly all commissions took some part in occupations. But these moderate commissions did so less often, and nearly always for housing rather than for party headquarters or public facilities. Their activities reflected the PCP's attitude toward mass mobilization: its purpose was to support the constituted authorities, as long as they represented the interests of the working class.

The neighborhood commissions' political orientations did not derive from prior ideological commitments but grew out of the effort to solve their problems. Like workers' commissions, neighborhood commissions first organized to meet limited goals, but success opened up greater possibilities. As a result they demanded not just minor improvements but major political restructuring and finally socialist transformation.

This development influenced participants, whatever their initial political views. It was an empowering experience which liberated them from the everyday ideology to which they had been subject. They had the sense that they could accomplish anything by their own actions, that the future was open, and that there were no defeats in sight. If everything seemed possible, it was partly because many things *were* possible. This new perception seemed to be confirmed by the forces of order, which either were incapacitated or had become eager participants in activities normally seen as illegal and which they would normally be expected to repress. Especially in the occupations, the armed forces were acting not to defend capitalist private property and repress the people but, quite the contrary, joined in and encouraged their attack on private property.

The Portuguese—and not just those who were politically active—were breathing a heady atmosphere. Activists were particularly affected, and in a dramatic moment—a "moment" that lasted more than a year—their consciousness was transformed dramatically. This heightening of consciousness made many popular movement activists imagine that socialist transformation was possible; and not only socialism, but a socialism based on the political organizations that they had created and responsive to their demands.

7

Seizing the Commanding Heights

On March 11, 1975, Spinola and his supporters attempted a coup. They gathered early in the morning at Tancos Airbase and ordered its paratroopers' regiment to attack the base of the First Light Artillery Regiment, next to the Lisbon international airport. This was the "Red Regiment," disdained by the Spinolists as "Tupamaros," whose soldiers, when dispatched to control the anti-NATO demonstration in February, had instead supported the demonstrators. The paratroopers from Tancos bombarded the base at noontime, killing one soldier. But almost immediately, huge numbers of civilians gathered outside the base, and the paratroopers stopped their bombardment. A mutiny by the National Republican Guard in Lisbon, coordinated with the attack on the Artillery Base, was also quickly put down.

Weeks of organizing among rightwing officers and leading capitalists had convinced Spinola that he had enough support in the military to depose the MFA. He miscalculated badly. Even though his allies within the Armed Forces had become more vocal, few of them were prepared to join a coup. When he learned that the attack had failed, Spinola fled from Tancos to Spain with his family and eighteen officers. Moving on to Brazil, he organized a "Democratic Movement for the Liberation of Portugal" (MDLP) in exile and claimed to be preparing for guerrilla warfare in Portugal.

Among Spinola's supporters implicated in the coup were several prominent businessmen; dozens of people were arrested, but most were soon released. Over the next months, however, many of them also left the country. Among those who fled with Spinola was Major José Sanches Osorio, Minister of Communication in the second provisional government who had been deposed with Spinola and had more recently surfaced as head of the Christian Democratic Party (PDC). From Spain, Sanches Osorio later claimed that the coup had been motivated by reports that the PCP was

141

planning an "Easter Massacre" against the right and had compiled a hit list of 500 people.

If the bungled coup had elements of comic opera, a soldier had nevertheless been killed and several others wounded in the bombardment, and the right had given notice that it would resort to violence to halt the leftward move of the MFA. Rumors of CIA involvement were rife, and Otelo, as head of the COPCON, announced later in the day that he could not guarantee the safety of U.S. Ambassador Frank Carlucci.

On the Socialist Path

The coup attempt temporarily restored unity among the factions of the MFA and made them determined to assert state control over the economy. Having accepted the moderate Melo Antunes plan only for tactical reasons, out of fear of moving too fast, the MFA abandoned it entirely after the unsuccessful coup. In a series of night-long meetings, the officers made decisions with dizzying speed, institutionalizing the MFA and nationalizing the banks. Formally, institutionalization meant establishing the Council of the Revolution (CR), consisting of the members of the junta and the MFA Coordinating Commission, as the supreme governing authority. The choice of name was symbolic. Some officers had called for a council of the revolution after September 28, but it had been rejected as premature. Now, those in charge clearly believed that the time was ripe.

But the creation of the CR was not just symbolic: for the first time, the MFA was formally vested with the power that it exercised in fact. The Council of State, which had some civilian members and was nominally the highest authority, was dissolved, and the CR assumed its powers. The CR's membership remained in flux for a few weeks—the MFA members first appointed were all leftists, but later in March Melo Antunes and some of his moderate allies were added. Second in importance to the CR was the MFA Delegates' Assembly. The MFA had officially declared a revolution. Now the young officers moved rapidly to make one. Constantly on the go, they became known as *os homens sem sono* (the men who never sleep).

The main target was the economy. The new program would nationalize banks, the monopoly groups, and basic industries, and expropriate the country's large landholdings for agrarian reform. All domestically owned banks were in fact nationalized on March 14; all insurance companies were likewise nationalized the next day. The banks' position at the center of the monopoly groups and their historical role as the principal source of investment capital meant that they owned outright or controlled large shares of firms in many industries. Their interest in these firms therefore passed to the state as well.

The MFA's new economic strategy consisted of seizing the commanding heights of the economy, to break the power of big capital and build socialism. This was essentially the strategy of the PCP, with its preference for centralism over worker control. The official slogan changed: whereas the Melo Antunes program had referred to a "socializing path," after March 11 the CR spoke openly of a *via socialista*.

Officials repeatedly proclaimed that they would not take over small or foreign-owned capital. Once the state controlled credit and basic industries, they assumed, it would not be necessary, since economic planning would give the state sector such a commanding role in the overall economy that small capital would have to adapt to the national plan. The PCP believed this antimonopoly strategy would appeal to broad sectors of the population. The MFA hoped that by respecting small capital and freeing it from the unfair competition of the monopolies, they could win over the petty bourgeoisie. The petty bourgeoisie, however, was not consoled.

A plan to expropriate large agricultural landholdings was also announced in April. The announcement stimulated farmworkers to occupy many of the latifundios of the Alentejo and turn them into cooperatives even before agrarian reform was officially enacted. Recognizing the duality between the large properties in the south and the peasant smallholdings in the north, the MFA hoped to incorporate small and medium farmers into the antimonopoly coalition. It announced projects to benefit small owners and declared that agrarian reform would only affect large properties. But the programs were not very effective, and peasants, fearing expropriation of their land too, turned strongly against the revolution.

The nationalization of the banks was highly popular; but it had been carried out without consulting public opinion. The MFA could not claim to represent a majority, except by making the same assumption which had traditionally governed military intervention in public life: that the armed forces were above politics, a "savior army" with interests identical to those of the nation. According to the centralist model, the MFA did not have to work actively to win people over and create a broad political base of support for the new policies, it only had to make the right decisions and popular support would follow. So it chose to move decisively before civilian politicians could mount opposition.

Nor did the PCP attempt to broaden its base or cultivate an alliance with sectors of the population who were not so eager to build socialism. Instead, it counted on its traditional base of support in the working class, especially in the heavy industries which were to be taken over. More importantly, the party subordinated itself to the MFA and relied on the dominant Gonçalvist faction (supporters of Prime Minister Vasco Gonçalves) of the MFA to put the program into effect.

MFA moderates, while accepting the main lines of the new policy, still feared alienating the middle class and losing it as part of the revolution's "social base." They urged that the MFA await the outcome of the election and respect its commitment to a pluralist society governed by the will of the majority. Instead, the CR hardened its position in its negotiations with the parties for a political pact. With the veiled threat of postponing elections indefinitely, the officers demanded that the parties accept the new measures. Elections would still be held, but the parties were hardly free to promote their own programs. Even parties represented in the cabinet, the PS and the PPD, felt they were being marginalized, and their support for the MFA was beginning to evaporate. The MFA's failure to cultivate civilian support would soon bring major problems.

The new government (the fourth provisional government) was sworn in on March 26. It was not exactly an afterthought, but the fact that the cabinet did not take office until nearly two weeks after the major decisions had been made reflected the government's complete subordination to the MFA. Economic ministries were reorganized and a powerful Ministry of Economic Coordination was created to oversee the economy as a whole. The same parties which had taken part in the previous provisional governments (the MDP, the PCP, the PPD, and the PS) remained in the coalition and nominally supported the new program.[1] To appearances, the PCP was no stronger in the new cabinet than it had been before. But the new ministers in economic posts, while not Communists, shared its policy of nationalization and central control.

The commanding-heights strategy was promptly put into effect. All banks and insurance companies were nationalized so that the state could take charge of the capital and credit markets. Similarly, all the firms in some industrial and service sectors were taken over. Within two months, electricity, oil and petrochemicals, steel, railroads, the national airline TAP, long-distance bus lines, cement, shipbuilding, heavy engineering, wood pulp, and tobacco were all nationalized. In principle, complete nationalization of a sector permitted unification of the firms and rationalization of their activities. But, as we will see, successful unification turned out to depend on the outcome of a political struggle by the workers of the sector.

Other firms, however, were nationalized because they were owned by the monopoly groups. It was widely felt that the monopoly groups had to be nationalized, because their concentrated economic power was inconsistent with social justice and allowed them to subvert democracy (as the monopolists had demonstrated by supporting the rightwing coup). But the diversity of each group's holdings made it difficult to integrate them into a coherent planned economy.

The state came to control most of Lisbon's daily newspapers, for example, because they were owned by banks; since television was already a state monopoly, the state now controlled all the major news media. But no program called for state control; it was apparently an unintended consequence.[2] Similarly, many small firms owned by the monopolies—small manufacturers, restaurants, travel agencies—came under state control. Conservatives complained that the MFA was nationalizing barbershops and florists; but it was the concentrated ownership of capital inherited from fascism which dictated these takeovers, not a vision of socialism which required state control of all economic activity (quite the reverse, since the policy explicitly rejected taking over small, independently owned businesses).

In all, 117 firms were nationalized, and the state controlled an additional 219 in which the nationalized firms had had a controlling interest. Most of the nationalized firms were large and highly capitalized. With an average of 700 workers in 1974, they owned 21 percent of gross fixed capital formation (while employing only 6 percent of the labor force—they were among the most capital-intensive firms in the country). The public sector share of total employment, 18 percent in 1974, rose to 24 percent by 1976. Its share of value added rose from 12 percent to 25 percent, and its share of investment (gross fixed capital formation) from 18 percent to 45 percent. The state's share was not appreciably greater than in such countries as France and Austria, but its complete control of the banks gave it, in principle at least, much greater powers of intervention.[3]

Firms were considered to be nationalized if the state took them over completely. But there were other firms in which the state's share was significant. It had invested in some of them before April 25, though it had not usually taken any active role in managing them. Others were firms in which the banks or monopoly groups had an interest, which now passed to the state.

State control of small capital also increased through the war on economic sabotage. Many capitalists, skeptical of the MFA's promise not to seize small or foreign-owned capital, curtailed operations and allowed their firms to slide into bankruptcy. If mismanagement or illegal financial dealings could be proven in such a firm, and it was large enough that its workers could argue that the health of the economy required its financial survival, the state—more frequently after March 11—invoked the Economic Sabotage Law and "intervened." Most of the 206 firms in which the state intervened were relatively small, but a few were large; in total they employed more than 55,000 workers.

Intervention meant that the state did not take over formal ownership, but appointed administrators who controlled the firm's bank accounts and could purchase, sell, pay salaries, and seek short-term credit. Many of these firms had for all practical purposes been abandoned by their owners; administrators had to take over and have the legal power to take urgently needed action.

If the diversity of the nationalized monopoly groups impeded rational control of the economy, firms in which the state intervened were even more heterogeneous. They were targeted because of their economic straits and because their workers were well enough organized to demand intervention, not because of their centrality in the economy. The movement for worker control further confused the structure of ownership, as workers took over other firms which were in danger of going out of business but were too small to justify state intervention. In them, however, the state did little more than recognize worker management.

The government also took some measures to redistribute income: it decreed a minimum wage in May and froze high salaries in September 1974; in June 1975, it raised the minimum wage and set a maximum salary limit. Price controls were established in the summer of 1974 and were quite effective. During the last six months before April 25, inflation ran at an annual rate of 40 percent; this was cut to 23 percent between May 1974 and March 1975, and to 7 percent between April and August 1975 (figures are for Lisbon only). Purchasing power, which had declined by 6 percent during the last six months before April 25, rose by 12 percent between then and September 1975. The share of wages in national income rose from 48.0 percent in 1973 to 56.9 percent in 1975 (*Economia e Socialismo* 1977: 14–18; Rosa 1976: 130–38).

Production and investment, however, fell off. Between plant closings, capital flight, and postponement of investments, private sector capital formation fell severely in 1974 and 1975. The economic ministers, notably Mario Murteira, minister of economic coordination, repeatedly warned the CR and the MFA Assembly of the dangers of economic stagnation.

Government planners called on Portuguese workers to rescue industry from its low productivity. Low productivity could be attributed to many factors, including lack of capital, technological backwardness, poorly qualified workers, and sabotage; but the government attempted to overcome it by raising workers' consciousness and enlisting them in a "battle of production." Prime Minister Gonçalves had successfully called on the nation to spend a Sunday working the previous October after the victory of September 28, and he attempted to revive the spirit shown then. He announced the program at the Sorefame railroad car factory on May 17, in a speech which virtually equated productivity with patriotism (Gonçalves 1976: 307–19). The government called on people to work an extra day once again on June 10.

The Communist Party, too, loudly trumpeted the "battle of production," and tried to enlist workers in the effort. But repeated calls to workers and managers alike to stimulate production went largely unheeded. The stagnating economy was the greatest failure of revolutionary economic policy, especially since the productivist rhetoric of the government and the MFA invited that they be judged by their ability to promote growth.

Workers' Power in Nationalized Industry

The nationalization program answered the demands that workers had been making for months, and they rushed to support it. But they discovered that they could not simply support the new policies passively. The way in which nationalization was implemented depended very much on how active a role the workers in the nationalized firms took in the process. They had to reject halfway measures and demand that the policies be carried out completely.

While the MFA and the PCP claimed to be seizing the commanding heights of the economy, workers made the seizure real at the point of production. The MFA did not have the resources to take direct charge of individual firms. The centralist model could be implemented only because the workers carrying it out at the base were practicing popular power, even if they did not explicitly acknowledge it. The workers and workers' commissions were the foot soldiers of the battle against capitalism.

Most firms remained under private ownership and control. Workers continued to deal with the workplace issues of recognizing workers' commissions, wages and hours, and unsafe working conditions, and demanded that companies open their books and make investments to maintain employment—much the same demands that they had been raising since April 25. In nationalized firms, too, workers' commissions sought job security and adequate wages and working conditions. On the whole, these were not major issues, at least during the initial period. In later years, with threats of closing or massive layoffs in many nationalized sectors, the workers had to worry more about their conditions of employment.

But with nationalization workers' commissions took on new tasks and sought to institutionalize workers' power within the nationalized firms. The large size of the nationalized firms inhibited direct worker participation. Instead, the commissions sought to set themselves up as channels for that participation and to have a recognized voice in management.

The workers' commissions sought to get all the firms in a given industry integrated into a single entity so that, exercising a monopoly, it could operate rationally and without internal competition. They also wanted to make it difficult, if a capitalist government returned, to dismantle a nationalized sector and return individual firms to the monopoly groups which had owned them.

This restructuring required negotiation with the state, particularly with the Ministry of Industry. It also required coordination with other firms which were in the same sector or were members of the same monopoly group. The process therefore had to be carried out at a level higher than that of the firm itself. It also required technical knowledge and detailed information about the firms' structure and economic condition.

While the new state policy also envisioned the restructuring and merging of firms, these did not take place without a political struggle by the workers. Such industries as oil, chemical, and transportation were restructured, but not the banking and insurance sectors. I will argue that the critical distinguishing factor was that in the first group the workers' commissions were politically cohesive and vigorously pushed for restructuring; in the financial sectors, workers were more involved in internecine political battles.

Workers' initial contribution to nationalization was greatest in the banks. On March 11, as the news of the coup attempt spread after midday, workers at the many branches of the banks throughout Lisbon closed them and refused to reopen until the banks were nationalized. For the next few days, they occupied the banks around the clock to keep them closed. On March 14 they planned a general assembly where they would vote on a demand for nationalization; but the CR announced nationalization that morning, and the bank workers prepared to reopen the next day.

The bank workers had a militant political tradition stretching back before April 25. There were three regional bank workers' unions, covering the north, center, and south of the country (the last was the Bank Workers' Union of the South and the Islands, including the Azores and Madeira). The southern union, which included Lisbon, had been a founder of the Intersindical in 1970.

Unlike most unions, the bank workers' unions were nearly vertical; most workers belonged to a single union. As a result, new workers' commissions were not formed there after April 25, because most workers were already represented by the union delegates' commissions. These commissions led the bank workers' struggles, presenting demands and pushing for *saneamento*. The banks readily met the early demands for raises and new fringe benefits, and there was no danger of a strike in the days following April 25.

As white-collar workers, bank workers were less supportive of the PCP than were most industrial workers. In January 1975, in an election for the northern bank workers' union executive board, the pro-Communist slate (headed by Avelino Gonçalves, who had been minister of labor in the first provisional government) was defeated by a slate led by Socialists and Maoists. Communists would lose in many more white-collar unions in the coming months, reflecting not only the low level of support for the Communists among white-collar workers, but also opposition to the PCP's attempts to dominate the unions, to control the nationalization process, and to impose its model on the revolution as a whole.

Supporters of the Intersindical still led the southern union, which led the campaign for bank nationalization at the beginning of 1975. So when the coup attempt came on March 11, workers were ready to take advantage of it. As one bank worker and union activist told the story: "The banks closed at lunchtime, and at 2:00 they just didn't open. (We had done the same thing several times, on April 25, for example.) We bank workers felt we couldn't let them open again until they were nationalized. Those were good days. We occupied the banks. . . . Thousands of bank workers took part, guarding the branches day and night."

Nationalization occurred on March 14. For the next few days, banks had no official management, and during those days the union delegates ran the banks: "The union opened or didn't open the bank to the clients. It gave instructions to the workers: this check can be paid, this one no; this account is a PIDE's account, it's frozen; that one belongs to a boss who fled, it can't be touched either. We were the ones who said what could be done. On March 11, the union decided that we wouldn't open again until the banks were nationalized. The workers were practically unanimous for nationalization; that's the only way it was possible." Even when the government named administrators for each of the banks, the union was consulted on the nominations, and many of the new administrators were themselves bank employees and enjoyed the confidence of the union.

After nationalization, politically active bank workers combed bank records for evidence of "economic sabotage" by the former directors. Workers of the Banco Espirito Santo e Comercial (the Espirito Santo family controlled one of the largest monopoly groups) published a dossier claiming that the owners had committed extensive illegal acts (Comissões de Delegados Sindicais 1975). There and in other banks, workers claimed to have evidence that the banks had made huge unsecured loans and unjustifiably expanded credit rapidly after April 25, despite the liquidity difficulties stemming from the energy crisis of the year before. Further, it was charged, they had facilitated decapitalization of firms, arranged the transfer of assets to foreign accounts, and financed rightwing political groups.

The banking system cried out for restructuring. All the banks operated nationwide; there were no banks with main offices in smaller cities and remote regions, and in towns where operations were unprofitable there were no banks at all. In the major cities, however, they competed fiercely for commercial business, with an enormous number of small branches throughout the metropolitan areas. The banks were virtually the only source of credit, but they made few loans to small businesses. Bank workers proposed to restructure the banks to eliminate some of the duplication and provide banking services where they were lacking.

But because of political divisions and battles among parties for control of the unions, the workers exercised no influence over the restructuring of the banks. The Communists' defeat in the northern bank workers' union forecast losses in the other two unions too. A slate organized by the PS and the MRPP defeated the pro-Intersindical leadership of the southern union in an election in July 1975. Both before and after the election, the Union Delegates' Commissions were torn by political disputes, and the winning slate, though it supported nationalization of the banks, was hostile to the Gonçalvist government.

Competing political factions differed on how the banks should be restructured. Communists called for essentially technocratic management, with the role of workers' commissions limited to "control," or monitoring management performance. For some Socialists, the ideal model was comanagement, in which workers' commissions would elect some bank directors. Some on the far left rejected all forms of worker participation in management as long as the state remained capitalist. In addition, the heavy-handed domination of the nationalization process by the union when it was under Communist leadership became an issue. So the commissions did not actively demand restructuring and unification of the banks, and without their efforts, no restructuring occurred. The banks remained separate and competing entities, even keeping their old names (in some cases, the names of the monopoly groups or even of the families of their former owners). The Communists remained strong in heavy industry. The support they had regained in workers' commissions in the winter was reinforced by the nationalizations, which appeared to vindicate the party's policy of moderation and support of the government. (Some far leftists, in contrast, had argued that the MFA represented the bourgeoisie and would never nationalize banks and industry. Without a genuine revolution, they thought, nationalizations would make no difference anyway.) The PCP used its newly recovered strength to support centralist restructuring in nationalized firms where it dominated or strongly influenced the workers' commissions.

In the oil industry, workers' commissions of the four Portuguese-owned oil refining and distributing companies had demanded nationalization of their sector and had begun meeting together before March 11. On March 12, workers held assemblies in the separate companies and demanded nationalization. All four companies were partly state-owned, and the government had already planned to restructure the industry. With the nationalization of the banks, the state controlled more than half their capital. The companies were nationalized (along with bus lines, the merchant marine, and the electric power industry) on April 16.

The Ministry of Industry appointed a restructuring commission for the oil industry, with a representative from each company. Meanwhile, the workers' commissions of the four oil companies formed a joint workers' commission, which was determined to influence the reorganization. This body was politically heterogeneous: each member was elected from a particular section within one of the original companies, and while it contained many Communists they were not the majority; several members were from the far left, and white-collar workers in the north elected a representative who was on the right.

From the workers' commission and the union delegates in the separate firms, a "parallel commission" was chosen (parallel to the ministry's restructuring commission), which met with the restructuring commission and consulted with the workers in the various workplaces. It also nominated workers to the working groups that were set up to study particular topics.

The major objective of the parallel commission was the complete fusion of the four oil companies. The restructuring commission initially proposed that four separate state companies be created, but in the end the pressure of the parallel commission was effective: a single firm, named Petrogal, was created, although not until the following year, after the revolution had been halted.

Beyond fusion, the parallel commission worked for a common set of work rules and salary scales for all workers, and a formal voice for workers in the management of the new company. It claimed success in both. It successfully opposed the restructuring commission's proposal that the new firm be subject to a General Council which would include, in addition to management and workers' representatives, representatives of the government and the public. The workers objected that this would both dilute their own influence and make it difficult to reach decisions.

The process which led to the creation of a unified chemical company was similar, though one of the firms, CUF, was so huge that its workers played the preponderant role. Dominated by the Melo family, the CUF empire had grown from a chemical fertilizer company, founded in 1907, to the largest monopoly group in the country. It was headquartered in Barreiro, on the south bank of the Tagus, the terminal of the railways to the south. Largely because of CUF, Barreiro became one of the most industrialized cities of the country, with a long tradition of industrial struggle and Communist Party activity. Among the most active in the struggles were the women workers, employed in large numbers in the firm's textile factory.

The CUF group owned not only the fertilizer company but a total of 186 firms in various sectors, which together produced one-tenth of Portugal's gross national product. Like the other monopoly groups, CUF owned a bank and an insurance company. Their nationalization meant that the state controlled a large share of the capital of the group as a whole, and CUF workers demanded that all CUF's assets be taken over. Jorge de Melo, principal CUF owner, was briefly jailed after March 11 and shortly thereafter fled to Brazil (in what the workers widely interpreted as a tacit admission of collaboration in the coup), but the CUF group was not nationalized until August 13.

Two other manufacturers of chemical fertilizers were also nationalized, so chemical workers' commissions pressed for a merger. As in oil, the struggle for unification of the chemical industry was drawn out, completed only with the formation of a new company, called Quimigal, in 1977.

Worker pressure did not always succeed in getting firms nationalized. Heavy manufacturing was a diverse sector which produced a variety of products. Among the most important firms were Sorefame, the railroad car manufacturer, and Mague, which produced heavy construction equipment. Sorefame came under state control because the social insurance fund

(*Previdência*) had invested in it to save it from bankruptcy some years before, but a French firm held a minority interest; Mague was privately owned and highly profitable. Other firms were smaller and more marginal. Some of them were intervened because of their financial weakness, but there appeared to be no advantage to be gained by nationalizing them.

The metalworkers were well-organized and militant, and they met with the Ministry of Industry to demand nationalization of the entire sector. But they were unsuccessful, the ministry promising only to monitor production levels in the separate firms to detect sabotage.

The process of nationalization illustrates the conflict between the centralist and popular power models of revolution. The oil and chemical fertilizer industries were restructured according to the centralist model, in which the power of concentrated capital had to be confronted with equally concentrated political power, not only formally, by expropriating, but also in substance, by reorganizing the firms to facilitate collective direction of the economy.

But the centralist model also imposed limits to workers' autonomous action. Because it did not make worker participation in the restructured firms a major goal, but instead concentrated on restructuring sectors and institutionalizing the power of workers' commissions, the process inevitably became bureaucratic and state-oriented, even where pressure from workers was most effective. The experience was therefore less empowering for the workers who took part.

The same process, however, demonstrates that the transition to socialism, even on the centralist model, requires worker pressure. Government-sponsored restructuring worked only when it was accompanied by support and involvement from below. It is difficult to demonstrate that worker pressure was what made the difference between successful and unsuccessful restructuring. But if pressures from below had not had a major effect, one must presume that restructuring would have been most complete in the banks, for several reasons: the banks were nationalized first; they were most widely agreed on as targets for takeover; and their concentration of economic power was recognized as a major obstacle to any redirection of the economy. Banks were not restructured, however, despite all these factors favoring their merger. It was in the sectors where workers exercised effective pressure that restructuring took place. In other words, where nationalized industries were restructured successfully, it was an exercise of workers' power, even if it was not in the service of workers' power.

An Election in Liberty

As revolution was being made in the economy, the political parties were preparing for an election. The MFA program had promised that within a year a free election would be held for a civilian Constituent Assembly which would write a new constitution. The MFA had often justified its refusal to take long-term measures on the ground that the decisions should more properly be left to freely elected civilian rulers. But by institutionalizing itself, it claimed a special governing role at the expense of representative institutions. At the same time, the nationalizations and other major economic measures, with no explicit popular mandate, clearly preempted the authority of a future civilian government. Some leftists in the MFA urged that the election be postponed, perhaps indefinitely, out of fear that the voters might reject the new course. Still, the MFA repeatedly stressed its promise to turn power over to a democratically elected civilian government as a point of honor.

The prospect of an election, scheduled for April 12, 1975, aroused tremendous public enthusiasm. Turnout for voter registration was high. All the major parties had held congresses the previous fall and winter. At the beginning of March, fifteen parties and coalitions announced their candidates and prepared to campaign. Some parties mobilized international support: the PS took advantage of its close ties to the Socialist International and especially the German SPD, and was also funded covertly by the CIA; the PCP received covert support from the Soviet Union.

Some leftists disrupted the campaigns of the rightwing parties which they accused of ties to fascism. MRPP militants took the lead, blockading or disrupting CDS rallies. Other leftist parties joined too, and the PPD and the PDC were also sometimes targets. The most serious incident occurred in Setubal on March 7, when a leftwing demonstration challenged a PPD rally. Police, called in to quell the demonstration, shot into the crowd and killed a demonstrator. The rally then turned against the police and besieged the police station until army troops were brought in to restore order.

Some defenders of pluralism wondered whether the MFA would be willing to respect democracy and relinquish power to a civilian government. On March 18, three parties were forbidden to run—the PDC because its secretary general, Sanches Osorio, had participated in the March 11 coup and fled the country, the MRPP and the AOC for their attacks on rightwing parties (or, as some accused, to make the banning look evenhanded). As the CDS had announced a coalition with the PDC, it had to reorganize rapidly and find candidates to fill the positions on its slates which had been occupied by PDC nominees.

The next day, the day the campaign was to begin, the election was postponed for two weeks, to April 25, the first anniversary of the coup, with campaigning to begin on April 2. Finally, on April 4, the CR announced the conclusion of negotiations with the major parties over the political pact, by which the parties accepted the institutionalization of the MFA and agreed that the constitution would affirm the transition to socialism and grant the MFA a major role in choosing the president and overseeing the legislative process. The parties had won some minor concessions, but the pact meant that the most important decisions were already made, and the Constituent Assembly would have only details to decide.

Of the twelve parties running in the elections, six signed the pact: the four parties in the government coalition, the CDS, and the FSP. All the six parties refusing to sign the pact were small; ironically, five of them (all but the Monarchists) were on the far left and undoubtedly were more enthusiastic about the MFA's recent moves than were some of the signers, but they refused to acknowledge any obligation to the state they still regarded as bourgeois. In any case, none of those parties was expected to win many votes. The parties committed to the pact were expected to win an over-whelming majority in the assembly, so the election would (in theory at least) represent popular ratification of the MFA's decisions.

Some critics feared that pact really meant that the MFA would simply ignore the election. But the moderate and rightist parties consoled them-selves that the election was to be held at all, and clung to the hope that by doing well in the popular vote they would establish at least a claim to influence the decisions of the MFA.

Despite the constraints, the campaign generated tremendous excitement. Rallies were held throughout the country and from the largest cities to the smallest hamlets, walls were plastered with posters and painted with grafitti. The television campaign had the biggest audience and the greatest impact: all the parties were allowed free (and equal) time on the national network to present their cases.

The parties of the far left viewed the election as a violation of direct democracy and a tool of bourgeois domination. Arguing that voters were not prepared to make a free and informed choice after five decades of fascist obscurantism which still reigned in much of the country, the far left denounced the election in which they were running and decried the cam-paign as a marketing exercise. Some parties, most notably the PRP, disdained to participate. But most of them planned to run, in part to take advantage of the opportunity for free television time. Their harsh anticlerical and Marxist rhetoric alarmed many viewers, and since several of them claimed the name Communist or used the hammer and sickle as their emblem, they fed the anticommunism of much of the rural population. Even with the growing tension of recent months and uncertainty about the democratic future, voting was for many an affirmation of their support for the new democracy. The year since April 25 had been the most open in living memory and probably in Portuguese history. Election day itself was a celebration, a reminder of the joy that had accompanied liberation the year before, and the culmination—if also the end—of the "civic orgy." The event was hailed as Portugal's "first free election in fifty years" (more accurately, as Wheeler [1975: 2] points out, the first free election ever). A newsweekly article about election day was headlined "The Elections were a Festival." Conservatives and some radical intellectuals could disparage it, but for those who knew the difference between the repression of fifty years and the freedom of the year just ended, the election was the symbolic capstone of liberation: "*O Povo sabe empiricamente o que ela [a liberdade] pode representar* [the people know empirically what liberty can represent]" (Palla 1975: 53).

At the last minute, the MFA promoted a campaign for blank ballots. It urged those who could not make a choice among the parties to cast blank ballots to express support for the revolution, democracy, and the MFA. But the campaign had little effect. The moderate parties won handily; the PS won 38 percent of the vote, the PPD 26 percent, and the PCP came in a poor third with 13 percent, while its ally, the MDP, won 4 percent. The UDP elected one deputy from Lisbon, but the far left as a whole won only 4 percent.

The election also showed the striking geographical polarization of the country: the PCP came in first in the district of Beja and second in the districts of Evora and Setubal, all in the Alentejo. It won three-quarters of its votes in Lisbon and south of the Tagus, even though less than 40 percent of the electorate lived there. Votes for the conservative PPD and CDS were equally concentrated in the north. Equally striking was the class polarization of the vote: within regions, the PCP was strongest in zones of industrial and agricultural wage labor, the PPD and the CDS in zones of small agriculture. The PS, on the other hand, was strongest in cities and zones where service-sector workers lived.[4]

The election gave a large majority to parties, including the PS, which were at best reluctant participants in revolutionary transformation. It revealed that despite the popular movement's high visibility in the cities and in some rural areas, most of the population did not endorse rapid revolutionary progress.

The meaning of the PS victory was ambiguous: many unpoliticized voters appeared to choose it because the MFA had now officially endorsed "socialism" (President Costa Gomes, in a nationwide television address on election eve, called on voters to support parties which did not block "the socialist path"; A. Rodrigues et al. 1976: 195). Publicly, the MFA interpreted the election as a victory for the left—the PS, the PCP, and the far left—and therefore as an expression of support for the revolution. But that interpretation was disingenuous: the PS and the PCP would not unite. The Socialists' commitment to parliamentary democracy and their desire to enjoy the fruits of majority were much stronger than their commitment to socialism. For its part, the PCP had stepped up its attack on the other parties after March 11.

In fact, many moderates were already hostile to the PCP for its sectarian behavior. It had taken key positions in local governments, trade unions, and ministries and won editorial control in several nationalized newspapers, and used those positions to push its policies and often to favor its own members and sympathizers. Moreover, it had used its control of the workers' commissions to steer the nationalizations according to its own model of socialist transition. It constantly pursued the double objective of implementing socialism from above and insuring its own institutional strength. Its flagrant disregard of the desire for genuine participatory institutions alienated many who might otherwise have sympathized with the revolution.

After the election, the moderate parties increasingly criticized the PCP's "assault for power" and claimed to fear an eastern European-style coup and Communist dictatorship. The PS took the lead of an anti-Communist coalition, which rapidly turned into a coalition against the revolution as a whole. Because the PCP was the principal source of policy advice and civilian support for the MFA, criticism of the PCP could serve as a cover for opposition to the process as a whole. The moderate and rightwing parties were increasingly disillusioned with the revolution, and the election gave legitimacy to their discontent.

Rivalries came to a head on May Day. The year before, May Day had been the workers' joyous celebration of the coup which had just liberated them. It was also a celebration of the (at least apparent) unity of the working class and the parties of the left. The 1975 rally, by contrast, was a vivid demonstration of disunity. The Lisbon rally was organized by the Intersindical, which invited representatives of five parties to speak: the PCP, the PS, the MDP, the MES, and the FSP. Mutual hostility between the Intersindical organizers and the PS broke out in the negotiations for the rally arrangements, with the PS demanding that the FSP and the MES be excluded; as a concession, the Intersindical decided to make the rally "nonpartisan," without speakers from any party. But the PS insisted on holding its own march to the rally.

The Intersindical's march (far bigger) arrived first and filled the stadium, leaving no room for the PS marchers. Soares attempted to mount the platform to speak, but was not allowed. The Socialists were convinced that the Communist-dominated Intersindical had deliberately excluded them.

The MFA attempted with increasing difficulty to hold the support of the civilian parties and to maintain a balance between revolution and pluralist democracy. The moderate parties claimed electoral legitimation, and in June the Constituent Assembly in which they had won a majority would meet, giving them a forum in which to air their views. They complained, accurately, that they were not being respected, but the MFA insisted that by signing the political pact they had acknowledged its authority to rule. The nationalization of the monopolies had created the objective conditions for socialization of the economy, but the election showed that the MFA did not have a solid popular base of support. It would either have to create one or accommodate itself to the parties which could claim to represent the majority.

8

Worker Control in City and Countryside

While the state took over banks and big industries, workers took direct control of many small firms, news organizations, and farms. As owners abandoned—or were expelled from—many firms, workers found themselves forced to take over simply to avoid unemployment. To keep these workplaces operating, they had to learn to participate, cooperate, and exercise responsibility. They succeeded beyond expectations, and in the process they discovered that work in a democratically organized workplace could be creative and challenging.

Worker control, therefore, was not part of an overall political program or an abstract ideological principle, but a response to necessity. Still, it would not have spread without the favorable political conjuncture and the growth of a new consciousness which saw unanticipated possibilities in that conjuncture. Though the struggle for worker control in small firms was independent of the nationalizations, both represented a rejection of workers' subordination to capitalism. Supporters of popular power saw in the takeover of workplaces the basis for a new form of social organization which would eliminate capitalist exploitation and allow all workers to control their workplaces.

While the government's centralist policy emphasized the commanding heights of the economy, most of the country's production and most of its workers remained in small firms in marginal industries. In the stagnant economy of 1974 and 1975, many of those firms were on the brink of bankruptcy. A number of them were badly managed; most had limited capital—either they were in the service sector or they used relatively primitive technology. Many owners, frustrated by the poor economic prospects and previously unheard-of conflicts with workers, virtually abandoned their businesses. Most of these firms were too small to expect the state to take them over, so the workers' only hope to save their jobs was to run the workplaces themselves.

Asserting Worker Control

In no case did worker control arise overnight; rather, it came at the end of a long process of conflict and negotiation. In the Hotel Baía, this process was particularly acute and drawn out. The Hotel Baía overlooks a splendid beach on the Bay of Cascais, a resort just west of Lisbon. Work there is seasonal, and before 1974 workers had earned a percentage of receipts rather than a fixed salary, so their income too was seasonal. In 1974 the hotel workers' union won an industry-wide contract which established salaries. The hotel, though fairly large (sixty rooms), was wholly owned by one man, who refused to honor the contract.

A protracted conflict followed. The workers went on strike—only for a few hours, but delaying the guests' dinner from 7:30 until midnight. Still the owner refused to pay the salaries. Soon he stopped replenishing stocks, pocketing the money instead. Workers discovered that they lacked food and drink to serve to their guests. With a Ministry of Labor delegate supporting the workers, the owner was "invited to leave" on June 9, 1975, and the workers' commission took over the hotel. The owner repeatedly attempted to return, thinking that he would simply walk in, assert his right to the property, and persuade most workers to accept his authority. The workers, however, mounted guard every night for several months.

Firms which entered into self-management in this manner asked for a "credential" from the Ministry of Labor, and normally received it, especially in the frequent cases in which the ministry had already been called on to mediate between a recalcitrant owner and workers demanding their legal rights. With rather uncertain legal justification, the credential authorized a workers' commission to transact the firm's current business and to draw on its bank account. It did not transfer ownership of property, so the commission could not sell any fixed property or (in effect) make any major long-range decisions regarding the firm. The ministry also saw to it that a commission was properly elected, if none had been, and that it understood its responsibilities. At the hotel it urged the workers to reduce the commission from twelve members to a more manageable five.

The transfer of control was more peaceful in a firm which installed air conditioning equipment. There, the workers had formed a commission of trade union delegates within a month after April 25 (that it was not an autonomous workers' commission reflected the strong influence of the Communist Party among the workers). The commission's first demands included salary increases, safety improvements, and import substitution— the firm only installed equipment, and the workers wanted to establish an assembly plant. The salary demands were met; the others were not.

The firm installed central air conditioning equipment in new buildings. But in 1975 the construction boom was over, and the company, like many others, had difficulty getting credit from the newly nationalized banks. Fearing bankruptcy, the owner attempted to liquidate his assets. When he returned from an unexplained absence in the summer of 1975, the workers' commission demanded that he not go away again without leaving someone to run the firm. He conceded, giving his proxy to two men, one whom he chose and one named by the workers, and disappeared. Later, the proxy was supplemented by a credential from the Ministry of Labor.

Limpa, a carpentry cooperative, grew of a construction company. With the recession in the construction industry, the owner of the firm could not pay back salaries. In the summer of 1975 he suggested to the workers that they form a cooperative, which would be eligible to bid on a project being put out by a leftist city council in a Lisbon suburb. He proposed to turn over the limited construction tools he owned if the workers would forgive him the back salaries, and he would remain as a member of the cooperative. They accepted the proposal.[1]

The process whereby firms came under worker control varied, but most commonly conflict would arise over some concrete issue such as wages, and the owner threatened to close the firm rather than meet the workers' demands. Confronting their boss invariably heightened the workers' consciousness and their solidarity until they were ready to take over. Sometimes the owner abandoned the firm; sometimes he was forced out; in some cases the distinction seems arbitrary. The support of the state and the general social climate made the actual takeover fairly easy. Moreover, a worker-controlled firm could claim a certain legitimacy since the takeover appeared necessary to avert unemployment and maintain the level of national production. One observer even said that the firms fell into the hands of the workers like "rotten fruit from an old tree" (Calado 1978: 10).

But once they took control, the workers' tasks were anything but easy. Most of the worker-controlled firms were small.[2] They had been managed directly by their owners, with the result that few workers had management experience. Those who did were often unsympathetic to the workers' takeover, since as professionals many of them had identified with the bosses. Social differences between them and blue-collar workers were often reflected in a political difference: production workers were much more likely to be Communists. In the air conditioning firm, some engineers who sympathized with the boss refused to collaborate with the workers' commission. The commission made some effort to win them over, but when the firm was unable to pay salaries for a period, they were the first to leave.[3] As a result, many ordinary workers had to take on management roles. (Almost all who did were men, even in firms that employed large numbers of women.) The most politically active workers, those who had led the workers' commission, generally took leading roles, and the workers' commission generally became the management committee and received the Ministry of Labor's credential.

Both for ideological reasons and to share work and responsibility as widely as possible, commission members encouraged all workers to take part in management. Consultation among them was intense: "I won't say we had a general meeting every day," reported a commission member in Corame, a metalworking factory in which the state later intervened (as described below), "but often we did. The commission hardly made decisions on its own. They were made in assemblies." But inevitably, some workers took leading roles—and they were blamed by their colleagues if things went wrong. Some commission members dropped out after suffering burnout from the intense effort and what felt like unfair criticisms from their less active colleagues.

Nevertheless, many described the initial period of worker control as the most exciting: everyone took an active part, learned various aspects of the business, and worked enormously hard. Especially at first, workers had to learn a great deal very quickly if the firm was to survive. As the president of UNOP, a large manufacturer of paper cartons, recounted: "We started right out by naming a workers' commission and looking for ways to resolve the crisis. Everyone went off, some to the customers, others to the suppliers, others to the bank, others to the government, the various departments; others to the union, the Ministry of Labor, etc. Others met with economists, sociologists, other cooperatives, companies, to gather information so we could figure out the best way to go." Especially at first, workers had to get a lot of experience very quickly if the firm was to survive. Many workers discovered that they learned in the process and developed the needed skills just by exercising decisionmaking power.

The first task was to make sure that production continued, and that required that the firm reestablish its credit, both literally and figuratively. Immediate, crucial negotiations began with creditors (who were usually also suppliers); the firm had to assure them that it would pay its debts, but at the same time persuade them not to demand payment immediately. Some found that their creditors were hostile just because they had taken over, as at UNOP: "The idea going around in a lot of companies was that we had occupied the company, . . . that the employees had kicked the bosses out, that we were savages, bad people, Communists. We were accused of everything. . . . It was hard work and took a long time to persuade them otherwise, that the bosses had just quit.''

But worker-controlled firms overcame that hostility. They argued, often persuasively, that if creditors forced them into bankruptcy, lien laws assured that wages and debts to the government (e.g., for social security taxes) would be paid before any private debts, so that the creditors would recover little or nothing; but if they continued to supply the firm, it might get back on its feet and pay the debts in full later. Some creditors accepted this argument. But they demanded cash on the line for further supplies.

Meeting payrolls was a priority. Workers took control to preserve their jobs, and in some cases they had gone with no or partial salaries for a few months. As we will see, keeping all members employed and paying their salaries remained a paramount goal in the cooperatives that survived to become economically stable.

Some conflicts between workers and owners led not to worker control but to state intervention. But intervention was not a goal in itself. In these firms, too, what workers wanted was to protect their jobs. They negotiated with management, often demanding new investments and other measures to save the firm. Only when negotiations failed did they seek intervention, and the government acceded only in medium-sized and large firms, those big enough that bankruptcy would cause a shock to the economy. Even so, a political struggle was necessary to get the state to intervene. Since it usually did so only after owners had abdicated, most of these firms were effectively worker-controlled for a while.

A lengthy conflict preceded the occupation of Corame, a light metalworking factory near Lisbon. Only three years old, it had 400 workers. A workers' commission was formed in May 1974, after a conflict between the administrative staff and the blue-collar workers. The commission demanded improvements in working conditions, investments to buy labor-saving equipment, and later a general salary increase. The owner attended a workers' meeting ("for the first and only time") to plead inability to raise salaries, and threatened to close the factory; but he did give in on the salary increase—though not on the new investments.

During the next several months orders declined, leaving workers idle.

Suspecting that the owner was turning down orders to drive the firm into bankruptcy, the workers' commission asked for a Finance Ministry audit of the firm's books. Such an audit was necessary to demonstrate "sabotage," which was the legal basis for intervention.

Matters came to a head in April 1975. When the owner announced that he would not pay a month's wages, the workers occupied the factory, expelled the owner, and called for state intervention. The workers' commission received a credential for ordinary management from the armed forces' leftist Fifth Division. This arrangement was even more irregular than Ministry of Labor credentials, but like many unsanctioned practices during the revolutionary period, it was effective. The state did not intervene until the following September, so for five months the firm was directly worker-controlled.

During that period, workers occupied the plant twenty-four hours a day. Here, as in other firms, occupying was an intensely politicizing experience. Everyone worked the regular day, and some (taking turns) stayed the night—passing time partly with cards and checkers, but also with heavy discussions: grievances about the old owner and capitalism in general, excitement about the course of the revolution. One night, after hearing a radio report about violence in Angola, the workers sent a telegram of solidarity to the MPLA.

In the textile firm Eurofil, part of the Borges monopoly group, a struggle broke out shortly after April 25 and culminated in intervention a year later. Management threatened layoffs, claiming that they could not afford to pay wage increases. Meanwhile the workers' commission, taking part in a joint commission of all the firms of the Borges group, discovered that the managers of the group had falsified invoices to decapitalize the firm. On February 4, 1975, the Eurofil workers voted to expel the management and demanded that the firm be nationalized. While they awaited a response, the workers ran the factory. Then in April the government, instead of nationalizing, intervened.

At Lusalite, the fiberboard maker discussed in Chapter 4, a long confrontation began with such bread-and-butter issues as end-of-year bonuses, and then was extended to issues of management. Workers in the firm's accounting department leaked the information to the workers' commission that management was siphoning away assets. A Finance Ministry audit demanded by the workers' commission confirmed this, and the state intervened in June 1975. The three-member administrative commission appointed included two who already worked as managers in the firm and a third who had been consulting with the firm on the ministry's inquiry.

Past financial irregularity was a common factor leading to worker control or intervention. The questionable practices that had been rife during the boom years of the 1960s and early 1970s probably escalated in 1974 and 1975 as capitalists, fearing takeovers, withdrew as much as possible in their own name or in tangible goods. Particularly for firms owned or controlled by monopoly groups (such as Corame, Eurofil, and Lusalite), opportunities for creative accounting and financing had abounded during the boom, and many such firms had been left in a precarious financial condition. Once workers got access to the books and discovered these practices, they made them the basis of the demand that the state intervene or provide a management credential.

The Economic Sabotage Law, though extremely vague, provided the legal basis for intervention and the appointment of an administrative commission to manage the firm. Its members were often from the firm itself. They were generally professionals or technicians, not line workers; but many of them had been active in the workers' commission or at least had the commission's confidence. The administrators had legal power over the firm's day-to-day affairs but could not sell its assets. Intervention in principle made the firms part of the social area of the economy and subject to government direction, but in practice they were relatively autonomous.

Sometimes the presence of appointed administrators meant a more restricted role for the workers' commission. This was true at Corame, for example, where one worker recounted: "After the intervention things changed. . . . The workers' commission was mainly concerned with the problems of the workers. But they also met with the administrators . . . and tried to influence their decisions. . . . Participation also became more organized, less spontaneous; [workers were less involved] in the day-to-day affairs of the firm."

But in some firms the workers' commissions continued to take an active role in management after intervention. In Lusalite, which faced a boycott by its usual suppliers of asbestos, the workers' commission negotiated a supply from the Soviet Union. It also organized subcommissions to deal with production, finance, sales, and social issues, each with a member of the administrative commission and one or more representatives of the workers' commission. Further, a general assembly of workers was held each month, but it dealt mainly with wages and other bread-and-butter issues.

The workers' commissions in worker-controlled firms and firms in which the state had intervened looked for outside support, both from the state and from other firms in which workers' commissions had either control or some influence. Some politically sympathetic firms and city governments gave them their business. The Ministry of Labor granted credentials freely, and offered at least minimal technical assistance, sometimes insisting on a reorganization of the workers' commission. Sympathetic military units supported them: when the workers at Corame learned that the firm's owner was fleeing the country to escape trial for fraud, a COPCON detachment accompanied them to the railroad station, delayed the Paris express, and pulled him off.[4]

In general, however, worker control emerged under very unfavorable conditions. The economy was stagnant, and most of the firms that workers took over were close to bankruptcy. State support was limited because officials were more interested in the nationalized firms which they controlled directly than in the small worker-controlled firms. Worker control nevertheless benefited from a favorable ideological climate which was at least partly encouraged by the state, for worker takeovers were part of a popular movement whose continued growth and enthusiasm would be necessary to sustain the revolutionary process.

How Worker Control Works

In the spring of 1980 I conducted a study of work organization in worker-controlled firms. Though this was several years after the revolution had ended, many of the firms which had been taken over were still run by their workers and some were thriving. I interviewed workers (current or former workers' commission activists) in six firms, ranging in size from 13 to 150 workers (some of them are discussed earlier in this chapter).[5]

Theorists of worker control maintain that it has many potential benefits for workers: it ends alienation by eliminating hierarchy and the detailed division of labor; it democratizes the workplace, giving all workers influence over decisions which affect them; it enables workers to exercise new capacities and to enjoy more rewarding social relationships among themselves; and finally, it increases productivity by increasing their motivation and commitment. I examined the internal organization of these six firms to determine whether their structure differed from that of capitalist firms and whether it achieved any of these effects.[6] The study is described in more detail by Hammond (1981).

Economic performance. These firms did operate on a somewhat different principle than capitalist firms: their major goal was not to maximize profits but to maximize and stabilize employment. These goals do not necessarily conflict, but if the goal is not to *maximize* profits, there will be conditions under which a worker-controlled firm will act differently. These firms pursued growth, but were reluctant to take risks which might endanger the position of the present members; no one was laid off when work was slack.

This emphasis is not surprising, given their origins. Workers took over primarily to stave off the immediate threat of unemployment; and though by 1980 several of these cooperatives were secure enough to raise salaries or distribute profits, they were cautious, retaining profits and allowing salaries to rise only slowly.

This emphasis on maintaining employment of members at all costs (and, secondarily, providing employment to new members) gave the cooperatives flexibility in mobilizing labor; if their salary was guaranteed, workers worked very long hours to ensure their firm's survival. Each of the firms that I studied reported that for a period they worked overtime every day and every weekend without extra pay.

All the firms emphasized, either as goal or as accomplishment, the reinvestment of their surplus to create more jobs, and those which succeeded reported the numbers proudly. All reported that the number of employees declined in the last months or years before worker control because the owner let the firm run down, and declined further in the first months of worker control because some workers became disillusioned and left. But all but one reported more members in 1980 than the peak under capitalist ownership, and in four of the six the number had at least doubled from the low point.

These firms could add more workers as the result of capital investment, almost exclusively financed from profits or created by voluntary labor. As a privately owned company and during the first years of worker control, the air conditioning firm only installed equipment. In 1979 it inaugurated a new factory, built with voluntary weekend labor, to assemble air conditioners under license from its former foreign supplier.

Members claimed that they worked harder and with greater enthusiasm under worker control and that their firms were more productive than they had been under capitalism. There is no systematic evidence on these firms' productivity. Productivity gains are certainly likely to follow worker control, not only because of greater commitment and longer hours, but also because strikes and petty sabotage are unlikely. Such gains have been found under worker control elsewhere, such as Chile under Allende (Espinosa and Zimbalist 1978: 163–74; Zimbalist and Petras 1976: 27–28) and in cooperatives in the United States (Bernstein 1976: 18–19).

Health and safety. Dangerous working conditions appeared not to concern either cooperative members or management committees very much.

Decisions about the cost-effectiveness of health and safety measures were apparently made either by design or default in favor of maintaining existing practices. Health and safety issues were raised with vehemence in many capitalist firms in the labor turmoil of 1974 and 1975. Yet concern seems to have been greater where changes in work practices could be won as concessions from capitalist employers than where workers had the opportunity to put them into practice themselves.

Authority and the labor process. One might expect worker-controlled firms to adopt a different division of labor to eliminate or minimize traditional hierarchy and job routinization, conditions which have been identified as alienating. Though these firms did operate very differently from capitalist firms, they nevertheless fell far short of any ideal standard. None reported any major change in the work process under worker control. The imperative of survival made them look for ways to keep going rather than to alter the work process to make it less dull or alienating.

All the firms had a dual structure of authority. Everyone who worked was a member and thus shared in ultimate legal authority. In day-to-day affairs, however, a traditional chain of command operated, in which section heads and members of the management committee made decisions and gave orders. But the chain of command was mitigated by informal relations. Those who had authority did not exercise it capriciously or harshly: they regarded the other members as colleagues, and the other members in turn knew that they ultimately shared in power. Yet it remained true that in these cooperatives, most members apparently did not care to take an active role in management and decisionmaking; they preferred just to do their jobs.

During the early stage of worker control, participation was more complete and more intense—the situation required that everyone take an active part, whether in lobbying government agencies or other potential sources of support, mounting guard, or simply keeping the plant operating. Presumably this active participation was accompanied by greater influence over decisions. As the firms stabilized, workers seem to have accepted routinization readily. Since the main stimulus to worker control was the desire to maintain employment, active participation slackened when it was less urgently needed.

In each cooperative, a general assembly (meeting annually in some cooperatives, more frequently in others) held ultimate power, and all members had an equal vote. To illustrate the sort of issue brought before its general assembly, a management committee member at the Hotel Baía gave the example of firing someone. The committee could dismiss a member for stealing, but for lesser offenses it sought the approval of all members. Twice the management committee had wanted to fire members (one who was habitually absent and another who circulated a petition calling for the hotel to be returned to its capitalist owner), but a majority of the members voted to keep them. Given the cooperatives' employment-maximization economy, the outcome is not surprising; that these were the major examples of issues referred to the entire body confirms how important the question of employment was.

Cooperative members, therefore, shared equally in formal authority, but were apparently happy to delegate that authority on a regular basis. As an administrative worker of the carpentry cooperative said, "When they're paid, they're happy." Gramsci argued that autonomous workers should come to see themselves as producers rather than as commodities on the labor market (1977: 98–111). For these workers, however, the conditions of work appeared less important than the fact of work.

Social and economic equality. Though the work process was governed by hierarchical authority, inequalities of income and status were much less pronounced. The salary range in all the cooperatives was smaller than in most capitalist firms; but most of the reduction was at the top. People in management positions received far lower salaries than did managers in private firms—as one administrator said: "When you decide to work in a cooperative, you've made a certain choice." Within the ranks of workers, something close to the traditional salary scale obtained, modified in some cases to raise the lowest salaries. The firms offered some fringe benefits which mitigated economic inequalities and others which, by being proportional to salaries, accentuated differences. Cooperativists with whom I raised the issue readily acknowledged both the goal of equality and the need to reward merit through salary differentials. This apparent inconsistency suggested that the issue was not very important to them.

Differences in status did not appear to be strongly reflected in deferential behavior. In most of these cooperatives, conscious efforts had been made to establish informal and equal social relations, most successfully where the management committee had at least some members who were ordinary workers before worker control. Deference was still visible in UNOP, the paper carton manufacturer, where the president had been the owner's deputy; his relations with other workers appeared paternalistic, but even so it was clear that deference was tempered by friendliness.

Especially at the beginning, but later too, the cooperatives required extra efforts that were likely to create commitment and enforce equality among members (indeed, it is hard to imagine that the efforts would be made by people who did not share commitment and equality). Since people from all hierarchical levels had shared the tasks of painting, sweeping, and standing guard, strong status distinctions were unlikely to survive.

Socialist socializing. The social atmosphere in these cooperatives was palpably friendly. Members got along well and genuinely seemed to enjoy being together. Some companies had an active after-hours social life too, with soccer teams, annual parties, and family picnics. Potted plants, birds in cages, pets, murals by members showing the history of a cooperative, all testified to the members' affection for their shops. Their willingness to do voluntary labor and overtime also indicated friendly relations.

Good social relations were at a premium in cooperatives, still-precarious institutions whose survival depended on commitment. Members knew how important this was; they were quite conscious of the value of an in-house lunchroom where people could get to know each other, of outings, and of annual parties. I found evidence of an extracurricular social life nearly everywhere; on discussion, it turned out that the members deliberately cultivated it and were aware of its importance. Why should good feelings be more abundant in a cooperative than in most workplaces? There are several plausible explanations: that the process of worker control encouraged people to get along well; that job security and relative social and wage equality eliminated a motive for competition; that members who did not get along left; or that these cooperatives survived and succeeded in part because of a fortuitous initial selection. Whatever the reason, the fact was palpable. Good feelings about the workplace and bonds of friendship among fellow workers were themselves signs of the success of worker control.

Overall, the achievement of democratic control in these firms was uneven. They came closest to equality in social relations not directly affecting work, did somewhat less well with regard to economic equality, and appeared to have done little toward eliminating the inequality of authority and the routinization and stultification of the work process. These limits were not imposed on the workers: cooperative members clearly could participate more fully and modify the labor process if they chose to (though economic constraints may have made them cautious about experimentation). It appears, instead, that they simply felt no strong motivation to exercise more control.

Although the literature on worker control does not cite it as a prominent goal, one achievement of these firms deserves emphasis: job security. As long as the cooperative survived (and the contribution their efforts made to survival was tangible), workers did not fear the loss of job and income. To that extent, their labor was removed from the market, and they were free of a major uncertainty of life. The significance of this accomplishment, which is also a major goal of trade unions in capitalist firms, went beyond mere economics. It was political: it gave the workers control over an aspect of their fate which is normally determined by capitalist imperatives without regard for their needs. Job security was a principal motive for founding worker-controlled enterprises and affected their operation in many respects, as I have shown. Theorists of worker control should pay more attention to it, as workers evidently already do.

These firms, in any case, changed enormously after 1974. Workers enjoyed job security. Authoritarian supervision had nearly disappeared. Social relations improved. Workers were routinely consulted before major decisions were made. The elements of worker control, however limited, made work in these firms much different from work in most capitalist firms.

Worker-Controlled Media

In 1975 two news media, *Rádio Renascença* and the daily paper *República,* were taken over by their workers. *Rádio Renascença* belonged to the Roman Catholic Patriarchate of Lisbon, and *República* was owned by people close to the PS, whose line the paper followed. The takeovers became important symbols for opponents of the revolution and international *causes célèbres.* They were heralded as evidence of a Communist drive to destroy independent media, though in fact both grew out of internal labor disputes and were not led by Communists or Communist sympathizers.

These worker-controlled media were important to the popular movement in a different way, regularly opening their pages and microphones to people engaged in the struggles for popular power in workplaces, neighborhoods, and military units, and providing them with instruments to communicate their views for the first time. Thus *República* and *Rádio Renascença* were not only examples of worker control of the media; they became voices for the larger popular movement as well.

Both struggles had been building up since the previous year and came to a head shortly after May Day. In part the timing of the takeovers reflected the political tension after the election, the moderate parties' growing disaffection from the government, and the political hostilities manifested in the May Day demonstration. Yet while national politics affected the struggles, each had its own dynamic: just as in other firms, worker control was a response to internal conflicts, not to an abstract ideological demand.

The dispute in *Rádio Renascença* had the longer history. Though the

Lisbon Patriarchate was the station's principal owner, the church had not interfered with programming before 1974. The station was run by a conservative business firm, and the only religious programming was the daily rosary. Management was closely tied to the old regime, and reporters had frequently protested internal censorship of news coverage.

Soon after April 25, a reporter forced the censorship issue. He interviewed Alvaro Cunhal and requested permission to broadcast the interview (rather than simply airing it without authorization, as he could have done). When he was refused, the station's workers struck. The strike was brief, but before it was over the workers had formed a workers' commission and made demands about working conditions as well. The workers' commission also voted to equalize all salaries—a revolutionary step taken in few if any other workplaces.

Hoping to end the conflict, the Cardinal, Dom Antonio Ribeiro, named a new management council for the station in July. But it refused to meet with the workers' commission. Worse, it established a new requirement for employment: newly hired workers would have to undergo a battery of psychological tests. The purpose of these tests was never clarified, but as it happened, a member of the Cardinal's management council ran a company which gave such tests, and eight recently hired workers were ordered to take them (even though they had been hired without any such requirement). When they refused, they were fired.

The workers' commission demanded that they be rehired, and a dispute simmered for months. Meanwhile, the national bishops' council, which had previously paid little attention to the station, declared on September 27 that programming should be "morally and spiritually harmonized" with the teachings of the church (*Expresso*, October 25, 1974). The hierarchy, which did not overtly oppose the revolution until the summer of 1975, nevertheless felt threatened by the demands for change from the station's workers.

In February 1975, workers at both the Lisbon and Oporto studios went on strike to defend their fired colleagues. The strike was still going on on March 11, but the workers returned to work the next day so that they could broadcast news of the crisis. Even after returning, they were paid late or not at all, and their relations with management remained at an impasse. Early in April the Communication Ministry intervened in the station and imposed a new management council, but it came no closer to resolving the issue.

On May 27, the Lisbon workers took control of the station. They described the takeover as an "occupation," but the state-appointed management council had already virtually withdrawn. Workers in the Oporto studio, who had joined the strike, did not go along with the Lisbon workers now. They continued to work as usual, and the management upgraded the Oporto station, buying a new transmitter powerful enough to broadcast throughout the country.

Still trying to drive the workers from the Lisbon studio, the administrators ordered in mid-June that the building's water and electricity be shut off and canceled wire service contracts. But the utilities workers refused to cut the station off, and the Reuters representative was persuaded to keep the wires open.

Since they were constantly reporting their side of the conflict, the *Renascença* workers kept the issue before the public. On June 18, the main newspaper workers' unions, the UDP, and Christians for Socialism, a small group of progressive Catholics, called a demonstration to support them at the Cardinal's palace. Supporters of the Cardinal called a counterdemonstration for the same day. A COPCON detachment arrived to intervene and prevent violence, but in ill-disguised support for the workers, it "protected" some of the pro-church demonstrators by carrying them off in army trucks. Many were elderly women or children from parochial schools, and some were roughed up on the way.

Under Otelo's leadership, the COPCON was emerging as the center of the far-left military. It supported the popular movement, in a growing split with the Gonçalvists, who attempted to maintain institutional legality. Not wanting the church to turn against the revolution, Gonçalves strove to settle the issue by returning the station, a position the PCP actively supported. On July 1, he met with the *Renascença* workers' commission. He told them that the government had decided to give the station back to the church, and asked them to leave peacefully rather than exacerbate the crisis.

The workers at the station rejected the plea. On the air, they asked the workers in general to decide whether they should comply. Predictably, they were flooded with phone calls, some of which they broadcast, urging them to hold on. The next day a massive demonstration gathered to support them. Despite the government's edict, Otelo refused to send the COPCON to break up the demonstration and dislodge the workers. The Council of the Revolution sided with him and named yet another administrative commission which would have nominal control but leave the workers in charge (Downing 1984).

Under worker control (both before and after the latest government–named commission), programming and broadcasting proceeded much as they had since the strike ended in March. Workers did not establish collective control over the content of broadcasting (as we will see, the situation in *República* was different, at least in intention). As at other workplaces, worker control did not change the work process much.

Programming did change in some ways. Portuguese folk music and international revolutionary songs filled the airwaves; although the announcers wanted to abandon Anglo-American-style pop music, they bowed to popular taste and continued to play it while explaining to their listeners the importance of the new kinds of music. They read the communiqués of parties, trade unions, and, most importantly, workers' and neighborhood commissions. This open policy made *Renascença* appear to workers as their voice; it gave them a chance to hear *their* news on the air.

The conflict over *República* blew up at the same time and over many of the same issues. *República,* an afternoon daily newspaper, had been the main voice of the antifascist opposition for many years. Shortly before 1974 it had been bought by a group close to Mario Soares and the political tendency which would become the PS. Its publisher, Raul Rego, was a militant of the PS who was elected to the Constituent Assembly in 1975. Since the paper was not owned by a financial group, it was the only Lisbon daily which was not nationalized after March 11. Advocates of press independence, angry at the PCP's domination of the state-controlled press, saw *República* as a bulwark.

In fact, *República* was hardly more objective or neutral than any of the other Lisbon papers; it presented the Socialist Party's point of view, which did not appear in the nationalized dailies. Many of its reporters wanted it to stay independent and present all leftist points of view. Its adherence to the PS line had caused friction between journalists and editors almost since April 25, and the following April several reporters resigned, including all who were militants of or close to the PCP.

The production workers, too, were increasingly opposed to the paper's monolithic political line. On May 2 they went on strike, demanding the right to veto any new journalists who might be hired. The strike prevented the publication of the PS version of the May Day dispute. Management rejected the workers' demand as an interference with *their* freedom of the press. The workers' commission then attempted to negotiate an agreement with the editorial staff to maintain an independent political line and treat all progressive parties equally. Failing that, it demanded that Rego, the publisher, resign.

The reporters still on the paper supported Rego and wrote stories about the internal struggle which reflected the PS position. On May 19, production workers refused to print an article which they felt misrepresented them. In retaliation, the journalists stopped writing. Faced with their implicit strike, the workers' commission claimed control of the paper and published an edition on its own.

That same day the PS called a demonstration to oppose the workers' takeover. Gathering outside the *República* building, the PS militants, led by Mario Soares, demanded that "their" paper be returned to them (an ironic confirmation of the workers' complaint that the paper was partisan). The COPCON sent a detachment to mediate the dispute, and then resolved to close the paper down.

Rego and the paper's directors demanded to have the paper returned and the PS threatened to abandon the government over the issue. On June 6, the Council of the Revolution declared that since the directors had asked to have the paper closed, they would have to request that it be reopened. But they demanded a guarantee of their freedom to run the paper without interference from the workers. With startling indecisiveness, the government announced the reopening for June 12 and then postponed it; on June 16, though the paper's directors had not agreed, troops reopened the office and let the workers enter. Once inside, the workers stayed. Civilian supporters of both sides, but especially of the workers, gathering outside the office more or less constantly, kept tension high.

Finally on July 10 the CR decided much as it had for *Renascença:* it named three officers to an administrative commission which would let the workers run the paper (Downing 1984). The workers then launched a unique experiment, in which intellectual and manual workers attempted to control an intellectual product jointly, and even to share that control with the popular movement as a whole, which they regarded as the paper's constituency.

For a newspaper, worker control meant something different than it did in production firms. Journalists and production workers alike assumed that *República* was to be the newspaper of the workers, and that "workers" meant members of the working class. As intellectuals, the journalists were there to serve them. While a few journalists remained from the old staff, most were newly hired by the workers' commission. (Several journalism students also wrote for the paper regularly.) So most of them owed their own jobs to the workers, and they all recognized that the production workers had made *República* a worker-controlled paper dedicated to the workers' movement.

But though the production workers claimed ultimate authority over its contents, they wanted journalists to write it—they did not challenge the customary division between mental and manual labor. Besides, the journalists were professionals with experience; they were better educated and came from higher social backgrounds than the workers, and the months of revolution had hardly destroyed the old habits of deference.

Relations between workers and journalists were therefore ambiguous (though generally harmonious). But the workers exercised final control through a political commission, chosen by the workers' commission, which approved each day's paper before it went to bed. While most of the stories were routinely approved, some were vetoed, and occasionally a decision on whether to print was referred to the workers' commission as a whole. Even more rarely, a story was held up for a day and referred to an assembly of all workers.

The paper's poor financial condition (it complained of an advertisers' boycott) meant that it could not hire a full staff; some reporters were student interns. These circumstances affected the quality of the writing (J.A. Fernandes 1980: 14). Stories often consisted of little more than the communiqués of mass organizations. Editing was limited, so each story reflected the politics of the writer. And though the entire staff supported the workers' movement, it included all varieties of leftist opinion, and all the left's internecine battles were fought out in the paper (unlike *Renascença*, where internal relations were remarkably calm and free of party-political conflicts). This created inconsistencies: two stories about the same topic, which reflected opposite points of view, might appear on successive days.

República as a whole felt a responsibility toward the entire workers' movement and saw itself as the movement's voice. In practice, this responsibility was met by opening its pages to the mass organizations; it printed their communiqués, reported their news, and interviewed their members in feature stories. The paper's workers themselves also participated actively in the struggles of other workers' commissions. They even became movement celebrities, speaking to other workers in their own workplaces and at rallies; some even went abroad on speaking tours when the *República* affair got international attention.

Many who saw worker takeovers of news media as a violation of freedom of the press attacked the *Renascença* and *República* workers as Communists. Others identified the station with the UDP because the UDP led the demonstration defending it. But the workers at both places—as in many other workplaces—denied identification with any party, insisting that their struggles were not political but labor-related, and were politicized only by management.

As with other commissions which insisted that they were "unitary," the claim to reject party influence was somewhat disingenuous. In the prevailing political climate, disputes within the media inevitably had political implications. But it was true that neither the station nor the paper presented a Communist line. A listener or reader, comparing the news erage in *Rádio Renascença* or *República* to the nationalized print press, would quickly conclude that they were far more independent of the PCP than most papers. Moreover, the Communist sympathizers among the *República* journalists had left in April, before the workers attempted to take over, and the PCP had tried to get *Rádio Renascença* returned to the church.

And even if *República* was affected by intra-left conflicts, party independence was an ideal which was widely shared by workers at both places. As the head announcer at *Renascença* said in an interview, in what I interpreted to be as much an expression of the unitary ideal as a specific criticism of the parties, "there are no parties that defend the interests of the workers."

If both groups of workers claimed to be independent of any party, however, they openly identified with the popular movement. Just as Lenin had argued in 1902 that the most important task facing the Russian workers' movement was to create an all-Russian newspaper, some at *República* hoped that their paper would be the spark which would ignite the flame among the Portuguese workers. They did not want to lead the movement; they wanted the paper to speak for the movement and (somehow) submit to its editorial control.

Some activists created a Secretariat of Support for the Struggle of *República*. Its members attended *República* workers' assemblies, offered advice and criticism, and raised money for the paper. But they were a self-selected handful. They did not represent the movement and they did not control the paper. Many of them were party militants, not independent activists supporting the nonpartisan goals of the base organizations, and were as eager to promote their own position as to let the paper speak for the movement as a whole.

The movement itself was not ideologically or organizationally coherent enough to speak with a single voice or have a single medium to represent it. Most activists were too busy with their own particular struggles to create a unified movement. The movement as a whole never proclaimed a coherent ideology: each of its components had arisen autonomously in pursuit of goals which were particular and immediate, and they only implicitly recognized themselves as all part of a common movement. Worse, any organization which claimed to represent the movement as a whole would be competing with other organizations and cease to be unitary. And while adherents wanted the movement to act in concert, they did not want it to be subordinate to a central authority. Thus there was no way for *República* to become the voice of the whole movement.

Agrarian Reform

In the countryside, farmworkers took over many of the huge farms of the Alentejo. They acted for the same reason as urban workers: to have work. Steady work had been the motive behind all their demands after April 25: the union contracts, the compulsory assignment of workers, the campaign for land expropriation, and the first occupations themselves.

Until the expropriation law was passed in July 1975, there were few occupations, because the PCP tended to oppose them until then.[7] Where the PCP and the union were weakest, however, occupations began earlier. The first occupations, described in Chapter 5, were led by tractor owners and tenant farmers afraid of losing their investment unless the farms were cultivated. Before July, some occupations were officially recognized under the Economic Sabotage Law. There were even cases in which the government appointed administrators of an estate, as it did with firms under state intervention.

But most early occupations occurred without state sanction and the occupiers ran the properties without state assistance. As in industry, their initiatives prodded the government to act. In February the Melo Antunes program had proposed compulsory renting or expropriation of undercultivated farms. But even before the Melo Antunes program appeared, farmworkers had demanded that all big farms be taken over, not just those which were not being farmed.

The government decided to expropriate all latifundios only after March 11. The new cabinet included a minister of agriculture, Fernando Oliveira Baptista, committed to land reform. Decree/Law 203-C, promulgated on April 15, nationalized some farms: those larger than 50 hectares (about 125 acres) which were served by state-funded irrigation projects (Barros 1979: 85, 160). In principle, nationalizations were automatic, but in fact they did not take effect immediately.

The same decree declared that all large farms were subject to expropriation. But it set only general guidelines: farms with more than 50 hectares of irrigated land or 500 hectares of dry land would be subject to expropriation, but actual expropriation would also depend on the potential yield of the land. Moreover, it did not set up a procedure for taking over expropriable land. It was not until July 29 that further laws defined eligibility for expropriation or nationalization by a complicated scoring system which took account of local conditions: any owner of properties whose size, fertility, and improvements were worth 50,000 points was subject to expropriation.[8]

Like the law requiring rental of empty apartments, the expropriation law did not explicitly allow occupations. But it signified tacit consent, and workers began to occupy in earnest. The PCP also put its full weight behind land occupations. Most were led by the Communist-dominated rural workers' unions, especially in the district of Beja, where the union was strongest. The union also played a major role in managing the cooperatives and recruiting members. Some farms were taken over by their own permanent workers. The farms which employed many permanent workers were large, fertile, and often highly capitalized. Workers occupied them (sometimes in collusion with the owner) to prevent union-sponsored occupations by unemployed workers from outside (Barros 1979: 115–26; Bermeo 1986: 90–91). Altogether, workers occupied some 450 large properties covering a total area of some 1.16 million hectares.

Agriculture Minister Oliveira Baptista recognized that the existing bureaucracy was too tied into the latifundio system to conduct agrarian reform, and that new institutions were needed. Beginning in June, Regional Agrarian Reform Centers were created in eight southern districts, and most of the agronomists they employed were leftists who supported agrarian reform wholeheartedly. Officially, the centers were to initiate expropriations and then assign workers to the expropriated farms (Baptista 1978: 140–41).

What each center actually did depended on the conditions in its district. Differences of topography, fertility, landholding and labor relations meant that the early occupation movement had proceeded very differently from one district to another. Where many occupations had already occurred, the centers' major task was to legalize them rather than to initiate expropriations. Their tasks were similar to those of officials who supported housing occupations: importantly, to certify that the property was eligible for expropriation and to oversee an inventory of goods—livestock, machines, and buildings—to establish the owner's presumptive right to indemnization and, more immediately (in the case of livestock and machines), to keep the owner from selling them off and decapitalizing the farm (Moreira and Simões 1982).

In Evora, for example, there were many early occupations, and the center could do little more than recognize them as *faits accomplis*. Manuel Belo Moreira, director of the Evora center, later complained that those occupations had produced many disputes between landowners and occupiers which the center had to spend most of its energy attempting to resolve, so that it was unable to direct agrarian reform in an orderly manner (Moreira and Simões 1982: 137,145).

In other districts few occupations had occurred before July, not because the union opposed them, as in Beja, but because more farmworkers had permanent jobs. In these districts the centers more often followed official guidelines. In the district of Setubal, for example, which contained some of the large nationalized farms, the center dissuaded workers from occupying on their own and instead initiated some expropriations officially and trained workers to run the properties once they took them over.

A second new institution was the Regional Agrarian Reform Councils. Set up in each southern district, these were composed of representatives from the Rural Workers' Union and the League of Small and Medium Farmers of the district and the MFA and the ministries of Agriculture and Internal Administration. They oversaw the process of expropriation and were meant to encourage direct action by occupiers.

The armed forces played a major role in supporting the occupation movement. Many units of the Southern Military Region, commanded by Colonel Pedro Pezarat Correia, a member of the Council of the Revolution, took part. The Artillery School at Vendas Novas, between Evora and Lisbon, was especially active, accompanying occupations and often providing vehicles. Along with the technicians of the Agrarian Reform Centers, officers oversaw property inventories and attempted to mediate in disputes which arose between occupiers and owners (Bermeo 1986: 66-68; Correia 1982).

The support of the armed forces deterred landowners from trying to evict occupiers. As in urban housing occupations, that support made clear that the forces of repression had been turned against the hallowed rights of property. Landowners had already lost a lot: the regime had changed; the National Republican Guard, which had traditionally repressed farmworker protest, had been disarmed, and the farmworkers' unions had imposed compulsory hiring. Now their very right to their property was denied by law and their farms were being taken over by the same farmworkers who had served them obediently in the past.

Both the armed forces and the centers were called in to adjudicate the many disputes that arose over occupations. Some landowners protested that their properties were too small to be expropriated and had been occupied illegally. An inquiry (conducted in 1976 by a government far less sympathetic to the agrarian reform than the revolutionary government) concluded that only about 2 percent of the land occupied was not covered by the law (Baptista 1978: 53–54). Many landowners complained that their farms were occupied after they had planted, and that they should be allowed to sell the crop to recover their investment; but the occupations were justified by Antonio Bica, later the PCP's deputy minister for agricultural restructuring, on the grounds that many landowners had borrowed money to plant and were preparing to sell the crop and leave the property encumbered with debt (Bica 1976: 19–20). Decapitalization was so common that new regulations were adopted making it illegal for landlords to mortgage expropriable farms or to sell off any movable property belonging to them.

The occupied farms were not divided up and distributed to individuals, but instead run as cooperatives by their members. The farmworkers, long proletarianized, did not seek to own farms individually. Most of them had always been casual laborers and had not even worked at any one place for very long. Besides, the farms were already organized on a large scale with extensive cultivation. It would have been difficult to divide up the equipment and the herds to create small farms, and they lacked the infrastructure of buildings and roads.

Some observers distinguish between two kinds of production units resulting from agrarian reform: cooperatives and collectives (*unidades colectivas de produção*). In principle, a collective was a single unit into which all the occupied lands (which in some cases meant virtually all the farmlands) of a *freguesia* were merged, with a single workers' commission (usually dominated by the union), and in which workers were paid a fixed salary. Most such mergers took place in 1976, after the occupation movement had ended. A cooperative was a smaller unit, generally a single farm. Workers did not receive a fixed salary but would share the surplus at the end of the year. The collective was the form encouraged by the PCP, and the cooperative was favored by the PS.[9] But this difference tended to disappear after 1976. Collectives generally incorporated as cooperatives, while cooperatives ultimately opted for payment of salaries rather than proportional distribution to members. For simplicity, I will refer to them all as cooperatives.

Each cooperative was governed by an elected workers' commission which was responsible for managing the farm. Farmworkers were on the whole even less well prepared than urban workers to manage cooperatives. An enormously high percentage of them were illiterate (51.4% in Evora, according to a survey; Estrela 1978: 249). Even of those who had rudimentary schooling, few had any work experience except as day laborers. Most of the leaders, therefore, came from the ranks of union activists or the leaders of the earlier occupations—small farmers, renters, or tractor owners with some experience in farm management, bookkeeping, and marketing.

Thus, though workers had formal collective control over the cooperatives, they took a less active part in managing them than was true in the urban cooperatives; workers were even more likely to do the work and leave management to the leaders. Bermeo's findings on the work process in agricultural cooperatives are strikingly similar to my own in the urban cooperatives: most workers took little active part in management but were satisfied with their level of participation, and social relations among workers were friendly and egalitarian (Bermeo 1986: 110–21). Active participation was lowest in the larger, merged collectives where the unions had a major role; smaller cooperatives were run more democratically (Baptista 1978: 77).

As in their urban counterparts, the cooperatives' main goal was not to maximize profits or productivity but to provide the greatest number of jobs. They sowed land which had long gone unplanted, increasing acreage by more that 20 percent over the previous year and allowing them to hire more workers and increase production substantially. The grain harvest of 1976 was far greater than it was for previous years—an extraordinary outcome in the first year of an agrarian reform. In part this was due to excellent weather, in part to farming previously idle lands. To sustain the higher employment levels, cooperatives made major improvements on their properties in 1975 and later, building ponds for irrigation and clearing fields of rocks—with pick and shovel—to prepare them for cultivation.

But much of the newly sown land was marginal and not very fertile. Baptista maintains that the cultivation of less fertile lands produced declining yields per hectare and suggests that labor productivity was also lower. Moreover, he argues, practices associated with employment maximization also produced problems for cooperatives competing in a capitalist economy. Employment maximization led to higher production costs, making the cooperatives uncompetitive and even economically unviable.[10]

A comparison of the worker control movement in urban workplaces and on occupied farms reveals some similarities, but also some major differences. They began in the same way: by the spontaneous actions of workers, without any initial state sanction and without any specific political direction. They also produced similar work relations and attempted to maximize employment.

But there were important political differences which made the land occupation movement far more homogeneous than the urban worker control movement. (It was also more homogeneous, of course, in that the cooperatives were all farms.) The state played a much larger role in agrarian reform than in urban cooperatives. The fact that it was such a hot political issue also forced the concept of agrarian reform into a single mold: discussions tended to oversimplify it. For the left the latifundio was a symbol of the concentration of wealth and power that had created economic backwardness and widespread misery. Agrarian reform was equally symbolic for the right, which counted among its principal supporters both large landowners and many small farmers who saw in agrarian reform a threat to their own ownership of property.

Urban workers took control of the firm where they were already employed, so they had some knowledge of how to run it—certainly more than most farmworkers knew about farm management. In addition, while urban workers could claim a right to a job which was specific to their own firm, most farmworkers had never had a fixed workplace—their claim was based on a general right to work, not any right to the property they occupied.

Finally, unlike the urban takeovers, agrarian reform had a single political leadership: even though many occupations still occurred independently, the PCP and the farmworkers' unions took a dominant role after the expropriation law was passed. No party took such a role in the urban movement. It was easier to dominate the rural movement because of the history of Communist leadership in the Alentejo and objective similarities among the farms which were the targets of the occupation.

This uniformity both in the process by which occupations occurred and in the political symbolism they embodied made it logical that the agrarian reform movement should lead to a general challenge to the latifundio system and the goal of eliminating it entirely. It also meant that agrarian cooperatives became a major target of attack, unlike worker-controlled firms. Governments hostile to agrarian reform destroyed many cooperatives in 1978 and later.

The agrarian reform has been criticized by those who thought that land takeovers should be centrally guided. The PCP did not support occupations before they were sanctioned by law. Even though it first demanded expropriation of all latifundios in the winter of 1975, it was suspicious of occupations which occurred without legal authority and which it did not control. It wanted expropriations to be directed by the state, and the farms to be turned into state farms. The similar criticism by Belo Moreira of the Evora Regional Agrarian Reform Center has already been mentioned: that the occupations which occurred before the expropriation law got in the way of the center's efforts to carry out land reform rationally.[11]

But experience suggests that if workers had waited for land to be legally expropriated rather than occupying it, the process would not have gotten very far. The early successes and the lack of reprisals against the first takeovers were due to a power *vacuum*. Though most occupations took place in August and later, after the law in effect authorized them and state institutions supported them, the law might not have been passed without the first occupations.

And for the most part farms were expropriated only after they had been occupied. The centers took the initiative only in districts with relatively little expropriable land (as can be seen from the figures in Cardoso 1976: 80). Far more land was taken over in the areas where the occupation movement had already begun or was carried on without the centers' stimulus. The expropriation law was decreed in July, but no land was formally declared expropriated until September, after many more occupations—and even then, for the most part, the law was applied only to land that had been occupied. When occupations were halted, about one-third of the farms legally subject to expropriation had not been occupied, and they were never expropriated. Even properties destined for nationalization were not taken over automatically; decrees nationalizing specific properties were delayed several months, and there were some properties which, while legally nationalized, continued to be run by their former owners. Unless workers had acted in advance of the law and then, after it was passed, exceeded its limits, little or no land would have been expropriated. Without direct action there would probably have been no agrarian reform.

Some scholars criticize the occupations not for having been insufficiently subordinate to central direction, but for having been too much so. As these critics recognize, the occupation movement, like the earlier mobilization of farmworkers immediately after April 25, was primarily motivated by a desire for steady employment. (The same was true, as they point out, throughout the First Republic and the fascist period; the history of farmworker protest from 1910 on included strikes but no land occupations.) From this, however, they conclude that the consciousness of the farmworkers must have been completely dominated by capitalist relations of production. They were workers, not farmers, and felt no "land hunger" (A. Barreto 1984a and 1984b; Cabral 1974; J.P. Pereira 1980, 1982, and n.d.).

If farmworkers did not themselves want land, these writers conclude, it must have been submission to the PCP which led them to occupy; the formation and political defense of cooperatives must have been unimportant to them. According to Pereira, the PCP had long espoused an agrarian reform which would divide the latifundios among individual farmers, and on discovering (only in 1975) that the farmworkers did not want to own land, it imposed collectivization on them. So convinced is he that the occupations were not the product of workers' own desires that he refers to the "so-called 'agrarian reform' " (1982: 186; n.d.: 157–86).

But the occupation movement was not inspired by the PCP; as Bermeo has it, the party "followed the landless onto the land" (1986: 59). Further, while the PCP came to dominate the occupation movement politically, and certainly won the sympathies of most of the occupiers, it was not able to impose its model entirely on the process: it wanted the latifundios to be turned into state-owned collective farms, but occupiers created cooperatives because the lack of state support forced them to act on their own.[12]

The anticommunist critics of agrarian reform, by attributing the occupation movement to outside forces, assume that workers' consciousness does not change in response to outside events and political opportunities. But as we have already seen, their consciousness grew and their demands changed progressively as opportunities opened up: they moved from the demand for compulsory hiring to occupations; when some occupations succeeded and were legitimized by the expropriation law, the occupation movement spread. Just as in urban movements, in the absence of repression each success bred further efforts and the escalation of demands.

If the land occupation movement did not owe its origins to the centralist model, however, it came to apply that model in two ways: first, as already mentioned, in the hierarchical organization of the cooperatives. Workers participated less in running them than they did in the urban cooperatives. Participation was in part limited by the lack of education and experience of most occupiers; but it was lowest in occupied farms merged into a single collective under the direction of the unions, where the large size inhibited active participation by all workers.

The agrarian reform was also centralist in that it came to serve the goal of destroying the latifundio system as much as the workers' immediate objective of job security. While there was no inherent conflict between liquidating the latifundio and providing the employment which was paramount to the workers, the former goal came from outside. In July and later, the PCP and the unions promoted occupations of all the property covered by the law, hoping to dispossess the latifundists entirely. The PCP believed that for the revolution to have a chance of success, the power of the latifundists had to be broken; and that the only way to accomplish that was to take away their land.

In this sense the critics are correct. While land occupations did not originate outside the consciousness of the workers, they were redirected to serve the centralist model. Because that model did not posit internal democracy as a key objective, workers' actual power in the cooperatives was limited.

So the conflict between the centralist and popular power models was felt in the agrarian reform. Worker control (or popular power more generally) can be an end in itself, or it can be reduced to a tactic in a revolutionary leadership's struggle for power. If internal democracy is neither deliberately cultivated nor imposed by necessity, it is not likely to flourish.

Worker Control and Popular Power

Worker control was due to the struggle to meet economic needs, not to a clearly formulated ideology. This spontaneity was in some respects a strength. Without a blueprint, workers had the audacity to try out possibilities which would not have occurred to them a short time before. They felt free to move beyond their original goals when the opportunity arose.

But spontaneity also produced problems: most important, a separation between the movement for worker control and the contest for state power. Worker control is fundamental to socialism if socialism is to liberate workers from oppression. But it does not fit easily into a revolutionary struggle. Neither the workers who practiced it nor the centralists attempting to lead the revolution recognized the need to link struggles in the workplace to the contest for the state. For workers running a workplace, day-to-day details demanded so much attention that they failed to see the larger perspective. They did not develop a clear conviction of workers' right to act autonomously and take charge of their workplaces, so the movement for worker control did not seek to spread beyond the affected workplaces; it did not try to guide the revolution toward the goal of universal self-management.

Because worker control was not defended as a model, centralists could use it for their own purposes. They rejected the diffusion of authority that local worker control requires. They did have a blueprint and they did not welcome a competing model of society. They welcomed worker control in small workplaces if it strengthened their attack on capital, but they recognized no reciprocal obligation to establish worker control more widely.

Workers who controlled their own workplaces ironically reinforced the centralists' desire to take advantage of them. They actively called on the MFA and the government for legal recognition, credit, and defense—political defense and sometimes physical defense in the form of troops to protect an occupation. Their precarious situation made that help necessary, but they deferred too readily to the centralists' definition of the revolutionary process as well. Most important, they expected the MFA to guarantee the advance of the revolution.

Workers for the most part did not recognize that to defend their firms, they had to defend the revolution. Most urban cooperatives, struggling to survive and not subordinate to any political leadership, abstained from public political mobilizations. The political course of the revolution was therefore set mainly by the centralists—to its detriment, as I will argue. The movement for worker control exemplified the failure of the popular power movement as a whole; it never matched its spontaneity and creativity with the organizational capacity to sustain itself.

Despite the eventual defeat of the revolution, the heritage of worker control remains. The worker-controlled sector itself survived. At one point it included nearly 130,000 workers, though the number declined after 1977 as some firms failed and unfriendly governments returned others to their former owners and worked actively to dismember rural cooperatives. In 1975, 70,000 farmworkers worked the 1.16 million occupied hectares of land (though by 1980 more than half the land had been taken away, and the number of workers remaining was only 26,000). In industrial production and services there were about 1,200 cooperatives and self-managed firms in 1978 (a small number of the cooperatives predated the revolution) with a total of about 59,500 workers, 2.9 percent of the nonagricultural labor force (Bermeo 1979: 5; Roux 1982: 20).

The experience of worker control survived in the memory of those who shared in it. Whether in factory or field, whether in a firm which was recaptured by its owners, one which went under, or one which remained worker-controlled, workers practiced autonomy and cooperation with fellow workers as they rarely do in capitalist firms. Though the motives for worker control were not ideological, and though many participants may not have been very concerned with the progress of the revolution in the abstract, they nevertheless exercised genuine power. Those in surviving cooperatives reported strong satisfaction with their work and with the good social relations with their comrades. To those whose workplaces reverted to capitalist relations of production, the experience nevertheless remained important. Some years later, the deputy editor of *República* told me that many of the paper's former workers had found the experience one of the most exciting of their lives; and would still say, ''I know I have to die, but no one can take this away from me.''

9

Direct Democracy
and the Neighborhoods

The movement in urban neighborhoods did not experience so dramatic an acceleration after March 11 as the movements of industrial and agricultural workers did. It did not need to, because it had already demanded revolutionary solutions to the housing problem before then. Moreover, there was no new housing policy comparable to nationalization or agrarian reform. So the neighborhood commissions continued in the course they had already set.

The neighborhood commissions raised the most explicit demands for popular power. As a result of their adversarial relation with the government, the conscious coordination of activities among themselves, their concern with issues of the quality of life, and their connection to the far left, they came to see their own movement as the model for an entirely new political system, based on direct mass participation and linking all the base organizations in a society-wide structure of popular power.

So when concrete proposals for new political organizations were presented, they originated in the neighborhood commissions. So too did the popular assemblies, which attempted to coordinate the popular movement and wage the revolution and were intended to be the embryonic governing structures of the future liberated society.

Inter-Neighborhood Organization

The SAAL commissions continued to develop the plans for their new housing projects. The *caderno reivindicativo* drawn up by the Lisbon Coordinating Commission in February—demanding subsidies, low interest loans, and land near existing shantytowns and rejecting self-help construction—was discussed in all the neighborhood commissions and presented to the government on April 7. The other coordinating commissions presented similar lists of demands. Getting no response, the various coordinating commissions began to plan for what would be a major demonstration on May 17, bringing together the commissions in poor neighborhoods working with SAAL and the commissions which were organizing housing occupations.

The commissions involved in occupations in Lisbon formed their own coordinating council, the Autonomous Revolutionary Commissions of Occupiers (CRAOs; later the word *moradores* [dwellers] was added to the name and it became CRAMOs). This council was heavily influenced by the far-left PRP and UDP. The Lisbon Tenants' Association, a long-standing organization which provided legal assistance to individual tenants, embraced the occupation movement and took an active part. The occupying commissions were dissatisfied with the law regulating empty apartments and demanded a new law which would protect occupiers better.

While a new wave of occupations took off in Lisbon on February 18, immediately after the expiration of the time limit for rentals, it started more slowly in Setubal. There, the moderately sympathetic, PCP-dominated city administrative commission wanted to keep the occupation movement under its own control. On March 2 it convoked the city's first municipal assembly to discuss the city's social problems, and with the encouragement of the president of the commission, the assembly resolved that neighborhood commissions should undertake housing censuses in their respective areas and report empty dwellings to the city. Commissions and *freguesia* councils together would then receive applications and assign the houses to needy families.

But the climate changed after the March 7 demonstration at which the police fired into the crowd and killed a demonstrator. The demonstrators marched on the police station, and the army had to be called in to break them up. The brutality of the police angered the population, which forced the authorities to respond. The main police station was temporarily closed, and one police post was soon closed permanently. The agitated atmosphere stimulated activists, and the demobilization of the police removed the only possible restraint. Occupations went into high gear and accelerated even more after March 11.

While the far left vigorously supported and stimulated housing occupations, the coalition parties were appalled at the breakdown of order and defiance of authority. Both the Socialist and the Communist parties condemned occupations and forbade their militants to take part in them (as did the FSP, which had split off from the PS after its December congress). The decision did not sit well with many of those militants—the PS's ban on occupations was announced just days after the Socialist Youth had occupied a building for its headquarters, and it was forced to abandon the building. The PCP's ban was ignored by many Communists who participated eagerly in the occupations and in the neighborhood commissions which promoted them. On this issue as on others, militants often acted independently of their parties. Communists especially may have deferred to the party line in principle, but many of them got caught up in the enthusiasm of the popular movement and did not honor the party's insistence on moderation.

Housing occupations did not just divide the political parties; they were also a major issue dividing the progressive wing of the MFA. United against the moderate officers during the winter's debates on economic policy, it split in the spring. The Gonçalvists, aligned with the prime minister, were centralists, in favor of imposing structural change by government decree. To their left was the faction centered in the COPCON which wanted to base the revolution on the popular movement.

The factional differences mirrored those in the political parties—the Gonçalvists generally allied with the Communist Party, the COPCON with the far left, and the moderates with the Socialists—but officers came to identify with each faction as a result less of party influence than of their respective assignments. The COPCON officers came to support popular power largely because of their contacts with civilian organizations which sought help from the units in the cities. They embraced "revolutionary legality" and believed that the armed forces' main role should be to support those movements.

MFA officers working in ministries or government agencies, on the other hand, lacked contact with the popular movement. From their bureaucratic positions, they relied on the power of the state to bring about social change; they were likely to be Gonçalvists. The Fifth Division, which designed the dynamization campaign for the benighted north from desks in Lisbon, was staffed mainly by Gonçalvists. Those who remained in operational commands had neither the bureaucratic experience nor the civilian contacts. Most of them stayed moderate and wanted to limit the armed forces to military duties.

Outside Lisbon, the split between the two left factions was not so deep as in the capital. Especially in Oporto, Gonçalvists had closer contact with base-level movements. They did not always follow the PCP line faithfully; in the last months of 1974, while the party was still espousing moderation, the officers who later became the Gonçalvist faction were arguing for acceleration of the revolution.

But in Lisbon, the division between the two factions hardened. One issue separating them was a new law to regulate empty housing. Early in April the Council of the Revolution debated two bills to deal with the occupations. One was a COPCON proposal which placed few restrictions on occupations and gave the neighborhood commissions the power to enforce compulsory renting. This proposal was rejected in favor of a law (Decree/Law 198–A/75 of April 14) that left the power to rent empty houses with the *freguesia* councils and established a series of conditions exempting properties from compulsory rental (and therefore from occupations, though the law did not explicitly mention them). Occupiers were to be evicted from the protected properties. According to the widely publicized claim of the neighborhood commissions, the new law made illegal 80 percent of the occupations which had already occurred.

Like the government's response to the political strikes of the summer before and its passage of the strike law, the housing law revealed the divisions within the government and the ambiguities of its commitment to revolution. At the same moment that the fourth provisional government was taking over virtually the entire financial system of the nation, it refused to recognize openly the neighborhood movement's right to occupy empty houses. But neither did it interfere with the occupations. Unwilling to delegate any of its power to the base-level movements, it was also unwilling to side openly with property owners.

The CRAMOs and sympathizing commissions denounced the law, calling it the "anti-occupation" law. Still, occupations continued—less frequently, because the choicest properties were already occupied. But until September they occurred fairly peacefully and no occupiers were evicted.

The SAAL Coordinating Commissions in Lisbon, Oporto, their suburbs, and Setubal began preparing for major simultaneous demonstrations on May 17 in Lisbon and Oporto. SAAL commissions declared their solidarity with the CRAMOs against the "anti-occupation law," and the two groups planned a joint demonstration under the umbrella slogan of "decent housing for everyone." They demanded revocation of the law and financing for SAAL. One of the Oporto commissions' main demands was final approval of the long-promised law regulating subleasing. The law was published the day before the demonstration, and the commissions claimed it as a victory. The law applied only to Oporto, but it made subletting illegal, and rents were reduced an average of 50 percent (although, of course, the living conditions of subtenants in overcrowded apartments did not improve as a result).

At the same time, a major dispute was brewing between SAAL commissions and the Oporto Administrative Commission. At an April 5 plenary, Oporto neighborhood commissions reiterated their demands for subsidies, low interest, and no self-help construction for SAAL projects. They went further, demanding that they be recognized as legitimate local authorities and, still more audaciously, that all urban property be nationalized and that they be authorized to manage it in the name of the people. Finally, they demanded that the Administrative Commission be replaced. Shortly after the plenary, the first land for SAAL projects was expropriated, a move which the neighborhood commissions saw as a response to their pressure.

The dispute between the SAAL commissions and the Administrative Commission was complicated by a strike by some city employees which began on May 5, triggered by the hostility between SAAL commissions and the city government. Hired on consultant contracts, SAAL workers were not subject to the same pay scale, but SAAL authorities justified their higher pay because they had no fringe benefits or job security. The city employees demanded the same salary as the SAAL workers. They also demanded that a section head who was supported by SAAL commissions be dismissed. They agreed with the SAAL commissions on one thing: they called for the dismissal of the president of the Administrative Commission. May 17, the day of the neighborhood commissions' demonstration, arrived with no resolution of the dispute.

In Lisbon, the demonstration drew some 50,000 people and won its major demands. At São Bento Palace, the seat of the government (and soon to be the meeting place for the just-elected Constituent Assembly), the demonstration was addressed by Captain Cabral e Silva, Adjunct Prime Minister and a close ally of Gonçalves. Cabral e Silva promised the SAAL commissions a subsidy of 60,000 to 90,000 escudos per dwelling unit, loans at 3 percent over twenty years to pay for the balance, and that in any case the cost would not be greater than 10 percent of a family's income. He did not mention self-help construction, nor did he say anything about the law regulating empty apartments.

Some 20,000 people demonstrating in Oporto heard an even more dramatic announcement from Brigadier Eurico Corvacho, military commander of the northern region and a Gonçalvist: the city's Administrative Commission would be dismissed and replaced by a military administrative commission, a major victory for the neighborhood commissions. The new military commission cooperated closely with them after it took office on May 28, giving them considerable de facto power in running the city for the next several months.

The Progress of SAAL

Publicity about the apparent success of the May 17 demonstration stimulated more shantytowns and slums to organize SAAL projects. The joint commission of the shantytowns of Outorela and Portela, just west of Lisbon, was formed on May 18, followed by the formation of other commissions shortly thereafter.

Each commission had to incorporate legally as a cooperative or association which would be responsible for further improvements. SAAL provided legal assistance in getting the organizations recognized. This was a complex and important task, as the commission had to decide the procedures for administering the new houses and assigning families to them. The most important decision was whether homes would be individually owned or would remain the property of the association.

Incorporation required choosing a name, which would become the name of the new community. Some projects retained the name of the old neighborhood for the new project, but others chose a politically inspired name: the People's Struggle (Setubal), Unity of the People (Lisbon), and 25th of April (Linda-a-Velha). They wanted the new community's name to symbolize the fact that the revolution had made it possible.

A project could not actually be undertaken until financing was assured. The Ministry of Public Works soon presented a housing program which affirmed most of the promises Cabral e Silva had made at the May 17 demonstration, but the promised decree on financing SAAL projects was never issued; financing was granted only case by case.

The communities all demanded that they be rehoused on sites near where they already lived. In fact, the best arrangement was to find a site adjacent to the existing shantytown, so that once construction began and some families were rehoused, the land of the shantytown itself could be used for further construction. Consistent with the practice of giving the commissions most of the responsibility but none of the authority to carry out their projects, each commission had to find its own site and demand that the city expropriate the land and turn it over to them.

The laws of eminent domain provided for compensation for owners at essentially market value. These laws were attacked by the several coordinating commissions because they dated from the period of fascism, and the organizations claimed that revolutionary right entitled them to unused land, and the land's owners to no compensation. Still, practicality dictated that they find land that was expropriable. This meant that land already publicly owned was preferred, and failing that, privately owned land which was not in use. The request to the city government for expropriation entailed inevitable delays—especially if city officials were hostile to the SAAL process.

Some commissions occupied land to protest the city's delay. In the summer of 1975 the commissions of Quinta da Calçada and Quinta das Fonsecas in Lisbon, for example, which had a joint construction project, occupied land which had been designated for a parking lot for the University of Lisbon. The commission that united the residents of nine small shantytowns in Linda-a-Velha, Oeiras, won approval for the expropriation of its land. When the declaration of expropriation was published in the government newspaper, on September 6, 1975, the commission organized a symbolic occupation ("because the people didn't really believe the land was ours," according to a commission member). Many SAAL commissions also occupied empty buildings near their shantytowns for their own headquarters, until a community center could be built in the new project.[1]

Each commission developed plans for its own housing project with its SAAL brigade. Within the limitations of financing and location (which were, of course, major), each new project was designed uniquely and to the specifications of the commission. Residents came into conflict with the brigades of technicians, especially the architects, over the design of the projects. Many of the architects considered themselves a vanguard of the built environment and wanted to incorporate the political and social goals of the revolution into the physical design. In the architects' vision of revolutionary housing, the property would be collectively owned and emphasize community facilities and common open spaces, and the buildings themselves would be multifamily units rather than individual houses. Many commissions were more interested in housing suited to their families' needs as they themselves interpreted them. They did not share the architects' belief that their preferences were warped by exposure to bourgeois ideology.

The SAAL process called for extensive consultation between designers and future inhabitants, and it is to the credit of the architects that they did not try to impose their own preferences. Instead, they made mock-ups and spent considerable time meeting with the commissions and residents to discuss the projects and incorporate features that the residents wanted. Most shantytown residents, at most a generation removed from rural origins, preferred one-story, single-family houses with land for kitchen gardens. (In some parts of Portugal, especially the Alentejo, villages are composed of individual houses built to the front property line and abutting adjacent houses on both sides. A similar design of separate but closely packed houses was adopted for many SAAL projects.) But the choice of design depended very much on the kind of neighborhood: the older slums, unlike the shantytowns, had existed for decades and their populations had never lived in rural areas. They were much more ready to accept multistory, multidwelling buildings.

Residents accepted the social criteria of the architects on some questions. One was ownership. Most commissions chose to maintain the houses under collective ownership: the commission would be responsible for further improvements on the properties, residents would pay monthly fees, and they would not be able to sell their houses on the open market but only return them to the association and be reimbursed for their investment. Nearly all projects were designed with ample provision for social facilities—community centers, daycare centers, medical posts, and greenery—which residents welcomed.

Each SAAL project also had to decide on the process of construction. The commission could let out contracts, or it could act as a small construction firm, hiring its own workers and administering the project directly. With housing starts especially low in the stagnant economy of 1975, firms and newly founded cooperatives of unemployed construction workers bid eagerly on these projects. However, just as their precarious financial situation and the lack of demand for more lucrative construction projects made them available for SAAL projects, many were close to bankruptcy and some firms failed before they completed the projects. Many SAAL commissions lost a large part of their initial investment before turning to direct administration of their projects.

Despite the repudiation of self-help construction by most SAAL commissions, there were a few which undertook it systematically. In the Algarve (the south coast) where the better climate makes the housing situation less severe, there were only a few small SAAL projects. Far from the major cities, the political climate there was also less severe and the heated demands made in Lisbon, Oporto and Setubal felt less urgent; many residents were eager to lower their costs by building their own houses. Residents of the beach shantytown of Meia Praia actively participated in the construction of a forty-house project, also on the beach, and each family's cost was discounted in proportion to the work contributed.

If design was a contentious issue between brigades and residents, they were united in insisting that the government fulfill what they regarded as its obligations to the SAAL process. Both in the north and in Lisbon, brigade members elected assemblies of delegates. These assemblies met often to protest the brigade members' job conditions but, even more, the government's delay and neglect of the projects. They proposed modifications to the laws governing SAAL and protested the failure of the government to meet its guarantees of financing.

With all the difficulties that they encountered, actual construction did not get very far in 1975. By the end of the year 138 operations had begun, involving nearly 38,000 families, but most of them were still in the stages of design and expropriation. And the governments in office after 1976 were even less willing to provide financing, expropriate land, and approve designs. The projects which had begun to organize earliest were in almost all cases the ones which got the furthest in building houses: they benefited from the favorable period and the cooperation both of the brigades and (to a lesser extent) the ministry and some city governments, whereas those which started later began in an initially unfavorable conjuncture, one in which the prospects of SAAL projects continued to worsen.

There were also significant differences between cities, because some administrative commissions were enthusiastic about SAAL and helped it out, while others were more hostile. Among the most favorable were Oporto (after the military administrative commission took office in May) and Setubal. In Setubal the Communist-dominated local government saw SAAL as an opportunity to stimulate a cooperative relationship with the SAAL commissions and undercut the militant stance of other neighborhood commissions, and the SAAL commissions were eager to cooperate as long as cooperation appeared to promise results. Another district where SAAL was relatively successful, though more after 1975, was Oeiras, just west of Lisbon, where the city council and in particular one member, an architect, supported the projects. On the whole, the SAAL commissions survived the demobilization of popular organizations in 1976 better than most other neighborhood commissions: with a project under way, a lot of effort sunk into it, and a concrete task to pursue, they had a reason to keep going (as did many commissions which started daycare centers or had other ongoing activities) and thus survived.

Citywide Revolutionary Councils

The neighborhood commissions were more active than the workers' commissions in creating coordinating organizations, due to necessity and ideology—their relation with the government required it, and they believed that the organization of popular power had to transcend the neighborhood, even if basic decisions still were made locally. Workers' initiatives remained much more at the level of the individual firm, and the limited coordination which they achieved later in 1975 was largely either ad hoc or under the aegis of political parties, violating the popular movement's claims to nonpartisanship.

In Oporto and Setubal, citywide councils were formed to unite all neighborhood commissions. The Oporto military administrative commission, shortly after taking office on May 28, asked the neighborhood commissions to present a proposal for a formal link between the base organizations and the city government. In June the Coordinating Commission of Neighborhood Commissions and Associations of SAAL/North created the Revolutionary Dwellers' Council of Oporto (CRMP). The CRMP lasted for only three months, but its existence symbolized the military commission's enthusiastic cooperation with the base organizations. The council met with the military commission weekly, and while it lasted, the military commission consulted with it on major decisions.

Initially the CRMP represented only the neighborhood commissions, but it came to include representatives of the Intersindical's local organization, the *freguesia* councils, and the volunteer firefighters, and it was announced that commissions of soldiers and police would also be included. But neighborhood commissions from SAAL and the municipal housing projects were the most active participants and they benefited most from the CRMP's existence. For SAAL projects, land was expropriated and new construction plans were approved easily.

Setubal's neighborhood commissions also founded a citywide council, the Dwellers' Council. It was neither as active nor as effective as the Oporto Council. It took a highly confrontational attitude toward the city administrative commission, an attitude which did not sit well with the SAAL commissions, which found the city commission reasonably cooperative. The Dwellers' Council was superseded in July by the Committee of Popular Organizations of Setubal, founded under the stimulus of the local Intersindical affiliate to defend the position of the PCP.

Several Setubal neighborhoods united in a campaign to lower rents. Many activists decided that a campaign against what they called "speculative rents" would be a good organizing drive. They believed that confronting high rents would appeal to many people who were not otherwise politically involved by showing them the direct relation of the revolution to their own interests—high rents were a clear example of capitalist exploitation. It would also expose the city government and some of the neighborhood commissions as "reformist" if they failed to support it, and discourage speculative real estate investment.

Campaign organizers faced a strategic problem: should they demand a ceiling on rent, or rent proportional to family income? The former would be clearer and easier to carry out, but its appeal would be restricted to people living in more expensive housing. In May activists from three commissions in recently built, relatively expensive neighborhoods met and organized a çampaign to lower rent to 500 escudos per room, 300 escudos in the case of basement apartments. (Five hundred escudos was equivalent to $20. If that figure seems low, it should be remembered that a three-room apartment at 500 escudos per room would cost more than one third of the minimum wage. Rent was higher in only some 10 percent of Setubal's dwelling units.) Their manifesto recognized that rent proportional to income would be fairer, but they agreed on the 500-escudo limit as a beginning.

Commissions in the poorest neighborhoods were unsympathetic: one member of a shantytown commission compared it to a "struggle for swimming pools." Despite heated divisions, the Dwellers' Council supported the campaign, while the municipal government refused to take a position.

The rent reduction struggle did succeed in organizing commissions in neighborhoods of high rent and mixed class composition, and mobilized many otherwise uninvolved, moderately well-off families. Late in June, several hundred families decided to take part and unilaterally started to pay lower rents. Landlords generally refused to accept the payments, and the rents were deposited in an escrow account.[2]

Early in July the government declared rent reduction illegal, and on July 9 Setubal residents demonstrated in Lisbon to support the rent struggle. When a landlord sued a tenant, the judge announced that he supported the tenant and refused to find him guilty; he submitted the proceedings to the Ministry of Justice with an opinion that the charges should be dismissed. The Ministry of Justice soon suspended the proceedings, in effect reversing the government's edict; for the next several months hundreds of tenants continued to pay their unilaterally lowered rents into the escrow account.

Neighborhood Commissions and Popular Power

Like the workers' commissions, the neighborhood commissions emerged to meet a basic necessity—in their case, housing—but went far beyond it. Their rudimentary conception of their purpose gave way to an increasingly elaborate ideology which demanded socialist transformation of property relations and political institutions. They established formal organizations, adopted statutes, and developed links with other base-level commissions to raise common demands.

Eventually, activists began to think of their commissions as genuine local governments. The Oporto commissions demanded formal recognition, and elsewhere commissions exercised some de facto authority, either alone (as when the SAAL commissions controlled improvements on the shanties), or in collaboration with the armed forces (occupying houses and enforcing rules on neighborhood nuisances). Their apparent success in extracting material concessions, winning recognition of their authority, and creating political bodies to exercise that authority made it appear that they could claim to be the legitimate representatives of the residents. Increasingly they defined themselves in opposition to the constituted government.

The goal of the popular movement was a political system governed by popular power; the commissions were to be its vehicles. Activists believed that the commissions, close to their constituency and open to everyone, embodied direct democracy and foreshadowed a new society in which all would share in making the decisions by which they were governed. They rejected representative democracy as a tool of bourgeois domination and believed that the new organizations which had sprung up in Portugal and struggled to take control of their neighborhoods and workplaces promised a new type of socialism, one which was fully democratic in both political form and economic substance.

Neighborhood commissions adopted this position more than did workers' commissions. There were several reasons why neighborhood commissions were in the forefront of defining the struggle for popular power: their local constituencies and coordinating councils gave them, like the state, a geographical base; their direct relation to the state and their need to confront it made them readier to challenge legally sanctioned practice and custom. Most workers' commissions sought prior legal sanction for their objectives, such as nationalization, intervention, or worker control. Nationalization and intervention were inherently state actions requiring legal sanction, and they strengthened the central state to the—at least relative—detriment of the power of the workers in the workplace itself. The neighborhood commissions more often acted first and only sought authorization later, as in the housing occupations. Housing occupations, moreover, were acts which required mass mobilization for success.

The neighborhood commissions developed closer links to military units than did the workers' commissions, relying on them for material support and defense of occupations. If these contacts brought many in the MFA to identify with the popular power movement, the process was reciprocal: neighborhood movement activists came to sympathize more wholeheartedly with the political positions espoused by the officers and soldiers on whose support they depended.

Unlike workers' commissions, neighborhood commissions attempted to go beyond issues of economic necessity to questions of culture. By building parks, establishing daycare centers, taking children to museums or the beach, founding musical and theater groups, and similar activities, they worked to improve the quality of their members' and their neighborhoods' lives.

Finally, the greater influence of the PCP within the workers' commissions meant that many of them did not voice the popular power model—even if they practiced it unawares. Though the PCP claimed to promote and defend popular power, its centralist model was very different. The far left had more influence in the neighborhood commissions. For all these reasons, the neighborhood commissions embraced a broader political focus than the workers' commissions, and took the initiative in raising the demand for popular power.

The leading role of the neighborhood commissions was paradoxical, for it was taken for granted in the popular power movement that the sphere of production had priority, and that the major political initiatives should therefore come from workers. The power of workers at the point of production was the source of the working class's strength; it gave workers' commissions a legitimacy which the neighborhood commissions, incorporating members of various classes, lacked. The fact that the neighborhood commissions played the leading ideological role was partly responsible for the abstract and bureaucratic character of the proposals that emerged.

The formal statement of the popular power model, however, came not from the neighborhood commissions but from the MFA itself. Despite its deepening divisions, the MFA was still the only force in the country with the legitimacy to enforce decisions. That legitimacy derived not only from its role as the liberator of April 25 but also from older traditions of civilian deference to the armed forces in political crises.

The MFA Assembly held protracted and heated debates over the proper form of political organization and approved a series of documents that claimed to resolve the issue. These debates mirrored the MFA's factional splits, which in turn reflected the polarization of the society. Although the ultimate decisions rested with the military, civilian political processes were a significant magnet for officers throughout the revolutionary process.

Officers of all factions were in close contact with the political parties, while the parties were willing to leave the debate in the hands of their allies the MFA, knowing that the armed forces would have to enforce any resolution.

For officers on the far left, contact with the popular movement provided a reference point; they wanted to base the revolution on the popular organizations and turn the MFA into a national liberation movement modeled after the movements they had fought in Africa. They were close to the far-left parties, especially the MES and the PRP. Gonçalvists espoused centralist principles similar to those of the PCP. The moderates were close to the PS, and believed that decisions on political structure should be left to the newly convened Constituent Assembly and its popularly elected civilian members.

All the factions compromised on a Political Action Program, passed by the MFA Assembly and ratified by the Council of the Revolution on June 21, which declared the MFA to be the "national liberation movement of the Portuguese people"; but it also endorsed pluralism and promised to honor the rights of the political parties (the text appears in *Monthly Review,* September 1975: 27–38). It appeared to guarantee respect for the winners of the April election and acknowledge that the voters had chosen pluralism and a moderate parliamentary constitution.

Although they endorsed the Political Action Program, both the Gonçalvist and far-left factions were reluctant pluralists, fearing that interparty conflict could cause the revolution to founder. They particularly saw the new Constituent Assembly, which had convened on June 2, as a threat, since it offered the moderate parties a forum for their dissent from the revolutionary process. The officers viewed that as a violation of the implicit pledge to respect the supremacy of the MFA, which the parties had made when they signed the pre-election political pact in April.

The neighborhood commissions' unitary ideal called for organizations which were nonpartisan, open to all, and devoted to solving concrete problems. The far-left faction, along with workers' and neighborhood commissions, endorsed that ideal in a new political proposal, the "Guiding Document for the Alliance of the People and the MFA" (the text appears in Peoples Translation Service 1975: 4–8), which was approved by the MFA Assembly barely two weeks after the Political Action Program and published on July 9.

The People/MFA Document proposed an entire new structure of popular power which would build from base-level commissions to unitary organizations called popular assemblies at the local, citywide, district, and national levels. The popular assemblies were envisioned as new channels for citizens' political participation, in effect replacing the political parties. They were to include delegates from all the base organizations, military units, and local governments in an area. Their leaders would be elected in assemblies (by show of hands, not secret ballot, as the document spelled out), and could be dismissed at any time.

These new organizations were intended not only as a model for the future. Creating them would push the revolution forward: they would simultaneously coordinate the political struggle, exercise state power, and prefigure the future society.[3] The People/MFA Document warned clearly of the immediate need "to defend the revolution from the attacks of reactionary forces," a reference to the moderate parties. The embrace of the unitary bodies as the basis of revolutionary political organization completely contradicted the Political Action Program's promise of pluralism, which moderate officers and civilians counted on as a guarantee of the survival of the parties.

But the leftist officers' espousal of popular power was not just tactical. They genuinely hoped to find in popular power a solution to interparty rivalries and a way to keep the revolution moving forward. Even leftwing officers liked to think of themselves as above partisan conflict and servants of the whole nation. The unitary bodies, they hoped, would express the will of the people unmediated by political factions. Some officers evidently believed that the conflicts among the parties could be overcome through a unitary structure, as if the existence of competing parties were a cause of political differences rather than an effect.

The alliance of the Gonçalvists and far-left factions was nevertheless tenuous. Each faction read its own meaning into the document and believed that it established a popular power consistent with its model of the future society: for the far left, the power of a vigorous, autonomous popular movement; for the Gonçalvists, the power of a society directed from above and enthusiastically supported from below. The Gonçalvists were also confident that the PCP's capacity for mobilization would assure it a dominant role in the "unitary" bodies.

The short-term purposes of the two factions were also very different. For the far-left faction, creating popular assemblies meant stepping up the revolution to defend it against the right—the MES, in hailing the People/MFA Document, called for the dissolution of the provisional government, which it described as a government of "class conciliation," and the formation of a revolutionary government in its place (*O Jornal*, July 11, 1975). The Gonçalvists, however, supported the provisional government and its policies; for them, the popular assemblies were less the expression of a political model than a tactic to undercut the moderate parties that dominated the Constituent Assembly.

The People/MFA Document presented highly abstract principles and at the same time a design for new political structures which was full of petty bureaucratic details. In both respects, the document seems far removed from any reality. Yet base-level commissions had had real experiences of popular organization for over a year, and some popular assemblies had actually been formed. The one that advanced the farthest was in Pontinha, which met for the first time on June 29. Neighborhood and workers' commissions—more of the former than of the latter—sent representatives, as did the assemblies of officers, sergeants, and soldiers in the Engineering Regiment. Several other popular assemblies were created in the bailiwicks of leftist regiments, such as the Lisbon Artillery Regiment (RALIS, formerly the First Light Artillery Regiment), which had been bombarded on March 11.

Except in Lisbon, however, popular assemblies did not get off the ground. (One was created in Oporto in September, but it was a PCP maneuver and it never really functioned.) Whereas coordinating organizations that grew more directly out of the commissions' struggles were relatively strong elsewhere, these organizations had declined in Lisbon. The Shantytowns' Coordinating Commission, which brought together the SAAL commissions, became less active after the May 17 demonstration, because its major demands were met for a period and the SAAL commissions were busy with their individual projects; the CRAMOs were also inactive, since occupations were few and not repressed, and most of the activists of the CRAMOs were involved in their parties. This left a space for the MFA-inspired popular assemblies. Though not free of partisan conflict, their MFA auspices made them less subject to interparty quarrels than were the coordinating councils in Oporto and Setubal.

Inspired by the MFA's endorsement, some assumed that the popular movement now had the capacity to claim state power. But that was an illusion, and a symptom of the growing dissociation between the movement and state-level politics. Popular power could not be enacted merely by MFA approval of a document; it required solid organization at the base. Organizing and expanding at the local level would take time, but it would allow the movement to continue to take advantage of its strength to exert pressure on the government for material concessions.

Instead, the popular power movement tried to supersede the state. Operating on the illusion that it might be able to seize power, it abandoned the work of building its bases and instead waged an ultimately futile struggle for state power during the late summer and fall of 1975.

Evaluating the Neighborhood Movement

Although the popular power movement never achieved state power, the neighborhood commissions had major effects on their neighborhoods, their cities, and the country as a whole. First, they gave the working class the political organization that it had previously lacked. They were formed more commonly in working-class neighborhoods than elsewhere, and even within neighborhoods (at least in Setubal), elected members of commissions and active participants were predominantly manual workers, out of proportion to their numbers.

Some will consider the class bias a limitation. Others may see it as a triumph that the working class was able to create its own institutions despite the repression it had suffered for so long. But there were other limitations: the manual workers who were most likely to be elected members of the commissions were the same people who were politically organized in unions and workers' commissions. They were also nearly all adult males, since the women and young people who were very active in the work of the commissions were rarely honored with its offices.

As a model for political institutions, popular democracy contained unresolved contradictions. The neighborhood commissions claimed that they represented their neighborhoods effectively because all residents were entitled to participate. Their legitimacy, therefore, depended on high and continuous participation. But base organizations and popular assemblies were far from achieving universal participation. No base organizations (except perhaps some workers' commissions in worker-controlled firms and neighborhood commissions building SAAL projects) mobilized anything close to a majority of their potential constituents. Moreover, participation was highly sensitive to the political climate. It was greatest when political events were most heated and optimism about the possibility of political change was highest. It fell off almost to nothing when the revolution ended. Few people stayed active in the face of the meager possibility of accomplishing anything.

But political participation of any kind was a new experience. Relative to the almost total demobilization under fascism, its level was extraordinary. It was a signal accomplishment of the neighborhood commissions that they were able to extend political participation to many who evidently wanted it.

People eagerly seized the opportunity and rose to the demands of participation: through sometimes difficult experience, they learned to cooperate and work together for common goals. An activist from Oeiras told me about the relations among cultural groups: ''Those groups lived by begging, and [before 1974] if they knew someone from the city council, they used pull to get a little bit more than the other group. Everyone pulled for his own sardine. . . . [But when the neighborhood commission brought us together] we worked to agree on a position among ourselves and present the proposals as the consensus of all the groups that were represented. That was an education! They were pieces, tiny little pieces for an education in living together.''

Neighborhood commissions also achieved results. Nearly all defined the housing shortage as their major problem, and they provided housing to many. SAAL projects were under way at the end of 1975 to house thousands of shantytown families. Other homeless people had found homes in apartments that had stood vacant. A significant number of people in Setubal were able to reduce their high rents for a time. And many commissions undertook major physical improvements for their neighborhoods, installing electricity, sanitary facilities, and other necessary infrastructure. Many neighborhood commissions improved the quality of collective life by establishing daycare centers, pharmacies, and medical posts, improving schools, and providing other social amenities.

The effect of neighborhood participation on the consciousness of activists was dramatic. One might assume that only people who already had strong political views would take part in the militant and often illegal activities of the commissions, and that therefore participation itself would have little effect on people's ways of thinking. But for the commissions as a whole, it is clear that the party line of the members did not determine their political orientation. The reverse was more often the case. Some tasks—SAAL projects, for example—required a militant orientation (as I have already argued). Similarly the rent reduction struggle in Setubal: it made sense only in the newer neighborhoods where rents were high; despite the large number of middle-class people in those neighborhoods, their commissions also adopted a militant stance. In both cases, physical conditions determined the needs, needs determined activity, and a strong stance was adopted to justify that activity. In Setubal, SAAL and the rent struggle explain the orientation of thirteen of the fifteen commissions which Downs characterizes as militant (1980: 432). Housing occupations (at least those in 1975) were initiated by political activists whose ideological commitments preceded their activity; but most who won houses by occupying them became radicalized and active in the commissions because they had a direct material reason to do so: to establish and protect their right to remain.

The popular power movement had another major effect on the consciousness of its activists, one which is less tangible. During the revolution, life was lived differently, more intensely; people were more integrated as individuals and with each other. I have already referred to the growth of neighborliness in urban residential areas where most people had lived anonymously before then. These changes are by definition hard to measure, but as a foreign observer in Portugal several times during the revolution and after, the effect of the revolution on the quality of everyday life was clear to me. Social networks were much more dense and intense in 1974 and 1975 than they were in later years: people were in constant contact and ready and available to talk. I had never been to Portugal before 1974, but all accounts agree that people were private and spontaneous social life was limited to small circles. After the revolution of carnations, "poor people were allowed to smile and Portugal learned to say *tu*" (U.T. Rodrigues 1977: 64).

Even more intangible, but surely important, were the effects on people's self-esteem and sense of power. People who participated in such activities grew and changed, learned to create and experience a world which they had not imagined themselves able to grasp. A social worker for the city of Oeiras commented with awe on how people with only primary education (at best) and limited resources had learned to handle the technical and bureaucratic details of constructing SAAL projects. Women active in workers' commissions, subjected to years of oppression in a highly sexist society, found that their worlds and their consciousness opened up (J. Rodrigues 1979). Other women and men too, in worker-controlled firms and many other situations, found that they could exercise powers greater than they had imagined.

According to a neighborhood activist who was part of the Christian left, "It was the kind of experience you don't forget. For me, that experience gives me the feeling that the idea [of socialism and worker control] is really possible." For those who experienced the revolution, this was one of its most enduring lessons.

10

The Hot Summer

In the summer of 1975 it became clear that the popular movement, which had been the driving force behind the advances of the revolution, would not be able to consolidate those advances. Mass movements are blunt instruments. They can raise issues; they are less able to determine outcomes. By summer the popular movement's demands went beyond the local concerns of workplaces and communities to call into question the entire structure of the state. The movement could not resolve these issues by itself.

The issues would have to be resolved by the government, the political parties, and the armed forces. But all of these became more and more divided. Among civilians, antagonism between the Communist and Socialist parties drove the coalition government apart. Divisions within the MFA also grew deeper, until two factions withdrew their support from the prime minister. Rumors of a coup—from one side or another—spread. Political tension and uncertainty grew through the summer, and some began to fear a civil war.

On July 9, the MFA Assembly approved the People/MFA Document; the next day the Council of the Revolution allowed *República* to appear again under the control of its workers. The PS opposed both decisions, reading in them the threat of its own extinction. It quit the government on July 11, followed in less than a week by the PPD. Independent cabinet ministers who were not identified with the Communists also quit, and the fourth government fell.

These conflicts stimulated violent confrontations among civilians, and riots swept the rural north. On July 13 a mob destroyed the PCP headquarters in Rio Maior, beginning a wave of anticommunist attacks that lasted for over a month. The cities, too, were disrupted: huge demonstrations, although usually free of actual violence, provoked the fear of chaos in much of the public. It appeared that those in power could neither remain united nor keep order.

The *República* affair revealed the seriousness of the divisions within the MFA, only a part of which now supported the government. Vacillation and division over *República* by the government and the MFA exacerbated the crisis. Insisting on interminable "negotiations" between the irreconcilable parties and announcing several times that a solution was at hand, they raised expectations and then could not fulfill them. By drawing more attention to the dispute, they strengthened the position of the Socialists, who were eager to take advantage.

República also attracted attention abroad. In June *Le Quotidien de Paris* offered *República's* deposed editorial staff four pages, which they used to publish an alleged Soviet plan for seizing power in the West (later shown to be a fabrication). Its allusions to Portugal were pointed: it called for an alliance with the armed forces, control of labor through a single trade union movement, destruction of the private economy, and control of the mass media.

República came to be a touchstone of relations between the French and Italian Communist parties, and between them and the other parties of their respective countries. The French Communist Party, which had signed a common program with the French Socialists in 1972, generally supported the Portuguese Communists (causing the French Socialists to challenge the PCF's commitment to pluralist democracy). The Italian Communists, who were pursuing a "historic compromise" with the Christian Democrats, had already condemned the PCP on trade union unity and the suspension of the Portuguese Christian Democratic Party from the April election; in the wake of the *República* shutdown they attacked the PCP even more harshly for sectarianism (MacLeod 1983). The attitude of the other Communist parties to the Portuguese revolution became a litmus test of their commitment to what would soon be called "Eurocommunism."

The PS used the issue to drum up fears, abroad as well as in Portugal, that the PCP was destroying freedom of the press. *República* was the overt issue which brought the government down, but it was something of a pretext for the PS: the party genuinely wanted to keep the paper, but Soares himself acknowledged that the Communists were not behind the paper's takeover. The more fundamental issue was the PS's charge that the PCP was excluding it from power even though it had won the election.

Gramsci argues that revolutions in the late twentieth century must be at least as concerned with ideological hegemony as with seizing power, and in fact, it is not surprising that the news media themselves became a major issue in Portugal. The media have a double significance. On the one hand, they are capitalist property, and in Portugal the *República* and *Renascença* workers' challenge to that property took the same form as it took in other capitalist firms. At the same time, the papers represented (or so many people thought) access to, perhaps control over, people's minds, and thus potentially a major force—for either change or reaction (cf. Pimlott and Seaton 1983). The relative lack of violence in the Portuguese revolution left a prominent role for ideological disputes—not only over the media, but also on the occasions when the publication of a document became a major political event.

Rural Counterrevolt

Shortly after the moderate parties resigned from the government, violent incidents did break out. The right wing organized a series of rallies in the center and north of Portugal and its Atlantic Islands. Many of them culminated in attacks on the left. More than one hundred headquarters of the PCP, other left parties, and unions were assaulted, and many were burned down (SIPC 1976: 35). Several people were killed in the violence.

These riots occurred in rural towns in areas where small farms predominated. Most participants were poor peasants, who saw no promise in the revolution, partly because their traditions of devout Catholicism and anticommunism made them hostile, and partly because the MFA and the revolutionary leadership did not address their concerns adequately. The revolution appeared to be imposed on them from the city and to threaten order and discipline; even worse, agrarian reform made landowners, even of small properties, fear expropriation. All this occurred at a time when their economic circumstances, always precarious, had deteriorated sharply, because the safety valve of emigration to northern Europe had virtually closed with the recession of 1973–74.

The leaders of the revolution hoped to appeal to these small farmers, and certainly did not intend to threaten them. The MFA had declared that just as it foreswore nationalizing small and medium capital, it would not take over small farms, hoping to assure small and medium farmers that they stood to gain when the unfair competitive advantage of the latifundios was eliminated.

The provisional government also took several steps designed to benefit small farmers directly. The most important was the Rural Rent Law (201/ 75) of April 15, which guaranteed renters the right to renew annual leases; required that rent be specified in fixed sums rather than as a share of the crop;

and required written contracts with copies deposited in a local office of the Ministry of Agriculture. However, this law was enforced only where renters were politically organized, and after a year very few contracts had actually been signed (Rosa 1976: 103).

In May, an emergency agricultural credit was announced. At first available only to small farmers, the measure offered loans for seeds and fertilizer at low interest and without collateral. The small farmers who most needed credit got little of it, however, because they were linked to traditional client networks for credit and were not prepared to deal directly with the state; when the measure was later extended to cooperatives they got most of the loans (Mansinho 1980).

To provide technical assistance to small farmers in the north, and especially to enforce the rent law, the Ministry of Agriculture created the Agricultural Development Support Service. Like the Regional Agrarian Reform Centers, this agency was designed to circumvent the inefficiencies and conflicting interests of the existing agriculture bureaucracy. But the program did not get beyond pilot projects in a few dozen northern *concelhos* (Baptista 1978: 138–39).

The government abolished the *foro*, a form of residual feudal dues: it applied to lands where the de facto owner enjoyed all the rights of ownership but nevertheless had to pay an annual rent. The state itself was the major possessor of *foros*, collecting on more than 400,000 properties (Estrela 1978: 252). The government also announced the restoration of the *baldios* (common pasturelands), which had been taken from rural communities by the fascist regime in 1938.

In practice all these measures amounted to no more than symbolic gestures. The restoration of the *baldios* had little effect, because most who had depended on them in the past no longer owned livestock. Rent regulation and agricultural credit required organization and political support to be effective. If these policies had been offered as part of a coherent and credible policy for small agriculture, they could have made an important difference to the peasants. But as it was, they did not win the support of small farmers or allay their fears of expropriation. The Dynamization Campaign had already revealed that the MFA could not speak to people in the conservative rural areas even when it tried to offer them assistance and incorporate them into the revolutionary process.

That the revolutionary governments never really confronted the problems of small agriculture was not just a failure of imagination or will. The coexistence of a large peasant population and zones of extensive agriculture where farmworkers predominated created conflicting demands, making it unlikely that any agrarian policy could be devised to suit both. The revolution's rural political base was among the farmworkers, and many in the government regarded the small farm sector as a relic which was destined to disappear as capitalism penetrated the countryside. They therefore emphasized taking over the latifundios rather than improving the lot of small farmers (Malefakis 1980: 456–57).

Any hope of winning over small farmers was destroyed by the PCP's sabotage of the Leagues of Small and Medium Farmers. District-wide leagues were founded in the Alentejo in 1974, set up by many of those small farmers who saw a common interest with farmworkers and led the first occupations. But the PCP took them over and turned them into mouthpieces for agrarian reform, installing new leaders; some of them were not farmers at all but farmworkers, others were small farmers sympathetic to the PCP and completely unrepresentative of their nominal constituency (Baptista 1978: 36–37, 53–54; Cardoso 1976: 46–47).

This left no viable organization which could represent the interests of small farmers within the revolution. Disputes constantly arose over occupations: many small and medium farmers had rented parcels, bought rights of pasturage, or worked as sharecroppers either of crops or of livestock on many of the occupied or expropriable lands, and believed that the land occupations threatened their rights.

For a year, farmers in the north and center of the country had watched the revolution with an attitude which had gradually turned from bewilderment to hostility; in the summer of 1975 they fought back. Those who lived in zones where large and small agriculture existed side by side attacked the new cooperatives directly. In the districts of Castelo Branco and Lisbon hardly any occupations took place after August; these were mixed areas of large and small farms, and by midsummer opposition to agrarian reform had grown so great that further occupations were unsafe (Barros 1979: 69).

But in areas where there were few large properties and no farmworkers' organizations, hence no land occupations, attacks were directed at the visible presence of the left: the headquarters of the Communist Party, the MDP, the unions, and (although far less often) the far-left parties. The first attack took place in Rio Maior, fifty miles north of Lisbon, where farmworkers and farmers, latifundios and small properties, coexisted within close range. On Sunday, July 13, when the district League of Small Farmers called a meeting, townspeople, mostly small farmers, gathered to protest the meeting and a mob stormed and destroyed the headquarters of the PCP and the FSP.

On the same day, a rally was called in the coastal city of Aveiro to protest the workers' seizure of *Rádio Renascença* from the church. Despite the attacks on the church during the Dynamization Campaign, the hierarchy had remained quiet about the revolution. But in July the church became an active and public opponent. It is significant that the first major church-related protest outside Lisbon occurred on the same day as the first major protest by small farmers. Over the next several weeks, the church took a leading role in mobilizing small farmers against the revolution.

Protests flared for more than a month, spreading to new areas every weekend. Most occurred on Sunday, and some during the week on local market days, when many people were in town and could take part spontaneously. Many initially peaceful rallies (often addressed by the local priest or bishop) turned to violence and destroyed party and union headquarters. At the same time, people forced the resignations of the MDP local governments of many *concelhos* and *freguesias* which they had come to believe had been imposed on them. Most of these incidents occurred in the northern coastal districts of Oporto and Braga, with other coastal districts, Aveiro and Leiria, close behind (SIPC 1976: 35). Few riots occurred in the interior districts, the poorest of them all, because the left hardly existed there.

The most dramatic incident occurred in Braga, center of the conservative church and seat of the Archbishop Dom Francisco Maria da Silva, known as the most reactionary member of the episcopate. At a rally on August 10, tens of thousands heard his scathing attack on the Communists and immediately assaulted the headquarters of the PCP. When party militants inside refused to surrender, shots were fired and troops were called in to quell the mob. But the mob maintained the siege overnight and ultimately broke through the line of troops, drove the party members out, and burned the headquarters down. Some thirty people were injured.

At the same time, two shadowy organizations claimed to be preparing armed intervention to overthrow the Communists: the MDLP, founded in exile by ex-President Spinola, and the Portuguese Liberation Army (ELP), said to be based in Spain. The MDLP openly distributed anticommunist literature in the north and claimed to be preparing an invasion (Calvão 1976). The ELP was accused of bombing a radio beacon in Vilar Formoso, near the Spanish border, in July. Accusations that these organizations provoked the riots were never proven, but at a minimum they took advantage of the same hostile climate which gave rise to the mob violence.

Before the end of August the protests died down as quickly as they had arisen. The abrupt halt showed that the protest movement among the peasants had a very different political character from the mobilizations in the rural south and in the cities. It was based on the peasants' symbolic concerns, and did not address their real grievances or promote an alternative program. What the protest movement demanded was simply a halt to the revolution, and the riots served the goals of the right.

That the right was able to use the peasants is not to suggest that they were manipulated like puppets, with no consciousness of their own. The revolution symbolized the long-term decline in the peasants' condition. It aroused their fears of Communism, loss of land, and opposition to religion, and thereby seemed to be the very enemy the church and the fascist regime had warned about for so long. They would hardly have responded so forcefully if the mobilization had not spoken to their real concerns. But it did not arise from them, and therefore did not produce any concerted political action.

Divisions in the MFA

Events in the capital and events in the countryside often seemed oddly out of joint with each other (confirming the oft-cited distinction between the *país real* and the *país político*). But if the violence in the north contrasted with the maneuvers behind closed doors in the capital, they were aimed at the same target: the prime ministership of Vasco Gonçalves. After they withdrew from the government, the PS and the PPD loudly demanded that Gonçalves resign. On July 18 and 19 the PS called its supporters out to demonstrate in Lisbon and Oporto. Demonstrations by the moderates were rare, but the huge turnout in both cities showed that at least on occasion they could match the left's numbers.

But the decisive political battle was in the armed forces. The battle broke into the open with the People/MFA Document, which violated the compromise that leftists and moderates had reached on the Political Action Program. Gonçalves still had the support of the majority of the MFA Assembly, especially the left-leaning navy and many delegates from his own branch, the army. But the moderates went into open opposition when several moderates on the Council of the Revolution boycotted a crucial meeting of the MFA Assembly on July 25 in a gesture of opposition to Gonçalves.

At that meeting, President Costa Gomes gave a pessimistic speech calling on the delegates to recognize that while initially "practically the whole population was with our revolution, today . . . that is not true." He called for the revolution to slow down and reminded the Assembly that given Portugal's close economic and political relations with the West, "national independence will not be achieved in the short run by any path that alienates the West'' (Neves 1976: 80–81).

Gonçalves followed with a hard-line speech which revealed how far the two men's positions had diverged. Refusing to be swayed by the resignation of the PS and PPD, he insisted that the pace must not be slowed down—''History itself teaches us the rhythm. . . . A revolution develops in crisis''—and that still further sweeping measures to dismantle the capitalist system were necessary to keep the revolution going (Gonçalves 1976: 429–47).

In a desperate effort to harmonize these conflicting positions, the Assembly named Gonçalves, Costa Gomes, and Otelo as a three-person ruling directory, quickly dubbed the ''Troika.'' This appeared to demonstrate that the Gonçalvists and the far left were united and would hold on to power despite the growing disaffection with the government in the population at large and among the moderates themselves. But it was a sham: Gonçalves' power was already fading, and the antagonism between him and Otelo was well known. (Otelo, traveling in Cuba, was not even present when the Troika was created.)

Costa Gomes too, though agreeing to be part of the Troika, had already made clear that he thought the revolution had to broaden its rapidly narrowing support. Known as ''the Cork'' because he always bounced back to the top, Costa Gomes coupled a strong survival instinct with indefatigable efforts to stem the conflicts within the MFA. He evidently assumed that by joining the Troika he would be able to hold the factions together.

The moderates began organizing too. On August 7, nine members of the CR published a manifesto written by Melo Antunes and addressed to Costa Gomes, hoping to influence him to break with Gonçalves. The Document of the Nine, as it became known, claimed to present an alternative view of socialist transformation: it rejected both ''the East European model of socialist society,'' characterized by ''bureaucratic control,'' and ''the social-democratic model of society in force in many countries of western Europe,'' which would be an attempt to repeat ''the classical schemas of advanced capitalism in our country.'' In implicit accusation of Gonçalves, it rejected ''the Leninist theory of a 'revolutionary vanguard' imposing its political dogmas in a sectarian and violent form'' and called instead for ''forming a broad and solid social bloc of support for a national plan of transition to socialism.'' Though the program was vague, the message was clear: opposition to the government.

Melo Antunes' position was consistent with the one he had already advocated as author of the MFA program and the economic plan of the previous winter. He wanted the revolution to seek the broadest possible base of support. He genuinely hoped for independence from the superpowers. His disavowal of the social-democratic model along with the model of bureaucratic socialism was meant to assert that independence, as was his emphasis on what he regarded as Portugal's special connection to the countries of the third world, making it a potential link between them and the developed countries (Milkman 1979: 65–68).

But Melo Antunes did not spell out his alternative development program clearly. And whatever his own intentions, he was forced to seek allies on his right. Within days, his manifesto was quickly endorsed by hundreds of officers, many of them rightists, eager to take advantage of his initiative. One of the most active organizers of support later wrote that his fellow supporters regarded Melo Antunes' views as "unrealistic," and that they never proposed him for prime minister because he was "too far to the left" (Mota 1976: 101–2, 141).

The Council of the Revolution reacted by suspending the nine original signers on August 9. Some CR members (including some who opposed Gonçalves) felt that by going public the Nine had committed a serious violation of military discipline. But other CR members supported them; Otelo argued against suspending them, and afterward distanced himself by reaffirming the confidence of the COPCON in Pezarat Correia and Franco Charais, signers who were military commanders, respectively, of the southern and central regions.

These divisions within the military were exacerbated by a breakdown of discipline within the ranks of the soldiers, fomented by factional rivalries. On July 17, troops sent from RALIS to control a demonstration called to support the People/MFA Document instead joined in and even gave rides to civilian demonstrators. A far more serious incident occurred in the Amadora Commandos' Regiment, a stronghold of rightist officers, on July 30. Its commander, Colonel Jaime Neves, and ten other officers and sergeants were expelled by a soldiers' assembly for having allegedly obstructed a popular assembly in the area, site of the Sorefame railroad car factory whose workers issued a statement supporting the *saneamento*. The COPCON initially supported it as well, but a few days later Otelo intervened in the unit and insisted that Neves be reinstated.

Otelo's actions seemed contradictory: he was identified with the far left of the MFA, he had insisted that housing occupations be legalized, and he frequently refused to obey the orders of the CR if he believed they required sending the COPCON to repress workers; yet he defended the Nine and Jaime Neves. Late in August he ordered the Commandos to close down the headquarters of the Gonçalvist Fifth Division, which had been turning out propaganda against the Nine at a furious pace. He was given to sweeping statements: in July, returning from his trip to Cuba, he said that it might soon be necessary to "round up the counterrevolutionaries" in the Lisbon bullring, and that it now seemed "impossible to carry out a socialist revolution by completely peaceful means" (FBIS July 31, 1975).

The Stillborn Fifth Government

Armed with the endorsement of the MFA Assembly, Gonçalves had been struggling to form a new government. The fourth provisional government had collapsed utterly: not only had the two biggest parties and the moderate officers, led by Melo Antunes, quit, but so had some independents close to the far left (including the minister of industry, João Cravinho, and his deputy minister, João Martins Pereira, who had played major roles in the nationalizations).

Gonçalves' efforts to put together a new cabinet faced growing opposition. Many refused to serve. He hoped to form a strong government, for which he hoped to win the support of the COPCON faction. Its members agreed that the pace of the revolution must be kept up. But they rejected the influence of the Communist Party. That along with Otelo's mercurial nature and the personal rivalry between him and Gonçalves prevented any alliance. Otelo refused to accept the post of deputy prime minister, even though the request came from Costa Gomes, not Gonçalves.

So when the new, fifth provisional government was announced, it had the narrowest of political bases: the PCP and its allies. Nominally the cabinet was nonpartisan: Cunhal resigned just as the leaders of the PS and PPD had done, and all the ministers entered it as individuals. But they all more or less adhered to the PCP line. The cabinet was sworn in on August 8, the day after the Nine went public. At its swearing-in Costa Gomes called it a "transitory measure" until a broader government could be formed which included the political parties (Neves 1975: 106–107).

Gonçalves' effort to form a new government in some ways seemed an idle exercise: it was not the government that ruled but the Armed Forces Movement, which had in fact exercised veto power over the government many times. Most recently, the Council of the Revolution had overruled Gonçalves when he had wanted to return *Rádio Renascença* to the Patriarchate. The new government's weakness ironically confirmed its subordination to the MFA: if it had required a significant political base to form a cabinet, the fifth government would never have been sworn in.

But the exit of the moderate parties meant that no one in the government tempered Gonçalves' insistence on keeping up the pace of the revolution. The fourth government during its last weeks (still in office after resigning until the new government could be formed) and the fifth government during what would be the few weeks of its life passed an avalanche of progressive legislation, including the agrarian reform laws (according to Agriculture Minister Fernando Oliveira Baptista, the PS had vetoed them while it remained in the government; Baptista 1978: 154), the nationalization of CUF, and the laws abolishing the *foro* and restoring the *baldios* to their communities.

In the midst of this political turmoil, the country was falling deeper into economic crisis. Investment stagnated while unemployment and the balance of payments deficit grew. The crisis was due largely to events outside Portugal: the international economic collapse following the oil price increases lowered world demand and closed northern Europe to emigration (which fell from 120,000 in 1973 to 45,000 in 1975); the energy crisis hit Portugal especially hard, due to an Arab oil embargo in retaliation for U.S. use of its Azores airbase during the October war. Decolonization deprived the Portuguese economy of raw materials and a preferred market; it also brought home some 150,000 demobilized troops and 700,000 white settlers (perhaps one-third of whom were in the labor force). The returnees and the closing off of emigration exacerbated unemployment, which rose to 15 percent (OECD 1976: 9, 15, 35).

Production also suffered because workers and workplaces were so often mobilized for political activity. Exhortations to the workers to maintain production (under the slogan ''the Battle of Production'' while Gonçalves remained in office, and then with appeals to ''discipline'' by his successor) fell on deaf ears.

Real GDP grew by only 4 percent in 1974 and fell by 3.5 percent in 1975. It did not fall even more only because workers' wage raises increased their purchasing power. In agriculture, as already noted, grain production increased remarkably in 1975 as a result of good weather and the sowing of occupied land which had been uncultivated; agricultural production as a whole, however, fell off. The declining level of production cannot be attributed to political factors alone, for the economic crisis was worldwide and other OECD countries did just as badly. But the Portuguese economy did not particularly benefit from the upswing in world trade which began later in 1975.

Exports declined steadily because of the loss of the colonies (which had accounted for 18 percent of exports), increased domestic demand, the worldwide recession, and what the OECD described as "lack of confidence on the part of foreign importers, with consequent cancellation of orders"— others called it a boycott of revolutionary Portugal. There was a similar boycott by tourist agencies. Emigrants, anxious about the political situation, withheld remittances. The trade balance, regularly in deficit, worsened in 1974 and 1975: while exports fell, imports increased in 1974 because of increased purchasing power (they declined slightly in 1975 because of declining investment and an import surcharge imposed on nonessentials in June). The balance of payments position, once very strong, was reversed. The growing deficit was met by foreign borrowing and drawing on Portugal's soon-to-be-exhausted reserves of gold and foreign currency (OECD 1976: 10, 21–23; Rosa 1976: 30).

Investment was hurt hardest. Worker militancy, wage increases, and general uncertainly about where the revolution was heading led capitalists to postpone investment and even withdraw investments already made. Many branches of multinationals closed down. Private-sector gross domestic fixed asset formation fell 3.4 percent in 1974 and 15.8 percent in 1975 (at constant prices; OECD 1977: 44–45).

The revolution produced some economic gains: nationalizations and land reform brought greater equality in the distribution of wealth and expropriated the economic base of the large landholders and monopoly industrialists who had been politically dominant in the old regime. Income distribution also became more equal, but continuing stagnation soon undercut working-class wage gains.

Most importantly, the fourth and fifth provisional governments failed to redirect the economy as they intended. That failure may have been due to their short life, only a few months, during a period of constant political turmoil. Some have argued, however, that regardless of political circumstances, the government's economic strategy was inadequate. Martins Pereira (deputy minister of industry in the fourth government) and French economist Serge-Christophe Kolm both criticize the government for not acting decisively enough to control the economy, even under Gonçalves.

Kolm argues that the fourth and fifth governments followed a classic scenario of strong reformist economic development, granting workers immediate economic benefits to garner their support, but failing to enact the structural reforms needed to reduce dependency and generate investment capital. As long as the economy remained dependent on private investment and imported goods, it was counterproductive to increase real wages to bolster political support. Real wages could continue to increase (and, to the extent that political support depended on them, it too could last) only if the government exerted strong control over the overall economy (Kolm 1977). In theory, the fourth and fifth governments attempted to do this through the nationalizations; but though they nationalized firms, they did not exercise real central direction. Most importantly, they did nothing to raise the level of investment.

Martins Pereira, too, argues that the revolution could not have succeeded unless the workers had been convinced that the government supported their interests, but its vacillation even under Gonçalves demonstrated that it frequently did not. The revolutionary leadership hesitated to take control of crucial sectors of the economy—especially foreign trade—and was insufficiently imaginative and too beholden to party politics in applying the measures it did enact (J.M. Pereira 1976: 219, 229–45).

The problem, however, was more political than economic. The population as a whole lacked the consciousness and the MFA itself lacked the coherence and unity necessary to sustain the revolution. The MFA's strategy for the transition to socialism could work only if it were applied consistently over a long time. But that required political unity in support of the strategy; if the orientation of the government changed, its measures could be turned to the service of private capital (as they were; see Chapter 12). In any case, the lack of political unity within the MFA prevented the effective execution of the policy the MFA officially endorsed. And the economic stagnation which resulted undercut the revolution's popular support from workers suffering from or threatened by unemployment.

At the same time, the government was subjected to mounting pressure from abroad. The United States and its allies opposed the leftward turn of their strategically located NATO partner, and intervened overtly and covertly to reverse its course. U.S. Secretary of State Henry Kissinger repeatedly bemoaned the advance of Communism; NATO expelled Portugal from its nuclear planning group because it had Communists in its cabinet; while the Common Market promised economic aid only if the political course changed. (In August the United States did the same when asked to help airlift refugees from Angola.) The CIA and the West German SPD financed the PS (as the Soviet Union assisted the PCP). The AFL-CIO's Irving Brown meddled in the dispute over the trade union law. Multinational firms closed their branches or curtailed operations while Western importers boycotted Portuguese products.[1]

Materially and symbolically the Western powers made clear their dissatisfaction with Portugal's threat to capitalist interests and attempted to eliminate it, while Portugal's traditional dependence on the Western bloc for imports, export markets, capital, and labor markets made it highly vulnerable. The right was strengthened by material assistance from abroad, and moderates, citing the need for external assistance in the economic crisis, bowed to foreign pressure.

On top of economic crisis and foreign intervention, Portugal faced a deepening crisis in Angola. The MFA was founded in large part to bring an honorable end to Portugal's colonial empire. But its internal divisions prevented it from leaving a stable government in the richest and most important of the colonies. The transitional government (including all three Angolan liberation movements, FNLA, MPLA, and UNITA) formed in January 1975 fell apart and the conflict degenerated rapidly into a civil war, with the CIA and South Africa supporting UNITA followed by Soviet support and Cuban troops for the MPLA. On August 14 Portugal formally suspended the January agreement and claimed authority over the territory once again, requesting Western assistance to evacuate the white settlers and preparing to return its own troops to Angola.

The Gonçalves government steadily weakened through August. Armed forces support for the Nine, though growing, was not strong enough to defeat Gonçalves until the far-left military went into open opposition as well. On August 13 officers from the COPCON faction (not including Otelo) published a response to the Document of the Nine which commended the Nine's ''patriotic and democratic intentions,'' but criticized their ''right-wing palliatives,'' arguing that the Nine's position ''will lead to the recovery of the right, and will open to it a field of maneuver for the destruction of the revolution.''

The COPCON document proposed instead a revolutionary program, spelled out in the economy, agriculture, housing, health, education, and other areas (Peoples Translation Service 1975: 16–19). It severely criticized the revolution's path so far, and signaled the far-left officers' final withdrawal of support for Gonçalves and the provisional government.

Throughout the summer, rumors of coups abounded, as officers of each faction suspected that their rivals were laying preparations. While everyone denied preparing any military move, all cautiously counted the units that could be relied on and encouraged their civilian allies to remain on alert and be prepared to take to the streets if necessary. While no one moved decisively, each faction's ''defensive'' preparations were seen by the others as evidence that it was preparing to take the offensive.

The Nine and the COPCON group, while they could not unite on a program, agreed that Gonçalves had to go. Otelo dealt the death blow in mid-August, when he wrote Gonçalves to forbid him to visit the military units under Otelo's command, and urged him to take "a prolonged and well-deserved rest" (Neves 1975: 230–31; the letter was sent to Gonçalves privately but leaked to the press). Soon Costa Gomes too withdrew his support. Although he never came out openly against Gonçalves, he stated publicly on August 20 that the government would last only a few more days.

The MFA was determined that the new government would again have the façade of a coalition of civilian parties, and that required agreement among the PS, the PPD, and the PCP. It took several weeks to put together the sixth government, as it had the fifth. At first there was not even agreement on a prime minister. After Army Chief of Staff General Carlos Fabião attempted and failed to form a government, Admiral José Baptista Pinheiro de Azevedo, seen as acceptable to both the Communists and the moderates, was asked to take on the job.

For a while Gonçalves stayed in office only because no one could agree on a new government. But even without an agreement, his position became untenable, as more and more officers supported the Nine. Costa Gomes hoped to allow Gonçalves a relatively graceful exit by naming him chairman of the Joint Chiefs of Staff (a post which Costa Gomes held along with the presidency). But too many officers refused to countenance the possibility, including Fabião and Air Force Chief of Staff General José Morais e Silva; even some of Gonçalves' allies decided that they had to oppose the nomination. The MFA Assembly was to meet at Tancos Airbase on September 5; on the morning of that meeting, bowing to the inevitable, Gonçalves resigned as prime minister and announced that he would not seek the chairmanship. Most of the Gonçalvists from the army and air force were voted off the Council of the Revolution, leaving supporters of the Nine with a clear majority.

Party and Union Battles

The battle over the course of the revolution waged by the military factions was mirrored in civilian battles, in the violence in the rural north and in the struggle to control organizations, especially the trade unions. The trade union unity law, promulgated in April, called for new elections in all unions. The PCP hoped to consolidate its strength in these elections, which began in the summer, but supporters of other parties offered strong challenges.

Most battles for union control were between the PCP and the PS.

Communists held on tenaciously in the unions in which they had a majority, and Socialists fought for leadership in the white-collar unions of bank, insurance, office, and retail workers where their base was strong. The Maoist MRPP was also relatively strong among clerical workers—the epithet of "petty-bourgeois radicalism" with which Alvaro Cunhal labeled the entire far left could without exaggeration be applied to the small but noisy MRPP, supported almost exclusively by students and white-collar workers. Rejecting the PCP as revisionist, MRPP militants were eager to oust it from union leadership. They believed that in the absence of a revolutionary situation (which they took for granted did not exist) they should support the PS and bourgeois democracy.

The Socialists and the MRPP forged an alliance (which the left gleefully dubbed the "Holy Alliance") to run joint slates in the union elections. They won in many of them, supported by the actively involved MRPP militants and the more numerous but more passive PS sympathizers. But most of the elected boards fell apart in bickering between the two groups; Communist union activists contributed to the disorder by packing union general assemblies. By November, the executive board of the Lisbon Officeworkers' Union had resigned in disarray, and the new election was won by the pro-Intersindical slate.

The PCP, while holding onto most industrial unions, was on the defensive in the country at large. It faced mounting violence in the north and the declining fortunes of the Gonçalves government. Instead of pushing for more revolutionary advances, it would have to fight to preserve those already made. To do this, it hoped to keep its working-class supporters in a high state of mobilization and at the same time to restore the alliance with the moderate parties (at least the PS). But the two goals were contradictory. The first required militancy while the second called for conciliation.

The PCP offered militant gestures to inspire its supporters. On August 17 it called a rally in Alcobaça (north of Lisbon, not far from Rio Maior), returning defiantly to where its headquarters had been attacked a month before—but it suffered yet another humiliating attack. At the same time it reached out to the far left. On August 20 it openly (but unofficially) joined a demonstration supporting the COPCON Document. It was one of the largest demonstrations yet and most of the marchers were poor people mobilized by workers' and neighborhood commissions. Communist participation was ironic: the COPCON Document was highly critical of the conduct of the revolution so far and signaled the COPCON officers' break with the Gonçalves government; one of the demonstration's slogans was "against imperialisms," Soviet as well as U.S. The PCP saw the COPCON document as the best available vehicle to mobilize support for the revolution. A week later it formed the Revolutionary Unity Front (FUR) with several far-left parties.

This show of militancy was mixed erratically with gestures of moderation. On August 14, in an open appeal to the PS, it called for an antifascist front to stem the violence. And it abandoned the FUR almost immediately after helping to found it and attempted to negotiate a new coalition government with the PS. This vacillation would continue for months.

Popular Power Defends the Revolution

As military factions and political parties competed to dominate the political course, the popular movement too faced a strategic dilemma. It had seemed unstoppable during the first year of the revolution, advancing from conquest to conquest on its own momentum and as if in a political vacuum. But as the moderate political parties and their military supporters organized against it, it needed to change course. Recognizing the new circumstances, the movement looked for ways to coordinate its base organizations and move to the terrain of state power.

But this shift weakened the movement's legitimacy, because it could no longer work exclusively at the base, in communities and workplaces, to empower people and meet their collective needs. As a movement of mass organizations, it could claim to be working for the aspirations of the whole people, arguing that its organizations were inclusive and open to everyone and that the spontaneity and dynamism with which the revolution had advanced showed that it transcended political differences. When the moderate parties aligned themselves against it, that claim came into question; with the decision to focus on state power, it was no longer credible.

The focus on state power also heightened party conflicts within the base organizations, weakening the movement's efforts at further base-building. Many so-called unitary organizations had been internally split by partisan rivalries all along. But when the goal of the popular movement became state power, not just particular gains for the neighborhood or workplace, the conflicts became more intense. The earlier partisan battles to control the base organizations had usually been between the PCP and the far left; now the supporters of both united to fight off challenges from the PS, again often allied with the MRPP. In some areas, party supporters even founded competing neighborhood commissions.

The decision to enter the contest for state power also presented the problem of how the efforts of the whole movement could be coordinated toward this end. The popular assemblies were clearly inadequate. They claimed to be the basis of the new state founded on direct democracy, but they were still embryonic, existed only in a few areas, and did not necessarily represent their bases. Nor were all the movement's strongest supporters organized into popular assemblies. Though their influence was substantial in some localities, they could make no credible claim to govern. The effort to turn *República* into a coordinating center also foundered.

The political parties of the far left presented the only possible coordinating mechanism. None of them claimed hegemony over the movement, for in their vision (and in fact) the movement was larger than they were. In practice, however, they now attempted to speak for it. But as parties, they could not even in principle claim the independence that the movement claimed. The election, moreover, had shown how small their support was. In order to unify the popular organizations into a single movement capable of leading the revolution, they needed some political base.

Some on the far left sought to build political strength by an alliance with the PCP, although any such alliance would have to bridge major differences over the nature of popular power and the mobilization of the bases. But by that time the PCP had appeared to recognize more clearly the importance of mobilizing its supporters to defend the revolution. The far left hoped that by allying with the PCP, they could pull it further to the left.

So the Revolutionary Unity Front (FUR) was born on August 25. On August 24, the MDP issued a call to the left parties to discuss how best to defend the revolution. That night, the PCP, the MDP, and five parties of the far left, including the MES and the PRP, reached agreement on a platform, which supported "the COPCON Document, popular power, and the fifth government as long as the conditions are not met for the formation of a government of revolutionary unity" (A. Rodrigues et al. 1976: 238). The UDP remained outside, still convinced that the PCP would never support a genuine revolution.

But of the three points of the FUR platform—the COPCON document, popular power, and the fifth government—only the fifth government represented a genuine center of power. The COPCON document was no more than that—a document—and the popular power movement's inability to consolidate itself was one of the very reasons which made the FUR alliance necessary. Even though the FUR's commitment to the fifth government was hedged, by entering the FUR the far left was in practice supporting the PCP and the Gonçalvists (and specifically Gonçalves himself).

There were tens of thousands of militants at the base who wanted to counter the threats to the revolution and preserve the gains they had made, and were therefore eager to take part in public shows of strength. This gave the FUR an important resource, a strong capacity for mobilization, and they brought massive numbers into the streets. The front was inaugurated with a huge show of strength in Lisbon on August 27. Like the pro-COPCON demonstration the week before, the FUR demonstration mobilized the PCP, far-left militants, and activists and supporters of the mass organizations.

But problems arose within the alliance immediately. Differences of political principle produced disputes over seemingly minor details. PCP supporters in the march violated the platform of the demonstration by shouting slogans supporting Gonçalves. The PRP reacted by abandoning the demonstration, protesting that the PCP was trying to take it over.

The PCP withdrew from the FUR almost immediately, in any case, to negotiate a place in a new government. As *República* summarized the FUR's vain efforts, the attempt to pull the PCP to the left was "an illusion" (*República*, September 1, 1975). The MDP remained in the FUR, but when the fifth government fell within days, it was clear that the FUR had failed in its initial purpose.

But the popular power movement had tested its muscle and shown surprising strength in the streets. Elections apparently did not have to be the final test of its numbers. With no tactical alternative, it would continue to mount huge demonstrations, mobilize tens of thousands, stop traffic, and disrupt public order regularly for three months. These mobilizations left many trembling in their homes, fearing that the violence that had swept through the northern villages was now overtaking the cities. To the demonstrators, the heady feeling of dominating the city imparted a sense of strength, a belief that they could actually take state power. But that sense was an illusion, because they had no means to move from disruption to consolidation of the revolution.

11

Counterattack

Throughout the fall of 1975, the popular movement found itself submerged in the battles of parties and government. A new, more conservative government succeeded Gonçalves, and the left, now in opposition, mobilized huge shows of force against it. Demonstrations were not only large but audacious—each one seemed to flout authority in some new and more daring way. For a while it appeared that the left had retaken the initiative and that only a revived left government could reestablish order.

The most important new element in the left's mobilization was the growing political activity by enlisted men in the armed forces. Soldiers refused to obey orders; they marched in demonstrations in uniform, usually violating specific prohibitions. Their politicization had apparently taken a qualitative leap, and officers seemed to be losing control of their troops. The armed forces, it appeared, could guarantee order no better than the government. Some of the moderate officers who had opposed Gonçalves tried to reach a new agreement with the left, both to reestablish social peace and to restore the revolution's momentum.

But the gains were illusory. Rightwing officers, witnessing the government's failure to keep order, were determined to reassert control in the armed forces and the country at large. On November 25 the military right moved against the leftist units in a show of force and won decisively. The blow was fatal to the popular movement, depriving it of the support of the armed forces which had been its main resource.

The Slow Gestation of the Sixth Government

Negotiations over the composition of the new government lasted from mid-August to mid-September. Admiral Pinheiro de Azevedo was appointed prime minister because he was acceptable to both Communists and Socialists. An original member of the junta after April 25 and later on the Council of the Revolution, Pinheiro de Azevedo was thought of as a leftist; he was from the navy, he had opposed the Nine (though he was not a Gonçalvist), and he pledged to continue the revolution.

But he could not put together a coalition without acceding to the demands of the PS and PPD for a halt and even a reversal of the revolution's advances. His program pledged to reinforce authority, disarm civilians, guarantee pluralism in the news media, and replace "illegally constituted" local governments (a reference to the MDP's continued hold on some northern local governments, though it had already resigned from many). The program implied that there would be no more nationalizations and proposed a clear delimitation between the public and private sectors of the economy, with guarantees and incentives for the latter. It conspicuously omitted any reference to popular power or to further advances of the revolution.

Pinheiro de Azevedo presented the program on September 14. But it took another week to agree on the ministers, and almost another before cabinet secretaries were named. In the negotiations, policy differences and the normal jockeying for cabinet slots were accentuated by accumulated hostilities between the Communists and the PPD; they refused to meet in the same room, forcing Socialists to act as messengers. The new government was a party coalition in fact but not in name. The three parties agreed to name ministers, but not as party representatives; rather they were to serve as individuals. And the party leaders were not in the cabinet.

Despite obligatory rhetoric proclaiming continued defense of the revolution, the cabinet's composition clearly represented a move to the center. The PS named four ministers, the PPD two, and the PCP one, and most of the military and independent civilian cabinet members were close to the PS and the Nine. The 4:2:1 ratio was touted as mirroring the popular will shown in the elections, but the ratio of votes had been almost precisely 3:2:1.

The PCP accepted the arrangement because it at least maintained its presence in the government, while the fiction that the government was not a party coalition permitted it to mobilize opposition in the streets and show its capacity for maneuvering (cf. Mujal-Leon 1977: 31–34). Through the fall it continued to alternate between active mobilization of opposition and attempts at reconciliation. While it was trying to keep all options open, it caused confusion among its supporters and hostility among its would-be allies on the left, while completely failing to win the confidence of the moderate military and civilian politicians. The latter criticized the PCP's "zig-zag politics." but believed that it would cause more trouble if it were openly in opposition (*Expresso,* August 30, 1975).

The PS and the right, having essentially won the government they wanted, supported Pinheiro de Azevedo unconditionally, while the left attacked him steadily. He was driven rapidly to the right. He hit hard at the left and angered many with his fiery temper. Mario Soares baptized him the "Admiral Without Fear," mainly because *"almirante sem medo"* rhymed with his name to make a chantable slogan which evoked the "General Without Fear," Humberto Delgado. But the fearless admiral was not able to control his troops, only to rail against their "indiscipline."

He and his government deliberately antagonized soldiers, the news media, and the popular movement, intending to provoke confrontations. But instead of rising to the bait, the opponents often simply ignored it. The first incident occurred even before the government took office. Most Gonçalvists had been ousted from the Council of the Revolution at the September 5 MFA Assembly and replaced by supporters of the Nine, who then had the clear majority. Early in September, the new Council of the Revolution issued an order forbidding newspapers and broadcast media to publish any military news from Angola. But they simply refused to comply; they disseminated the news freely. What was meant as an initial show of strength by the new CR turned out to be a striking demonstration of its weakness.

Mass Mobilizations Against the Government

From September on, base organizations concentrated even more on mass mobilization to challenge the government. Every struggle for land, for wages, for the narrowest grievance in a workplace or neighborhood became part of the struggle for state power. Not only were struggles taken over for partisan purposes—most were initiated for political motives.

When workers demanded higher wages, moderate supporters of the government resisted, partly because the raises would pose a very real danger to economic recovery, and partly because any victory for the workers appeared as a defeat for the government. By the same token, the PCP encouraged such demands both to secure the workers' support and to challenge the government. The year before, the PCP had generally tried to dampen workers' militancy over economic grievances. Now, however, the party tried to turn the workers' militant action to its political advantage.

Workers won many of these struggles, proving their power to impose their will on the government.

The metalworkers' struggle in September and October was a good example. Their union federation had been negotiating a new contract for months, and the Ministry of Labor had finally approved it at the end of August. The employers' association, even though it had won a two-tier wage schedule which allowed lower wages in smaller factories, refused to honor the contract, hoping that the new, pro-PS minister of labor, Captain Tomás Rosa, would let them renegotiate.

The previous contract, signed more than a year before, had never been enforced in many factories. But while Gonçalves remained in office, the strongly pro-Communist unions had protested little. Similarly, pro-Intersindical union leaders had not opposed a law, passed in July, that greatly relaxed the conditions under which an employer could fire workers: it specified that workers could only be fired for cause but left it up to employers to define what was a just cause. With the sixth government, many union officials, including the metalworkers, took up the issue to challenge the government and the new minister of labor.

At the same time the union leaders were fighting off challenges from their ranks. In the Lisbon union, the most important one in the national federation, two slates were challenging the leadership in an election scheduled for October 4: an MRPP slate and one sponsored by a far-left alliance including the UDP and the MES. Both opposition slates condemned the leadership's slack efforts to enforce the old contract and rejected the two-tier wage schedule in the new one. The opposition slates charged that the leadership was now demanding action on the contract only to undercut them.

To show its muscle to its left opponents, the employers, and the ministry, the metalworkers' federation called a symbolic one-hour strike on September 24, with assemblies in workplaces to air grievances. When the employers continued to balk, it called a second strike on October 7; in Lisbon workers massed outside the Ministry of Labor. Minister of Labor Rosa had met with the leaders of the federation the night before the demonstration and agreed to address the strikers. The assembled workers were so hostile that they hardly allowed him to speak. Still he gave in to practically all their demands. He promised to enforce the new contract and pledged that the law regulating firing would be revised to allow workers' commissions or trade union delegates' commissions in workplaces to determine what was a just cause for firing. But on television the next day, he seemed to contradict himself, criticizing the contract and the demonstrators and saying that it would not be so easy to revise the law.

Disputes over land occupations also escalated into opposition to the government. At Cujancas, an occupied farm in the district of Portalegre, on September 8, the former owner forcibly repossessed the cattle which the occupying farmworkers had taken over along with the property. Soldiers finally recovered the cattle and returned them to the cooperative some ten days later, but not before the dispute had mobilized farmworkers and land occupiers throughout the district and provoked a one-day farmworkers' strike which spread to the districts of Beja and Evora.

The striking farmworkers had other grievances. Cooperatives were short of cash. Until they could harvest and sell a crop, they could not pay salaries. They demanded that the Ministry of Agriculture grant them emergency credit for salaries. Hostilities between strikers and bank workers broke out at a demonstration in Evora when the strikers attempted to block the entrance to the Bank of Portugal (Mansinho 1980: 529–31). Strikers blamed the bank workers for the failure to grant them credit. The bank workers had no authority over the decision, but the Communist-dominated farmworkers' union charged that the new PS/MRPP executive board of the bank workers' union supported the government position.

The sixth government included a new minister of agriculture, Fernando Lopes Cardoso of the PS's left wing. He was a supporter of agrarian reform, despite the hostility of the PCP and the farmworkers toward him. He wanted to halt occupations and instead have the ministry expropriate and distribute farmlands, but he accepted the occupations which had occurred. On September 27, he granted a major demand of the occupying farmworkers: he agreed to expand the government's emergency credit program to allow loans to the cooperatives for salaries.

A dramatic upsurge in occupations followed. In Beja and Portalegre (two of the three districts where workers took over the most land), three times as much land was occupied between October and December as had been occupied before October. The availability of credit was only one reason— sowing time was approaching, and as they had done the year before, farmworkers wanted to occupy to ensure that land would actually be sown. And as in the cities, the political offensive created a go-for-broke determination in the countryside to push the revolution forward or at least to take as much land as possible before occupations were halted (Barros 1979: 70–73).

Pereira argues that the upsurge that resulted from guaranteed salaries proves that the occupiers were only seeking stable employment, not land, and that they waited for the state to take the initiative before acting. This timing, he says, "makes a 'revolutionary' interpretation of the 'agrarian reform' difficult" (J.P. Pereira 1982: 51). But he seems to imply that a movement is less revolutionary because it acts when its chances of success improve. It is not surprising that workers were more likely to occupy when their wages were assured; it is especially noteworthy that occupations stepped up when the political climate was shifting and one could expect that occupations not completed then might never be possible. And the farmworkers' willingness to defend the cooperatives and the agrarian reform generally, as they did in the strike over Cujancas, shows that they saw it as a political victory, not just an economic gain.

Neighborhood commissions also entered the lists against the government. In Oporto, the neighborhood commissions had had real political power, but only because they counted on the support of the northern military region and its commander, Eurico Corvacho. They had worked very closely with the Oporto Military Commission which had taken charge of the city government in May. Their revolutionary council (CRMP) had won a big role in city affairs, expediting city actions for SAAL and other neighborhood projects.

Opposition to the government was strongest in the north, not only among civilians but also among officers, who challenged Corvacho as soon as the Document of the Nine was published. The members of the city's military commission, recognizing that Corvacho was on his way out, submitted their resignations in August. When Gonçalves resigned, Corvacho was ousted from the Council of the Revolution, and shortly thereafter from his command as well. His successor, Colonel Antonio Pires Veloso, immediately took a hard line, demanding discipline of his troops and telling the base organizations that they could not expect assistance from the units, which would be restricted to military duties.

The loss of support had a devastating effect on the commissions in Oporto. Some activists wanted to declare the CRMP itself the city government. The Council had reached beyond the neighborhood commissions to include workers' commissions and other base organizations throughout the city. Instead of demanding to govern in its own name, however, it urged the Military Commission members to withdraw their resignations. But when Corvacho was removed, the Military Commission stepped down on September 12. The civil governor, a PS delegate to the Constituent Assembly, named three long-standing city civil servants to an administrative commission to replace the Military Commission. At the same time, he declared the CRMP dissolved.

Defying this order, the CRMP invaded City Hall and held a meeting. But the PCP chose this moment to create a popular assembly to compete with the CRMP. The old divisions emerged here, as they did on other occasions— even though the PCP, the far left, and independent organizations cooperated to support most of the mobilizations that fall, their alliance was always tenuous. But the PCP's effort to create a popular assembly was irrelevant, for neither the CRMP nor the popular assembly had much influence with the new commission. (In October, yet another administrative commission took office, with neighborhood commissions represented as well as the political parties. But the commissions' influence remained minimal: they had three seats, while the PS and PPD together had ten and the PCP two, and the civil governor reiterated that he would ignore the neighborhood commissions because they were not democratically elected.)

One of the demands of the PS and the PPD before joining the sixth government had been the return of occupied apartments to their landlords. When the government took office the neighborhood commissions stepped up occupations, which had slowed down since the rush in February and March. The government started eviction proceedings against occupiers beginning early in November; but the neighborhood commissions disrupted the proceedings in the name of "popular justice." When the first case came to trial, the neighborhood commission appeared in court and demanded to be tried in place of the defendant. Protesting the disruption, the judge refused to hear the case, so neighborhood activists convened in the hallway, held a mock trial, and found the defendant innocent. The same scene occurred at many more trials (Downs 1980: 146; B.S. Santos 1982: 371).

In factory, farm, and neighborhood, for more than a year, workers had been winning victories, many of them totally unexpected. They had found that they could act together and felt that they were masters of the society as never before. All of that was threatened by the retrenchment of the revolution. So they united and converted their local grievances into national challenges. The farmworkers' and metalworkers' strikes, the upsurge in occupations of land and housing, the struggles of the Revolutionary Council in Oporto and against housing evictions, all were turned into weapons to defend the revolution. Local demands were focused on a single goal: to topple the provisional government. At times, it appeared that it might fall. The popular movement repeatedly flouted the government and frequently forced it to give in. While not able to rule, the movement continued to prove that the government could not rule either.

The Soldiers' Mutiny

Soldiers, too, started to go into virtual open revolt. Deteriorating discipline was palpable, as soldiers "patrolled" in improper uniform and casually chatted with passers-by. Even worse was a steady escalation of acts of defiance and insubordination in units throughout the country. At the beginning of September the Lisbon military police regiment refused orders to go to Angola. Other units did the same, destroying any small hope that Portugal would be able to prevent a civil war there. To announce their refusal, the military police held a press conference in defiance of the military censorship edict.

Soldiers in Oporto provided a catchword which was to spread through the country. Two days after Gonçalves resigned, on September 7, masked soldiers appeared at a press conference and announced the formation of SUV (Soldiers United Will Win) to oppose the right turn in the Council of the Revolution and the government. The slogan caught on: a few days later, SUV organized a massive march of soldiers in Oporto, joined by civilian popular organizations. They hoped (in vain, as it turned out) to exert pressure to keep Corvacho as northern regional commander.

SUV rapidly spread to other regions. Its marches in several provincial cities were the biggest those cities had seen. It demanded higher wages and soldiers' commissions with power in the barracks analogous to the popular power of the workers' and neighborhood commissions; it demanded that reactionary officers be dismissed; and it was "against imperialisms." Its rhetoric placed SUV close to the FUR and to the left of the Communist Party, but the PCP tacitly supported it. Its politics were never clearly defined, and its spokesmen in different places adopted somewhat different lines. It became part (and, briefly, the leading edge) of the opposition to the sixth government.

SUV's greatest show of strength was a demonstration in Lisbon on September 25, calling for the release of two soldiers who had been arrested at the Infantry School in Mafra for distributing SUV literature, and imprisoned at Trafaria, across the river from Lisbon. The demonstration was unusually large, and when a speaker at what was supposed to be the concluding rally announced that there would be a protest at Trafaria the next day, the crowd shouted "Let's go today!" Leaving the park, close to midnight, marchers boarded city buses and announced to drivers and passengers that they would be taking a detour. The buses took the huge crowd to Trafaria, and before morning the authorities announced that the two soldiers would be freed.

In another dramatic protest, Captain Alvaro Fernandes went underground in September with 1,500 G–3 rifles from Beirolas armory and told friendly newspapers that he had turned them over to "the masses." (This was the largest "diversion" of arms to come to light, but some units publicly declared that they would distribute arms to the population against a possible counterrevolutionary coup, and there were reports that thousands of weapons shipped back from Africa had disappeared from the docks; *O Jornal,* September 19, 1975.) Rumor had it that Fernandes had given the rifles to the PRP, but both he and the PRP denied it. The PRP nevertheless announced that its Revolutionary Brigades were going underground, and warned civilians to arm themselves for an inevitable confrontation.

Soldiers by this time routinely disobeyed orders to restrain civilians' demonstrations. One occasion was a protest against Spain's Generalisimo Franco: in his dying days, Franco insisted on the execution of five political prisoners, provoking repudiation from all of Europe. On September 26, the eve of the execution, demonstrators in Lisbon sacked and burned the Spanish embassy and chancellery, and soldiers sent from RALIS refused to intervene.

This refusal to obey orders spread to other units. On September 29 the government attempted once again to censor military news on radio and television, sending soldiers to occupy the stations. Crowds of civilians quickly gathered outside each station and the Communication Ministry to protest. Within a few hours the occupying soldiers had voted solidarity with the stations' workers. News broadcasts not only defied the order but further embarrassed the government by telling the story of the "occupation."

Then in early October, a qualitative leap in the level of indiscipline occurred in Oporto. The founders of SUV who had supported Corvacho rapidly turned their fire on Pires Veloso, the new regional commander. When Pires Veloso ordered the military transport school in Oporto closed and its soldiers demobilized, the soldiers refused his orders and called a demonstration on October 6. Soldiers from many other units poured out to support them, and the demonstration concluded in the early hours of the morning by occupying the Serra do Pilar Artillery Regiment. Soldiers there welcomed the occupiers, who vowed to remain until their old unit was reconstituted. They held out for a week; on October 9 civilian demonstrators supporting and opposing them clashed, leaving one hundred injured. On October 14, Army Chief of Staff Fabião undercut Pires Veloso by traveling to Oporto to meet with the soldiers and agreeing to reconstitute their old unit (although the promise was not kept).

SUV was concentrated in the army, the most politically divided of the branches. The conservative air force officers brooked no indiscipline, and sailors did not organize against their officers because so many navy officers were leftists. While SUV was organized by enlisted men, leftist officers encouraged them. These activities appalled moderate officers, who feared that they were losing control of their troops. Officers of several units had to back down from threats to transfer SUV activists. Some officers (including the commander of the regiment at the Infantry School when the two soldiers he had ordered arrested were released) even resigned their posts, complaining that soldiers under their command refused to obey them.

What they were facing was not just "indiscipline." A new spirit had been growing in the armed forces since April 25. When combat did not end immediately, troops still in Africa refused to fight. Returning to Portugal, they demanded to share the popular power which civilians had won, and in some units the officers' own democratic convictions had led them to foreswear some of the trappings of rank. Soldiers watched their offices air disagreements in public, and decided to exercise free expression themselves.

What was at issue was not a breakdown of morale but political opposition. Soldiers in some units had become politicized by close contacts with the popular movement over the previous year. Everywhere party militants in the armed forces spread propaganda among their fellow soldiers. (Many political activists who had left the country resisting the draft had returned after April 25 and enlisted to fulfill their military obligation.) In some units where the upsurge of militancy was new, politicization was shallow—activism gave the young recruits a chance to strut, to be embraced at demonstrations, and to proclaim, in a popular slogan, that soldiers were "always on the side of the people." But even if many of the new activists in the troops had only superficial political convictions, their protest was clearly aimed at the sixth government's threat to undo the revolution.

The Heightening Challenge

Civilian leftists from parties and base organizations turned out in huge numbers for all the SUV demonstrations, and for demonstrations over neighborhood and workplace grievances. Almost every night—and almost all night long—tens of thousands marched in Lisbon. They caused huge traffic jams and felt that they had taken over the center of the city. In other cities, protests were smaller and less frequent but could be equally immobilizing.

New efforts were made to coordinate the base organizations. At the beginning of 1975, far-left militants had founded the Interempresas to coordinate workers' commissions. It organized the anti-NATO demonstration of February 7 but afterward became inactive. PCP militants in workers' commissions therefore began planning to fill the void in September, sponsoring the Secretariat of Workers' Commissions of the Lisbon Industrial Belt (the last three words produced the acronym CIL by which it became known) in Lisbon.

The CIL held its founding assembly on November 8, attended by representatives of 115 workers' commissions. The overwhelming majority were PCP supporters, but some far-left commissions were present as well. The assembly voted to condemn the government, especially its minister of labor, and passed resolutions on economic grievances and worker control. The purpose was not to express the common demands of the workers' commissions, however, but to mobilize them. The CIL was a direct arm of PCP strategy, and in the name of popular power, it called on the commissions to destabilize the government by repeated demonstrations in the streets.

In Setubal, a Committee of Struggle was founded to protest the occupation of the radio stations on September 29. It brought together representatives of workers' commissions, neighborhood commissions, and soldiers. For two months, it held several large meetings and undertook new projects—occupying land for a long-delayed public housing project and setting up direct sale of agricultural projects from Alentejo cooperatives. But its main purpose was to pressure the government—or to force it out of office.

The Committee of Struggle was more successful than other efforts to link workers, neighborhood activists, and soldiers, but the task remained difficult, and its effectiveness was ultimately limited. The committee was organized territorially to work more effectively on neighborhood-oriented projects, but most activists regarded the point of production as primary, and hence saw workplace organization as more important than neighborhood organization. Moreover, the ability of workers to halt production gave their commissions more political power, and they were more effective at mobilizing their members beyond the immediate neighborhood. Finally, the committee's neighborhood orientation gave it a far-left tone, while most workers' commissions were dominated by the PCP.

The various coordinating organizations claimed to exercise dual power, a claim that was certainly premature. Trotsky defined dual power as a situation in which the class seeking power, "although not yet master of the country, has actually concentrated in its hands a significant share of the state power, while the official apparatus of the government is still in the hands of the old lords. . . . By its very nature such a state of affairs cannot be stable" (1967: I: 203; cf. Lenin 1975). But the popular movement never reached that point. The confrontations increased the level of disorder and proved that the government could not govern. But dual power requires not only preventing the ruling class from governing; the working class must exercise authority itself. Only a few workers' and neighborhood commissions exercised positive power of their own. The popular power movement as a whole was not sufficiently strong or coordinated to claim sovereignty generally. Santos characterizes the situation as one not of dual power but of "dual powerlessness" (B.S. Santos 1982: 372).

The center and the right demonstrated too; but less often, and they mobilized their supporters less effectively. The PS did organize some very large demonstrations: in the summer, to support the *República* management and when the PS quit the government, for example; in the fall, a major demonstration on November 9 supporting Prime Minister Pinheiro de Azevedo, where he let loose an unbridled attack on the PCP (the demonstration was broken up by a tear-gas bomb, apparently thrown by a provocateur). But the middle-class constituency of the PS and the PPD was not easily mobilized. The left's demonstrations were indisputably bigger, not only in Lisbon but in several provincial cities as well, even where supporters of the PS and the right clearly outnumbered leftists.

The only demonstrations that consistently mobilized large numbers against the revolution were those called by the anonymous right in the rural north during the summer. These rallies continued in the fall, though they less frequently erupted into violence. Many bombings and other deliberate acts of destruction were attributed to the MDLP. Those who bemoaned the chaos that seemed to be overtaking the country usually directed criticism at the left—perhaps because the critics were in the cities, where the left was active, and were not directly threatened by the mobs in the rural towns. But though the left's mobilizations were disruptive, they rarely harmed people or property. Most of the real violence came from the right.

Some people in the cities who were hostile to the revolution provoked some minor incidents. Most important were the refugees who had fled the former colonies. Hundreds of thousands of settlers had returned, especially from Angola, where the political settlement was still not final and civil war threatened; where Portuguese settlers had been the longest and had the biggest stake, and from which they had fled in fear after some whites were massacred.

The Rossio, one of Lisbon's two main squares, became the returnees' favorite gathering place (it had been the habitual meeting ground for the left, and had seen many illegal May Day demonstrations under fascism). Lodged at government expense in the hotels surrounding the Rossio, returnees gathered in the coffee shops every afternoon. Handwritten wallposters were stuck up on a bus shelter on the square; most demanded that Portugal either reestablish its rule in Angola and allow them to return or (at least) take care of them now that they had been deprived of their homes and livelihood. One afternoon in September, a jeep of the leftist military police, the unit which had disobeyed orders to go to Angola, stopped at a red light, and returnees quickly surrounded it. The ugly atmosphere of confrontation was dispelled only when the soldiers fired shots into the air, sending the crowd scattering.

Rádio Renascença soon returned to the headlines. The troops who had occupied the station on September 29 did not close it down, but another unit occupied the transmitter, located on the outskirts of Lisbon, and took the station off the air. Later the transmitter was sealed by the police.

On October 21, a demonstration of *Renascença* supporters marched to the transmitter and surrounded it all night long. Early in the morning demonstrators broke in and turned it back to the station's workers, who began broadcasting immediately. For just over two weeks, the station continued to broadcast its messages urging the popular movement to solidarity and action. Then on November 7, before dawn, the CR ordered a squadron of paratroopers from Tancos to destroy the transmitter. The paratroopers, the same unit which had supported Spinola's coup on March 11 and bombarded the Artillery Regiment, ordered the technicians working there to evacuate. They then blew the transmitter up.

The paratroopers were an elite unit, specially recruited and trained, and assumed to be politically reliable; it was not for nothing that they were selected for the task. But after blowing up the *Renascença* transmitters, they revolted, claiming that they had been deceived into being a tool of the right. With rebellion brewing on the base, Air Force Chief of Staff General Morais e Silva went to speak to a soldiers' assembly, but he was shouted down and most soldiers and NCOs walked out on him. Recognizing that they could not control the troops, 123 officers abandoned the base, leaving it in the command of its sergeants and a handful of officers who remained. For the next two weeks, the paratroopers engaged in a war of words and mutual provocation with Morais e Silva, in which they demanded his resignation and he in turn declared the unit dissolved (though he could not enforce the order).

The CR intended the destruction of the *Renascença* transmitter as a show of firmness, but the act suggested that it could keep order only with dynamite. It also deepened the chasm between the government and working-class activists. Once again, the news media were themselves at the center of Portuguese events, and the opponents of the revolution refused to let the working class have its own media.

The destruction of the transmitter seemed all the more precipitate because confrontation had let up for a few weeks. The PCP wanted to keep things calm in anticipation of the independence of Angola, scheduled for November 11. The Communists hoped that lowering the pressure would encourage the government to recognize the MPLA as Angola's government or at least stick to its plan to withdraw all Portuguese forces by that date. Portugal did withdraw on schedule, but without handing over power to anyone.

The home front erupted again immediately, stimulated not only by the independence of Angola but by the *Rádio Renascença* bombing and Pinheiro de Azevedo's outspoken attack on the PCP on November 9. On November 12 a massive demonstration of construction workers turned into the left's most threatening show of force to date. The construction workers, on strike over their long-expired contract, marched to São Bento Palace, surrounded it, and trapped the prime minister, the cabinet, and the entire Constituent Assembly inside for more than twenty-four hours.

The construction contract was another case which became an issue with the change of government. The union federation had presented its negotiating position for the new contract the previous May, but the employers' association stalled and the ministry did little to force them to bargain, for fear that any salary settlement acceptable to the workers would only worsen the crisis of the construction sector. As long as the Gonçalves government was in office, the unions did not push the issue.

In October a group of construction workers' commissions, led by the PCP and the UDP, met and decided that it was time to act. They demanded a contract and more: they wanted government construction projects to relieve unemployment. The Ministry of Labor called the union and industry negotiating committees to a meeting on October 28; when the industry committee failed to show up, the ministry agreed to dictate a settlement within thirty days if the industry did not sit down to negotiate one.

But since the employers continued to refuse to negotiate, the workers went on strike and called the November 12 demonstration. The plan was to march to the Ministry of Labor, but the ministry had closed for the day, so instead the crowd marched to São Bento, the seat of the cabinet and the Constituent Assembly. The demonstration was huge. Over 100,000 people filled the plaza in front of the palace, and a negotiating committee entered to meet with the prime minister. He agreed to address the rally, but lost his temper and cursed the workers out, turning the crowd against him. At that point they surrounded the palace, trapping the members of the cabinet and the assembly.

The siege continued for more than twenty-four hours; President Costa

Gomes asked Otelo to send the COPCON to break it up, but Otelo refused. Finally Pinheiro de Azevedo gave in to the workers' demands. He agreed to impose higher wages on the employers, to undertake a program of public construction projects, and to conduct an investigation of the Ministry of Labor's handling of the case. The capitulation showed vividly both how weak the government was and the way in which a sectoral struggle could become a challenge to state power. The construction workers, supposedly seeking wage increases and employment guarantees, had practically pulled off a *coup d'état*.

From the numbers, it was clear that the majority of those who joined the siege were not construction workers at all but saw this struggle as yet another opportunity to challenge the government. The demonstration fit within the overall strategy of confrontation which had been laid down by the PCP and the parties of the FUR. They did not control the forces they were leading, however. The capture of São Bento had not been planned; the demonstrators had acquired a momentum of their own. The victory seemed to prove that continued pressure in the streets might bring the government to its knees.

But Pinheiro de Azevedo and his civilian allies learned a different lesson from the São Bento siege: that there could be no reconciliation with the left. On November 19 Pinheiro de Azevedo announced that the government was suspending activity—in effect, going on strike—until the president could guarantee the safety of the cabinet.

The São Bento demonstration was the beginning of two final weeks of escalating confrontation. The CIL held a major demonstration on November 16 to demand a new government. The day after the government went on strike the CIL called a three-hour general strike and a new demonstration, marching to the president's palace in Belem to demand that he dismiss the government. There a group of eighteen officers, from units in Lisbon identified with both the Gonçalvists and the COPCON, presented a "Manifesto of Progressive Officers" in which they called for the arming of the people (Almeida, n.d., II: 490–92). Uniting to resist what they saw as a probable coup attempt from the right, Gonçalvist and COPCON officers had at last forged the tactical alliance which had eluded them while Gonçalves was in office.

Otelo himself appeared ambivalent. He openly opposed Pinheiro de Azevedo's government and disobeyed the CR's orders to break up the siege of São Bento. Commenting on Captain Fernandes' robbery of rifles from an army depot, he said that it was a "satisfaction" to know that they had been turned over to the left, but in the same press conference he condemned SUV, "however well-intentioned," as counterrevolutionary (*Diário de Notícias*,

September 26, 1975). He defended the censorship order on September 29, addressing a hostile crowd from the balcony of the Communication Ministry. But he tried to invoke the protesters' sympathy, saying in a long speech that, if only he had more political culture, "I could have been the Fidel Castro of Europe" (quoted in A. Rodrigues et al. 1976: 245).

The mutual provocations were reaching dangerous levels. Many were worried that a civil war was brewing. Rumors of coups and countercoups flew with an intensity even greater than what had come to be regarded as normal. In October pro-Communist newspapers headlined an alleged "plan of the colonels," spelling out in great detail the marching orders for a rightwing coup. In November a "Commission of Revolutionary Vigilance" in the armed forces denounced yet another alleged rightwing coup plot. The right also accused the left of plotting a coup and speculated about how long a "Lisbon Commune" taken over by radicals could withstand a siege from the rest of the country. Many PS and PPD militants left Lisbon in fear for their safety; the Constituent Assembly threatened to move to Oporto.

Amid the mutual suspicions of plots, it was common belief in the military that *"o primeiro a saltar, come"* ("the first one to jump will eat it"; A. Rodrigues et al. 1979: 134), so each side was eager to provoke the other into acting rather than to take the first step. Officers who had endorsed the Document of the Nine had begun in August to plan a military show of force which would defeat the left once and for all. These officers were far more conservative than were the Nine. They formed a group which became known as the "operationals" (in contrast to the "politicals," the Nine themselves). The operationals were led by Lieutenant Colonel Antonio Ramalho Eanes, who had been removed from a post in the television station after March 11, suspected of sympathy with (though not participation in) Spinola's coup. Acting rather independently of the Nine, Eanes laid meticulous plans to respond to any move by the left. He could count on a few units in the Lisbon region, notably the Amadora Commandos; other supporters (including the officers who had abandoned the paratroopers' base at Tancos) reactivated the idle Cortegaça air force base near Oporto for their center of operations.

As I argued earlier, officers came to sympathize with the far left because their assignments brought them into direct contact with popular organizations, or became Gonçalvists because they held bureaucratic posts. Most officers whose politics had not changed through the political struggles had remained in line positions. They commanded the best-disciplined troops, ready to move on very short notice. This was now to prove to their great advantage. Determined not to jump first, they gathered their forces and waited for an opportunity to move against the left units.

Any military confrontation would have to begin in the Lisbon region. The left (Gonçalvists and COPCON, now acting together) controlled most of the bases in the region, and would be reinforced by civilians equally eager to defend the revolution if called on. But the balance in the armed forces as a whole favored the right. If a real military revolt occurred in Lisbon, it would be crushed by troops from around the country, although at the cost of enormous bloodshed.

Pinheiro de Azevedo's government was essentially a creature of the Nine. But while he was being driven to the right, the Nine, especially Melo Antunes, still hoped to come to terms with the left. They wanted to avoid a bloody conflict, but they also feared that a decisive defeat of the left would give their new conservative allies a free hand to reverse the changes wrought by the revolution so far. The PCP was also trying to keep a foot in both camps: to stay in the government despite the turn to the right, but at the same time to keep up the pressure in the streets and if possible bring the government down. So the PCP and the Nine began to negotiate to form a new government.

The tide appeared to be turning in the left's favor. The Nine were willing to negotiate, and the demonstrations had won some victories. President Costa Gomes himself had said on television, after the São Bento demonstration, that the government had to keep the workers' support. To the left, it seemed necessary only to keep up the pressure. But leftists deceived themselves. The negotiations with the Nine came to nothing after several meetings among key officers of the three factions. The Nine could never persuade the PS to support any government which strengthened the position of the PCP.

The Nine saw one last hope to stave off the confrontation: to remove Otelo from his post as commander of the Lisbon military region. They believed that Otelo had made himself and the COPCON a center of power which responded to no other authority. Even if his own politics were unpredictable, a clear majority of the Lisbon unit commanders under him were on the left, and their units actively joined the civilian left to mobilize against the government. To restore peace, the moderates on the Council of the Revolution knew, the leftwing units had to be neutralized.

On Friday, November 21, the CR named Nine member Vasco Lourenço the new commander of the region, allowing Otelo to save face by "promoting" him to vice chairman of the Joint Chiefs of Staff. But the leftist officers in the region recognized that this move would totally reverse the military balance between the factions. Despite Otelo's erratic leadership, their power would be severely undercut without him. They met the next day and refused to accept Lourenço as their commander.

Throughout a weekend of unbearable tension, coup rumors flew even faster. Everyone knew that something had to break soon. On November 24 both the left and the right showed their forces. The CIL called another two-hour strike and demonstration in Lisbon. At a farmers' convention in Rio Maior, scene of the summer's attack on the PCP, thousands of farmers from all over the north roundly condemned the agrarian reform and in effect called for its revocation. As the meeting ended, they poured onto the main north-south highway joining Lisbon and Oporto, stopping traffic. (Rio Maior farmers had done the same thing two weeks before during the construction workers' siege of São Bento.) The farmers closed off the rail line as well, "splitting the country in two," as they later boasted, and proving that they could cut off Lisbon's food supply (CAP 1977: 60–61).

November 25

Then the operationals got the opportunity to move. That night the Council of the Revolution met and reaffirmed Otelo's dismissal and Morais e Silva's decision to disband the paratroopers' unit. The paratroopers responded by occupying four airbases around the country. Moving in the early morning hours of November 25, and taking the bases completely by surprise, they captured them peacefully and imprisoned General Anibal José Pinho Freire, air force commander for the Lisbon region. Had operationals not reactivated the Cortegaça airbase and the Tancos officers staffed it, the paratroopers would have knocked out virtually the entire air force.

The operationals viewed this action as the long-expected leftist coup. They gathered at the president's palace to demand Costa Gomes' approval of their carefully laid plans to move, not just against the occupied airbases but against all the leftwing units which they suspected of plotting a coup. Once Costa Gomes agreed, Eanes moved to the commandos' base at Amadora where he directed the countercoup. Commandos were quickly sent to put down the uprising.

Few leftist units moved to support the paratroopers. The military police occupied the radio stations, and troops from the Military Administration School, commanded by Gonçalvist Captain Manuel Duran Clemente, occupied the nearby television studio. In the evening Duran Clemente appeared on television to introduce two paratroopers who read a statement demanding the dismissal of Morais e Silva, Pinho Freire, and two other CR members from the air force, then called on civilians to gather at the leftist military bases to support the uprising. Very shortly, however, the commandos took the television transmitter, cut off the Lisbon studio, and switched the transmission to the Oporto studio. Costa Gomes soon came on the screen to announce a state of siege, and by nightfall the paratroopers at all four occupied airbases had surrendered.

Though no leftist unit moved to any airbase, some remained in a state of alert on their own bases despite the threat of attack by the commandos. Commandos surrounded the military police base and some shots were fired the following morning, killing two commandos and one military policeman, but the unit surrendered the same morning. Mopping up continued until November 27 when the paratroopers who had remained at Tancos finally surrendered as well. Over one hundred leftist officers were arrested and imprisoned, and their units were disbanded.

When the civilian population learned of the action, thousands put down their tools, left their assembly lines, and either maintained a state of alert in their workplaces or surrounded the military units assumed to be friendly, ready to take up arms if the troops would distribute them. Hadn't the eighteen officers of the progressive manifesto promised as much? But no arms were distributed. Empty-handed, the civilians were powerless to resist. Costa Gomes later said that he asked the PCP to demobilize its militants (Gomes 1979: 91), and during the night of November 25 the PCP did so, sending couriers to factories large and small with the message that resistance was useless.

So the rising was put down quickly and easily, and with remarkably little bloodshed: the toll was three dead in the commandos' attack on the military police. As one veteran recounted it, ''Between the dead and the wounded, everyone escaped.''

But the defeat left many questions unanswered. Sources disagree over who ordered the paratroopers to occupy the bases. More important, and equally unresolved, is the scope of planning for a coup: did the left prepare a serious coup attempt, and were the paratroopers part of that attempt, or did the operationals take advantage of an isolated incident? None of the conflicting accounts is disinterested on these questions, and most are speculative.

As to who gave the orders, most claim that the paratroopers at Tancos received a telephone call in the early morning hours of November 25 ordering them to occupy the airbases. Sources of diverse political perspectives claim that the call came either from Otelo himself or the COPCON.

According to Dinis de Almeida, second in command of the RALIS, it came from Otelo (Almeida, n.d., II: 366); Vasco Lourenço implies that if Otelo did not personally convey the order, he approved it (A. Rodrigues et al. 1979: 288; cf. J.F. Antunes, 1980: 263–64). The official inquiry states that the orders came from the COPCON, but does not name an individual (*Relatório do 25 de Novembro*, 1976, II: 117); Duran Clemente, who went on television to urge civilians to join the uprising, suggested that it was the result of a collective decision taken in the COPCON (A. Rodrigues et al. 1979: 144).

A source sympathetic to Otelo claims that the phone call came from the former Tancos officers at Cortegaça, pretending to convey orders from the COPCON. In this view, the operationals provoked the paratroopers to create a pretext for their own coup.[1] Otelo himself denied that he or the COPCON was responsible. In 1976 he claimed that the paratroopers acted on their own, which is consistent with the paratroopers' claim that their only goal was to force the resignation of the four air force officers (Faye 1976: 41–43). Later, Otelo accused Communists within the unit of inciting paratroopers (Ferreira and Marshall 1986: 120).

The question of where the paratroopers' orders came from remains unresolved. Knowledge of who, if anyone, gave the orders would throw light on the more important question: was the occupation of the bases part of a coup plot? From the conflicting and highly partisan accounts of November 25, it is impossible to answer conclusively. But circumstantial evidence suggests that the paratroopers acted on their own, hoping to inspire sympathetic units to join them, as other military conspirators had hoped so often in the past.

In virtually all accounts appearing in the United States and northern Europe, the paratroopers' occupation of the bases is described as a "leftwing coup attempt" which was put down by the operationals acting for the President. But a leftwing coup attempt by whom?

The paratroopers' claim that their only purpose was to force the resignations was at best disingenuous. With the tension built up on November 25, an action like theirs could hardly have been interpreted as having only a limited objective—even though it was only slightly more drastic than many other events which had preceded it, notably the occupation of the Oporto artillery regiment. Still, they may have acted on their own; the occupation of the bases did not look like part of an elaborate plan.

Officers on the left undoubtedly anticipated the possibility of a coup, counted forces, and had contingency plans for action. Many leftist officers of the Lisbon region, both Gonçalvists and COPCON supporters, were gathered at the COPCON headquarters on the night of November 24 waiting to hear the Council of the Revolution's decision on ousting Otelo, and their presence there had been offered as evidence that they were preparing a coup.

The possibility cannot be entirely discounted, but their units responded on November 25 as if they were taken by surprise. Some of the units whose participation could have been expected in a planned coup did not act, and others did little more than go on alert until they saw that the uprising was going to fail. Except for the taking of the radio and television stations, there were no military movements which would indicate planning and coordination.

It seems most likely that if leftist officers had mounted a coup, it would have gone differently. Collectively, they enjoyed vast military superiority over the operationals in the Lisbon region, but they were outnumbered in the rest of the country. Leftist officers knew that they would have to strike a heavy and coordinated first blow. If they had decided to move to prevent Otelo's dismissal, the forces under his command would probably have acted, not the paratroopers, who were part of neither the COPCON nor the Lisbon region. The prevailing view that "the first one to jump will eat it," moreover, would have restrained the left from moving first, and especially from moving less than decisively.

Serge July, writing in *Libération,* the daily of the French far left (December 3 and December 6–7, 1975), charges that Gonçalvist officers were preparing a coup. When the paratroopers anticipated them, according to July, these officers rapidly concluded that the coup was not going to succeed, so they did not support it. This argument is also suggested by Eanes himself (in Mota 1976: 229). Rodrigues et al. (1979: 151–52) give it little credence, principally because no written documentation of such plans has ever been revealed and because there was little apparent activity on November 25 at the Gonçalvists' alleged command post. Though July's articles were translated in *República* in December, moreover, his thesis received surprisingly little attention in Portugal; no detailed refutation appeared, as one would expect if it had been taken seriously.

The only advance planning of military operations for which there is clear evidence was by the operationals (J.F. Antunes 1980: 211–21; Mota 1976). It seems most likely that the paratroopers' move was not the beginning of a planned coup but an isolated act of which the operationals took advantage to strike hard. Something similar had happened on March 11, after all: a coup attempt by a single unit (the same unit) did not receive the expected support, but the opponents who put it down used it as the occasion to consolidate their power.

The fact that civilians were not mobilized also argues against a coup attempt by the left. There were many who were eager to defend the revolution, many of them recent veterans with military training. In fact, they made efforts to participate: thousands of factory workers and others were ready to move when they learned of the occupation of the bases. But their actions show no sign of coordination. They secured nearby targets and took up positions near crucial military bases on November 25 much as they had in many previous emergencies, major and minor—September 28 the year before and March 11, when the revolution seemed seriously threatened; when coup rumors spread in the summer; and when the news media's premises were occupied on September 29. On all these occasions, the workers acted in concert with their mass organizations, but each time they were reacting to unanticipated events, showing that they could move without clear advance planning. Moreover, no civilians carrying the arms stolen in the preceding months emerged to defend the revolution on November 25.

The PCP itself was undoubtedly aware that its supporters in the military contemplated military action, and the party formulated contingency plans. Some cells and some organizations close to the party, such as the CIL, actively urged their members to be on alert. But the evident lack of coordination in the response indicates that they were not following carefully laid plans any more than were the leftist officers.[2]

Even if the left was not actively plotting a coup, however, it bore some of the responsibility for November 25. From August to November and especially during the last two weeks, base organizations of civilians and soldiers had provoked the government with little concern for the consequences. Military threats and counterthreats, the spread of visible indiscipline, and civilian demonstrations all sought to destabilize the government and create an atmosphere of crisis.

The PCP had been erratic: first claiming that the revolution could best be defended by acceleration, then pausing for consolidation; joining the government, then destabilizing it. Along with the PCP, the FUR parties and the popular movement in general had mobilized large numbers—their only resource, it often seemed—to prevent the government from governing. The strategy appeared to be working for a while—but it had its costs.

For one thing, continual disruptive actions produced a climate that encouraged violent solutions. Confrontation antagonized the right, and many who did not identify with the right nevertheless feared that the country was falling into chaos. The popular movement was responsible for very little actual violence: there was only one instance of major physical destruction, at the Spanish embassy, and most demonstrations proceeded in an orderly fashion. More violence came from the right, between the mobs throughout the north during the summer and the bombings by the MDLP. But because the left openly fomented disorder, it invited the brunt of the blame for the growing chaos. Many on the left argued that confrontation was necessary to prevent a Chilean-style repressive coup, but the strategy only made a military response more likely.

Even if it did not promote a coup from the left, the PCP continued this dangerous game on November 25 when a coup seemed in the works. The party was evidently unprepared for the paratroopers' action, but actively considered supporting them, with a view toward taking a leading role. Quickly recognizing that the paratroopers had no military support, however, the PCP bowed to the inevitable: it demobilized its civilian "troops" to avoid being implicated, and later announced that it would discipline some party sections which had violated the order to demobilize (Gomes 1979: 91; *O Jornal*, November 28, 1975). In the events of November 25, anticommunists on the right see proof that the PCP had attempted to take power by storm, but failed; while opponents on the left find confirmation not only of the PCP's lack of revolutionary courage but of its determination to stifle any revolutionary attempt.

For the popular movement, adopting the strategy of confrontation and attempting to force a new government rather then continuing to build the bases implied a centralist orientation, abandoning the popular power model which had inspired it. The movement also submitted to centralized leadership: it followed a strategy and carried out tactics set by the political parties which claimed to guide it—not just the Communist Party, which always had an ambivalent attitude toward popular power, but also the far-left parties which, while advocating popular power, nevertheless made decisions for the movement from above.

Seduced onto the terrain of partisan politics, the popular movement was diverted from the task of building popular power in workplaces and neighborhoods. Work at the base is slow and undramatic; confrontation was appealing because it appeared to offer quicker rewards. Mobilization in a common purpose with huge numbers of others gave participants a sense of unity and strength which was often heady and inspiring, particularly when it produced mammoth traffic jams and exposed the impotence of the coercive apparatus.

But that heady feeling led to extreme misjudgments of the movement's strength. In 1975 the support for the popular power movement was still too narrow to permit it to win state power. The movement could have put popular power into practice fully only by widening its support and strengthening the base organizations; the power to obstruct was not enough.

12

Conclusion

Following their decisive victory on November 25, the operationals consolidated their power over the next several days by occupying key command positions in the armed forces—Eanes, later elected president, became army chief of staff—and replacing the remaining leftists on the Council of the Revolution. They then turned their attention to their two major objectives, one declared, the other only implicit: to consolidate parliamentary democracy and to reestablish capitalist supremacy within the newly restructured economy. That required civil order, which in turn required control over the working class. To make clear that it would tolerate no more worker militancy, the government decreed the suspension of all collective bargaining on November 27.

The new leadership did not intend to revert to fascism. On November 26, Melo Antunes announced on television that the participation of the Communist Party was essential for the construction of socialism. His use of the rhetoric of the revolution made clear that there would be no wholesale repression, but the implication that the effort to build socialism would continue turned out to be hollow.

The new military leadership strengthened the parties of the center and right that dominated the Constituent Assembly. The Council of the Revolution signed a new agreement with them (and the PCP) on February 26, 1976, reversing the political pact signed with the parties a year before. It ratified civilian parliamentary rule as expected, laying the way for parliamentary and presidential elections in the spring. The CR agreed to dissolve itself after four years, although keeping veto power over laws it found unconstitutional until then. In a symbolically important change, the new pact omitted the first pact's guarantee that the socioeconomic transformations achieved in the revolution would be preserved.

The new Constitution, framed by the Constituent Assembly and promul-

249

gated on April 2, 1976, offered strong rhetorical guarantees of the revolutionary gains: it enshrined the proposition that Portugal is "engaged in the transition to a society without classes," declared the nationalizations "irreversible conquests of the working classes," and called for "the progressive transfer of control [*posse útil*] of the land . . . to those who work it." Further, it guaranteed workers' commissions and base-level popular organizations the right to organize.

The Constitution was touted as the most progressive in the Western world; deputies of the moderate parties in the majority had endorsed revolutionary goals in theory even as their parties attacked the revolution in practice. But most of the Constitution's rhetoric was never fulfilled. In the years following 1976, a series of moderate and conservative governments, most of them dominated by the PS or the PPD (later renamed the Social Democratic Party), held office. Committed to the modernization of the nation's capitalist system, they undid many of the structural changes achieved by the revolutionary governments. Even the PS, when in office, made clear that it had no intention of pursuing socialist policies.

For a decade the chief policy goal was integration into the Europe of the Common Market, finally consummated only in 1986. The principal legal milestone along this path was the constitutional revision of 1982 embodying the measures envisioned in the pact of 1976. The CR was dissolved, leaving the military without a formal governing role for the first time since 1974. The 1982 Constitution reaffirmed that the nationalized firms could not be returned to private ownership. But the 1976 Constitution had declared entire nationalized sectors of the economy off limits to private capital. After 1982 new, competing private firms were permitted in the same sectors, most importantly banking (Baklanoff 1987).

While nationalized financial and industrial firms remained under state control, most of the governments after 1976 adopted policies designed to reinforce private enterprise and weaken the state sector (the 1982 Constitution was only the culmination). In any case, no effective system of economic planning was established, as had been intended, so state-controlled banks were not run to serve the reorganization of the national economy; instead, like the nationalized industrial firms, they were run as capitalist institutions. In effect, capital was dispersed; the firms which had been integrated into monopoly groups were now run independently.

Virtually all the firms in which the state had intervened, and many of those under worker control, were returned to their former owners in 1977 and 1978. A 1977 law delimiting the public and private sectors returned to private control or management many activities which had been brought under virtually complete government control. Many small occupied firms, however, continued to operate under worker control, though in unfavorable economic circumstances and a hostile political climate.

The rural cooperatives suffered severely from government hostility: a 1977 law passed by the PS government with the cooperation of the PPD raised the minimum expropriable size, permitting many former owners to reclaim lands which had been taken over legally under the old law. In the next several years, many cooperatives were dismembered. By 1980, slightly less than half of the land which had been taken over remained in the hands of the workers (Barros 1982: 128). Especially the governments led by the PPD, which made political capital out of hostility to agrarian reform long after occupations had ended, made every effort to dismantle the rural coopera- tives and hinder the progress of those that remained. Even after the revolution was defeated, the symbolic significance of agrarian reform made them a target of attack. But some cooperatives survived and were still controlled directly by their workers. Other apparent advances in agriculture under the revolution, especially the rural rent law, had never been effective- ly enforced. The rent law itself was effectively annulled by a revision sponsored by the PPD in 1977.

The economic policies adopted in 1976 and after served the interests of the modernizing nonmonopoly bourgeoisie, both its technocratic and its small or medium-sized capitalist segments. This is the civilian class with which the moderate officers who took control after November 25 were by origin and current position most closely identified. The destruction of the power of the old oligarchy through the attack on the latifundios, the nationalization of the monopoly groups, and the liberation of the colonies had been undertaken in the interest of the working class. But in practice all those changes increased state control of the economy. The segment of the bourgeoisie which took power in 1976 could use the centralized economic control to its own advantage.

For that reason, the new regime did not reverse all the changes that had been enacted. The fate of the economic transformations of the revolution reveals a fairly consistent relation to class interests. Those that were preserved served the class interests of the nonmonopoly bourgeoisie, and those that were undone challenged those interests.

Technocrats gained from the expansion of the state's role in the capitalist system and from the establishment of a liberal political structure with social- democratic leanings, in which they could expect far more access to political influence and economic advancement than under fascism. The military too was to be reoriented in a way which would provide greater scope for technically trained officers.

Owners of medium-sized capital appear likely to benefit from the revolution's outcome as well, although less certainly. Their competitive position should be improved by the nationalizations, which eliminated monopoly capital's privileged access to credit, marketing mechanisms, and political influence. Without effective national planning mechanisms, the remaining holders of capital must play a leading role. The small and medium-sized capitalists favored will not be the medievalists of Salazar's day, however; integration into the Common Market will require that these capitalists adopt modern and competitive technologies and collaborate (as subordinates) with foreign capital (J.M. Pereira 1978; A.R. Santos 1978).

The efforts to promote the interests of the nonmonopoly bourgeoisie have not been entirely successful: economic conditions have been unfavorable, and the political capacity of the system remains weak, because democracy is not well consolidated and the alternation between governments of the two leading parties has prevented application of any consistent policy. Still, the major beneficiary of the Portuguese revolution is the nonmonopoly bourgeoisie, despite the rhetoric of service to the least favored classes.

The most important gains of the working class were reversed after 1976. The new, democratic political system is clearly a gain: overt and consistent repression was eliminated and workers won the right to unionize and strike. The cooperatives, too, were a gain. But the further gains which appeared within their grasp in 1975—an economy run in their interest and new forms of democracy that would prevent capitalists from recovering their power—proved ephemeral.

This reversal was brought about less by the deliberate abolition of the gains than by the demobilization of those who fought for them. The COPCON and the principal leftwing military units, those that had put their rejection of capitalist legality into practice by their collaboration with the base organizations, were disbanded after November 25; many officers were jailed briefly. They had been the main support of the popular movement; without that support, the sense of power which had animated it was destroyed. Base-level organizations with concrete tasks—a firm to run, a construction project in the works, or occupied land to farm—continued to pursue those tasks, with greater or lesser success but without the enthusiasm derived from participation in a larger revolutionary process.

But most base-level organizations quietly died or fell into inactivity without any further illusions of a revolutionary seizure of power. Some of these organizations continued to exist, but they were never granted the formal power promised to them in the Constitution. Moreover, the informal power which they enjoyed in 1975 depended on a favorable political climate which also disappeared. It was the popular movement's dynamic that had enabled it to win its many victories; once it wound down they could be reversed, and they largely were. The revolution was defeated.

The Two Models of Socialist Transition

Despite a dramatic leap in political consciousness and organization, the working class did not consolidate power in revolutionary Portugal. It did not create a socialist society or even maintain all the gains which it had made in 1974 and 1975. It was not sufficiently organized or united to transform its society.

The failure of the working class to consolidate its gains reveals the limitations of the two models of socialist transition, each of which inspired some of the forces attempting to build socialism in Portugal in 1974 and 1975. The centralist model proposes to take power in the existing state structure and build socialism by central decree. It adopts the point of view of state officeholders with a reformist program who believe that they can use the power of the state to implement the transition. The popular power model calls on the working class to create power for itself in local, self-directed institutions where workers practice, in anticipation, the political and social relations which are to prevail in the future socialist society. Its viewpoint is that of a mass movement which seeks to increase the power of the working class by confronting the state apparatus and challenging it from outside rather than using it from inside.

Each model contains major inadequacies, which were accentuated in the confrontation between the two models in Portugal. The centralist model concentrates on occupying the state apparatus, the popular power model on transforming it, each to the near exclusion of the other. Both are correct: the state apparatus cannot be transformed only from without; it must be occupied first, but then it must also be transformed.

The two models are similarly one-sided in their opposed views of power. According to the zero-sum conception of the centralist model, the working class can achieve power only by taking hold of the state and wresting power from the bourgeoisie. In the popular power conception, the working class accumulates power through self-organization. Again, both processes must operate, and simultaneously. The working class must create power for itself by organizing, but it must also wrest power from the class which holds it.

The contradiction between the reformist officeholders' attempt to concentrate power and the popular movement's struggle to create it autonomously was felt in Portugal both in the economy and in the political process. The economy offers the clearest example. The appropriation of the means of production occurred in two largely independent, and even contradictory, ways: state expropriation and direct worker takeover. As Korsch points out, socialization of the economy presents a dilemma: shall the power to make economic decisions be vested in the social collectivity or in the workers in each firm? The problem is one which will evidently be most keenly felt only after the working class has consolidated state power and the new institutions of a socialist state are being constructed (Korsch 1975: 72–73; cf. Nove 1983: 137). But even at the beginning, a transition to socialism must provide both for central coordination of the economy and for the exercise of power by workers.

In the centralist conception, the state would end exploitation by expropriating the means of production and managing them in the interest of the working class as a whole rather than allowing decentralized control by workers in individual workplaces. Centralism was symbolized by the major role attributed to nationalization of the basic sectors of the economy. Nationalization from the top was carried out with no real provision for transferring power to workers. Nationalized firms continued to operate with capitalist incentives. The labor process was not reorganized and authority relations were largely unchanged. Workers preserved the gains they had won in 1974 regarding wages and fringe benefits, job security, health and safety conditions, and even in some cases a share in making policy decisions, but nationalization did not increase their collective power over their conditions of work.

The worker-controlled firms exemplified the popular power model: their workers exercised genuine collective power. They discovered that they could learn rapidly and manage the firms, better even than they themselves had suspected. They also discovered the rewards of working together for shared goals. But the precarious economic condition of the firms made the struggle for survival paramount. Workers attended to their parochial interests more than to those of the working class as a whole, and took little part in the larger political process.

The two models implied very different approaches to political authority.

The centralists attempted to occupy the existing state apparatus as quickly and as broadly as possible and to use that apparatus to direct the transformation of the economy. The popular power model called for new centers of power in the base organizations and higher level coordinating organizations which would eventually supplant the existing state. The former model, therefore, called for rapid consolidation of power by the new officeholders even against challenges from below, while the latter called for continuing organization independent of the state and struggle against it.

The resulting tension is illustrated by the relationship between local governments and neighborhood commissions in the second wave of housing occupations in the winter of 1975. According to the law ordering compulsory rentals of empty apartments, *freguesia* councils were supposed to assign the apartments to needy tenants. But it was mainly the neighborhood commissions which found the apartments and organized the occupations. Even though the *freguesia* council members had been appointed under a revolutionary government, they were moderates. Respecting traditional legality, they would probably not have acted on their own. Only the neighborhood commissions' willingness to act without the councils' sanction made the occupations a reality.

The relationship between the *freguesia* councils and the neighborhood commissions makes clear that "the working class cannot simply lay hold of the ready-made state machinery, and wield it for its own purposes" (Marx and Engels 1972: 552). Instead, the state machinery must be transformed to serve the interests of the working class. Unseating fascist-appointed councils was an important step toward establishing a new regime, but it was not sufficient. Local governments had few resources, for their powers were still as limited as they had been under the old regime. To be effective, they would have had to create power for themselves by allying with the mobilized population. Some councils cooperated with the neighborhood commissions, certifying occupations and attempting, in a limited way, to prevent occupations of ineligible housing. In general, the only effective councils were the ones which sympathized with the base-level neighborhood commissions and used the pressure generated by their activism to make demands on the national government.

The popular power model proposed a complete transformation of the state apparatus. The proposal for political structure presented in the People/MFA Document, this model's main theoretical statement, was excessively abstract and bureaucratic, even though it was derived from the experiences of popular power in workplaces and neighborhoods during the previous year. The idea of direct democracy, moreover, was not sufficiently well formulated to provide for full participation, and neither the base organizations nor the popular assemblies mobilized anything like a majority of their potential constituencies.

According to the model, the base organizations of popular power would eventually simply supersede the existing state apparatus. But the model never made clear how this would happen. Workers' and neighborhood commissions were assigned diverse roles—as pressure groups, as a revolutionary opposition, and even occasionally as organizations exercising sovereignty—and some organizations attempted to play all those roles.

These functions appear contradictory. Historically, the resolution has been found in situations of dual power, situations of rapid change in which a government is too weak to rule and the base organizations supplant it at least in some places, while continuing to challenge it on a wider scale. In those circumstances, challenging a government and exercising sovereignty intersect.

In Portugal, however, the popular movement never achieved sufficient power to claim sovereignty. While a few base organizations exercised authority locally, the power of the movement as a whole was almost exclusively negative. The model offered the movement no means of winning the authority to govern: in short, no strategy for taking state power.

Models and Strategies

The conflict between the two models of socialist transition was expressed in the relations among three major actors in the revolutionary process: the MFA, the Communist Party, and the popular movement. The MFA began the process with a military coup, necessarily an act of central direction. As its purpose changed from toppling the dictatorship to constructing a socialist society, the leftwing officers who dominated it believed that they had to concentrate power to expropriate the capitalist class. Implicitly, they adopted the centralist model. They assumed that they could continue to direct the process even when the goal shifted.

But central direction would only have been effective if the military had remained united and in control of the state apparatus for a long time. Despite the sense of unity at the beginning, the MFA was politically heterogeneous: many in it did not support the centralist model of revolution while others wanted no revolution at all. So the leftist officers embarked on the socialist program without a strong political commitment from the MFA as a whole.

Equally important, the leftists themselves were divided over the issues of centralism and popular power. This division ultimately brought down the Gonçalvist government and ended the revolution. Since the MFA was not united around a common political project, the class position of the officers became the decisive factor in determining their loyalties: the majority of officers united behind a program which favored the interests of the nonmonopoly bourgeoisie. The Nine, whose social democratic project supported those interests, rapidly found the wide support among the officers that enabled them to take over.

The MFA was encouraged to assume central leadership by the acquiescence of the other two principal actors, the PCP and the popular movement. Both willingly let the MFA take the leading role because they assumed that continued progress would be guaranteed by the revolutionary intentions of the leftist officers. The reversal of November 25 proved them wrong. The military supported the revolution far less reliably than many assumed: soldiers were only superficially politicized and the officer corps was deeply divided.

The PCP relied on the MFA both to carry out structural transformation centrally and to guarantee the political power to make it possible. Along with centralizers in the MFA itself, the PCP conferred on the MFA the authority of a vanguard, the ''motor of the revolution'' and the ''national liberation movement of the Portuguese people.'' To win the confidence of the officers and to forestall potential challenges to central power, it obstructed base-level mobilization.

Ironically, though the popular movement emphasized mobilization at the base in workplaces and neighborhoods, it too placed too much faith in the MFA. Believing that the MFA did hold power, activists failed to acknowledge the need to counter the opposition among capitalists and in the military itself. The movement also allowed itself to depend too much on state support: worker-controlled firms and agricultural cooperatives relied on the Ministry of Labor for credentials or the agrarian reform centers for certification; on the COPCON for defense; and on the nationalized banks for credit. Neighborhood commissions similarly relied on the COPCON for protection and on local governments, which had ambiguous revolutionary commitments, for legal cover. The whole popular movement assumed that the favorable political conjuncture would last and that the revolution would continue from above.

In assigning the MFA the leading role, the PCP was at least consistent in its centralism. But the popular movement's dependence on the officers contradicted its commitment to popular power. Its inconsistency was due to its spontaneity; it had arisen in response to immediate necessity, and its long-range objectives were not always clear or conscious. Workers in individual worker-controlled firms offered no broad conception of a social system in which self-management would become universal and people would exercise collective control over all the institutions that affect them. So their experience was not incorporated into the ideology of the broader popular movement. Nor did neighborhood activists or workers in workplaces which remained under capitalist control bring their initiatives into a single coordinated movement.

The movement as a whole, moreover, was not confident of its own strength. Only the power of the popular movement had turned the coup into a potential revolution, and the movement's initiatives were responsible for the major steps forward. If the movement had recognized its own importance, it would not have confided in the ultimately unreliable military, instead reaching out to more and more of its potential constituency and developing their political skills and commitment. A stronger and more autonomous mass movement would have strengthened the revolution against its enemies.

Many activists recognized that the movement could have grown stronger only by involving the mass of the population in a long and slow process. But in practice, inspired by the initial explosion and steady growth of enthusiasm and by the tangible victories they won, they exaggerated their popular support. For example, they disregarded the results of the April 1975 election which clearly demonstrated that their revolutionary aspirations were not shared by the whole country and which became an ideological instrument legitimizing opposition to the revolution.[1] The desire to take advantage of the suddenly favorable conjuncture made them attempt to accelerate the process rather than building the movement from below.

Greater autonomy would also have strengthened the movement in the face of its defeat, as is clear from the contrast of the fate of the nationalized firms and those in which the state had intervened with that of the worker-controlled firms after 1975. Virtually all in which the state had intervened were returned to their former owners, while nationalized firms, which were now state property, were managed in the interest of the newly dominant segment of the bourgeoisie. Because the worker-controlled firms were independent of the state during the revolutionary period, in contrast, they could not so easily be returned to capitalist control. Many remained independent and controlled by their workers. Neighborhood commissions, too, were more likely to remain active if they had ongoing projects of their own. For the movement as a whole, less dependence on the state during the favorable political period would have left it better able to cope in the face of later adversity.

Finally, if the movement for popular power had been informed by a more explicit ideology, the differences between the projects of popular power and centralism would have been clearer, and the popular power movement would have put its ideas into practice more explicitly and consciously. Such an ideology might have developed if the revolutionary process had lasted longer, but it was cut short.

To say that the movement depended too much on state support does not imply that it could have done without it, or that it should have tried to. In a hostile political climate, base-level organizations face innumerable difficulties (as the worker-controlled firms and the rural cooperatives found after 1975). But the movement should not only have relied on the state for material assistance or assumed that the issue of state power was decided, but rather should have pushed those in office to promote popular power in order to strengthen the revolution.

While the popular movement relied excessively on the state, it did not coordinate its own diverse initiatives effectively. The struggles of individual base commissions for their immediate objectives must come together in a single revolutionary movement. The base organizations offered little real possibility of resolving potential conflicts among themselves or of coordinating the struggle against increasingly aggressive counterrevolutionary opposition. Nor did the popular power model acknowledge the need to coordinate the economy centrally. Movements for transformation must not only practice the new forms of social relationships which they hope to see spread through society; they must also begin to create the mechanisms necessary to coordinate the institutions of a complex socialist society. Even more crucially, they must provide for a coordinated struggle against those who resist transformation—a struggle for state power.

The popular movement also failed to take account of the complexity of power in the existing state. Its activists had an ambivalent attitude toward the MFA and the government, sometimes assuming that they were susceptible to pressure and at other times regarding them as enemies to be superseded. In either case, however, activists failed to recognize that the state apparatus was only partially occupied by forces relatively favorable to the goals of transformation.

The base organizations had arisen spontaneously and each one pursued its own immediate goals. They addressed their demands to the state institutions which had the capacity to respond to their problems and which could be counted on for a favorable response. Choosing the targets most likely to respond has some strategic advantages, for partial victories can increase confidence, expand mobilization, and thereby amass more power for the movement. By revealing the gains to be made by flouting prevailing legal constraints, such victories can stimulate further efforts to transform the state structure.

But concentration on more responsive targets led the movement to ignore the need for a coordinated attack on the power of capital. The ambiguity of the popular movement's conception of the state meant that it had no strategy for taking state power. This lack was revealed most poignantly in the escalating confrontation which preceded the denouement of November 25. When the PS and the PPD abandoned the government in July 1975, the revolution was in danger, and to defend it the popular movement saw no alternative but the de facto alliance with the PCP, even though the PCP offered no promise of acknowledging the initiatives of popular power.

And the only means available to the popular movement was a massive show of force in continuous street demonstrations, but that strategy violated the principles of popular power and subordinated the movement to the centralist model. The success of the popular power movement in defying the government and disrupting public order created the illusion that it had the power to rule. But exposing the government's incapacity to keep order did not advance its goals. Because it had no conception of appropriating power in the long run, the popular movement was unable to do so in the short run during those final months.

The centralist model correctly recognized the need to concentrate forces. Concentrated power had to be counterposed to the power of capital in order to take advantage of the unique opportunity presented by the revolutionary situation in Portugal. The centralist leaders did take advantage of it, and their accomplishments were remarkable: they expropriated the major means of production and broke the power of the oligarchical capitalists.

But the PCP, in applying the centralist model, also made mistakes. Some believe that it is irrelevant to analyze PCP strategy as if it were aimed at socialist revolution; they argue either that it was blindly following Soviet direction or that its behavior can best be explained simply as the pursuit of its own organizational advantage. But Western claims of Soviet influence on the PCP were highly exaggerated: Soviet officials never developed a consistent view of the Portuguese revolution. The Soviet Union made clear, moreover, that it would not rescue a Soviet-aligned Portugal from its economic crisis. Even Soviet financial support to the PCP was modest (Legvold 1977; Mujal-Leon 1977: 22–23; Szulc 1975–76: 9, 41–44).

While it can be argued that the PCP was opportunistic, its base forced it to be opportunistic in the interest of the working class and socialist transformation. The PCP's support for a single trade union federation is a clear example among many where its behavior was self-serving, but where its interests coincided with those of the working class. During 1975, the PCP acted on the assumption that a transition to socialism was possible, and it adopted the strategy and tactics which its history of political activity and its traditions offered as most likely to guarantee its success.

Some have argued that the PCP's error was in adopting a strategy of insurrection (e.g., implicitly, Poulantzas 1978: 86) and that the Portuguese revolution demonstrates the impossibility of revolution by insurrection in advanced capitalist societies. But this conclusion misunderstands the centralist model. Because of the association of centralism with a Leninist command structure, it is assumed that its goal is to "smash" the state apparatus.[2] In fact it is reformist: it aims not to overthrow the existing state apparatus but to seize it and to build socialism from within it. PCP strategy assumed that the MFA held state power and would use its position to embark on a transition to socialism. Even after the Gonçalves government lost power in September 1975, the PCP did not make or seriously attempt an insurrection—if by insurrection is meant a popular assault on the institutions of the state in defiance of its coercive apparatus. It contemplated that its supporters in the military might move to seize power, but it made every effort to stifle the apparent attempt at insurrection on November 25.

Eurocommunist critics of the PCP (Amendola 1977: 40–41; Hobsbawm 1977: 81–82) argue that the MFA and the PCP, by moving too fast in blithe disregard of objective conditions, destroyed a consensus which originally favored the transition. They criticize the PCP's "assault for power" in the trade unions, the media, and the government, regarding it as the equivalent of an insurrection. This behavior, they argue, condemned the revolution to failure because it alienated other political forces—especially the PS—which were equally committed to socialism but suspected the PCP of dictatorial tendencies.

This claim assumes genuine engagement in the struggle for socialism not only within the PS but among those who supported it against the PCP in the summer of 1975. Many who joined or voted for the PS supported the revolution, but the commitments of its leadership were elsewhere. The PS was allied internationally with parties which regarded themselves as socialist, but whose main concern was to combat communism; the PS itself turned *Rádio Renascença* and *República* into symbols of the PCP's alleged totalitarian intentions even though the PCP was not responsible for the workers' takeover of the two media.

The PS, moreover, led a coalition which extended far to its right, which opposed any move toward socialism, and which found a convenient target in the PCP's allegedly antidemocratic behavior. The anticapitalist policies of the government could not be attacked openly because they were highly popular, accepted (however reluctantly) by the Socialists themselves, and (crucially) carried out under the explicit aegis of the MFA, which for a long time remained sacrosanct from attack. If the PS had remained part of a revolutionary coalition, the forces of capitalist restoration would have found (or founded) another political organization to wage their battle. The weakness of the PS as the governing party from 1976 to 1978 demonstrated that much of its support in the summer of 1975 was due to its leading role in an anticommunist coalition (Milkman 1979: 96), and its policies in government—imposing austerity, undercutting agrarian reform, and reversing intervention—after 1976 and its willing subordination to international capital further belied its socialist intentions.

Still, Communist sectarianism undoubtedly alienated many who were genuinely committed both to socialism and to democracy. For some of them the problem was not that the PCP violated pluralism among political parties but that it thwarted mass democracy at the base. These critics argue that popular initiatives needed not to be controlled but encouraged; they regard the major flaw of the centralist model to be its failure to respond to the continuing pressure from the mobilized base organizations and to transform the occupied state apparatus. Hostility to genuinely autonomous organization was a contradiction in the practice of the PCP and of the centralizers in the MFA. Initiatives from the base were essential for every decisive advance of the revolution after the initial coup. Neither the MFA not the PCP would have been shaken out of its initial determination to steer a moderate course if the popular movement had not overpowered them.

But the centralizers saw in popular struggle a threat to their own power rather than an opportunity. Having only partial control of the state apparatus, centralists—particularly the PCP—believed that they had to concentrate power. They tended to regard the mobilization of the base as a mere tactic in the struggle against capital, a tool to help them to seize power, rather than a process which could transform people and the social order. Since they had to maintain social stability and govern society as well as extend their control over the state apparatus, they regarded any challenge as a threat to the revolution, even when it came from the sectors of the population in whose name they claimed to act.

Undercutting base mobilization and concentrating power, moreover, deprived the revolution of needed support. If the centralizers had encouraged the organizations to develop spontaneously and independently, support for the revolution might have expanded to build a strong and united working class and prevent the forces of capitalist recovery from enlisting a large part of the population on their side.

If the revolutionary process had had greater mass support, its contradictions might have been sharpened to turn it into a full-scale revolution and made it more capable of resisting when the military moderates attacked. With a stronger, more self-conscious and autonomous popular movement, a rightwing coup aimed only at leftwing military units would not have been sufficient to end the revolution.

While the contradictions between the two models had some special features in Portugal because of the role of the military, the problem of competing models is nevertheless common to all reformist projects of socialist transition. Miliband, drawing on the defeat of the Chilean revolution, argues that a mobilized base must push to expand the struggle beyond the bounds of the reformists' immediate intentions. It must create organizations of popular participation comparable to an apparatus of dual power, independent of the state and capable of exercising authority on their own, but with the difference that their purpose is to support the state against opposition rather than to confront it (1977a: 435–36; 1977b: 188–90).

This problem has been present, and unsolved, in every revolution in the twentieth century (at least). There can be no single, universal solution—not only because concrete conditions will vary from case to case but because those waging the revolutionary struggle at the base will preserve their autonomy only if they make the discovery anew at each opportunity.

Evaluating Popular Power

The goal of the popular power model, variously called popular power, direct democracy, or worker control, is a society in which all members have an equal share in the decisions by which they are governed, in the economic as well as the political sphere. Discussing the model's strategic adequacy only makes sense if that goal is itself feasible.

Some reject it as a utopian vision which is totally unrealizable, either in a transition process or in a future society. Perhaps surprisingly, those who reject the project are not advocates of the centralist model; centralists often appropriate the language of popular power, claiming to give due credit to popular initiative and to encourage full participation (e.g., Cunhal 1976: 57–64, 331–80). Rather, it is advocates of parliamentary democracy who offer the most significant criticisms: that direct democracy is structurally impracticable, that most people do not have the capacities it requires, and that it leads to totalitarianism. It is impractical, they argue, because decisionmaking in face-to-face meetings is ruled out by the size and complexity of today's societies.

More controversial is the claim that the average person does not have the knowledge and skills—or the interest and inclination—required for responsible participation in a direct democracy. Some advocates of this view go farther and claim that the political apathy prevailing among most citizens is necessary and functional for a democratic system to survive (Berelson et al. 1954: 305–23; Schumpeter 1962: 260–62).

Those who claim that the average citizen lacks political competence often conclude that democracy based on mass citizen participation may encourage demagogy and give rise to totalitarianism. Others predict the same outcome, but not necessarily because citizens are incompetent or easily manipulated. Instead, they argue that the size of a modern society imposes practical constraints on direct democracy, so that if all citizens participate, the only way to achieve coherent leadership is through demagogy. A related argument has it that direct democracy assumes that there is a general will; since, in this view, there is no suitable means for determining the general will, it can only be decided arbitrarily by some subset of people, hence by dictatorship (these arguments are made by Bobbio 1976; Poulantzas 1978; and Schumpeter 1962, among others).

These critics support representative democracy, which they regard as the best available system for determining the consensus of citizens on how they wish to be governed. But their version of representative democracy explicitly restricts the citizen to the passive role of choosing between alternatives posed by elites, with no voice in framing those alternatives. They apparently assume that human nature seeks to maximize material reward and to minimize effort and that political activity, like any other expenditure of energy, is costly rather than potentially satisfying; therefore the average citizen will not take the time or trouble required to participate responsibly, so participation must be restricted.

Defenders of direct democracy reject these criticisms, arguing that political participation is a fundamental and universal right; moreover, like other purposive activity, it is rewarding in itself and people exercise it responsibly when given the opportunity. Pateman (1970), for example, grants that responsible participation requires a certain level of skill and commitment, but argues that democracy must be understood as precisely the process through which they develop. The local community and the workplace provide a proving ground, and when people share genuine influence over decisions about matters of direct importance to them, they will develop the skills and knowledge which will enable them to exercise influence at higher levels, including the national level. In Pateman's view, any theory of democracy that disparages citizens' abilities or justifies limits on their participation implicitly offers grounds for rejecting democracy.

Pateman's rejoinder to the critics of direct democracy is well taken, but even she omits a fundamental issue. Mass participation threatens democratic stability in a way which liberal democratic critics do not always openly acknowledge: by allowing the majority to strive to realize its class interests, it threatens those of the dominant class. It has been argued that representative electoral democracy naturally supports a capitalist system, while a society of economic equality requires the full and direct political participation of all members (Macpherson 1972; Therborn 1977). The greatest danger critics see in mass participation is that it threatens the stability of the political system by "overload[ing it] with participants and demands" (Crozier 1975: 12). In the capitalist system, that is, too much deference to the demands of active participants will interfere with the needs of capital accumulation.

Representative democracy supports capitalism because people participate as individuals; the nature of participation does not encourage them to organize to pursue collective goals. Participating as individuals, they enjoy an illusory equality. The capitalist system claims to separate politics and economics and thereby to render irrelevant any preexisting economic inequalities, which are therefore unlikely to become the basis for common activity. But the effect is precisely opposite to what its supporters maintain: the system magnifies the political importance of existing inequalities by allowing the more privileged to convert their privileges into political resources and discouraging the collective organization which would be necessary for the less privileged to assert their demands. Finally, representative democracy creates obstacles to participation precisely by cultivating passivity (though, to advocates of representative democracy, this is an advantage).

The criticisms of popular power nevertheless deserve to be examined empirically. The Portuguese revolution provides a test of how well popular power worked: we can see to what extent base-level organizations established genuine popular power and created in embryo the forms of social relations of the future society, allowing people to participate on terms of equality. From the Portuguese experience, we can better understand the possibilities and limitations of popular power. It is worth examining not because popular power was achieved there in any complete sense but because it is so rarely attempted.

Representative democracy, too, claims to institutionalize universal and equal participation, but, as I have argued, its separation between the political and the economic actually magnifies in the political sphere differences which arise in the economic sphere. Does popular power do any better?

In the Portuguese revolution, people achieved through worker control and neighborhood organization a sense of real participation and an opportunity for political expression that representative democracy does not normally provide. They learned and grew; they showed in their collective actions that they could cooperate, define common goals, and act responsibly. Both by the numbers of participants and by the abilities they demonstrated, the Portuguese revolution shows that a greater measure of popular power than now prevails in representative democracies not only is possible but can produce greater equality of participation and of result. If under ordinary circumstances most people's capacity for participation appears limited, ordinary circumstances do not provide a proper test.

Participation was widespread—explosive, even. It overcame the obstacles imposed by the poverty and limited education of the majority and brought in many people who had never before acted politically. Nevertheless it fell far short of being universal. In the circumstances of 1975, joining a demonstration can be considered the minimal level of participation, but most people did not demonstrate. Surely even fewer attended or spoke up at meetings.

Equality of participation is limited by individual differences: some people are more interested in political activity and have more time for it than others. Different levels of persuasive skills will also give people unequal influence. Social movements in the U.S. that aspire to participatory politics have frequently encountered a major problem: they reject formal structures because such structures seem to institutionalize inequalities among people, but the lack of structure can generate inequalities of its own, as some individuals are attractive, speak well, or have other qualities which allow them to take leading roles (cf. Freeman 1973; Mansbridge 1973). In the Portuguese popular power movement too, particular talents allowed some people to dominate organizations. These differences did not necessarily reflect external economic inequalities, but they nevertheless meant that some participants' interests were less well represented than others'—and those of nonparticipants, whose interests were also at stake, even less so.

Only a lengthy process of mobilization would have built a fully participatory political culture and constituency—and one of the contradictions of popular power is that the revolutionary situations which stimulate such mobilization are by their nature ephemeral. Mobilization of the intensity felt in Portugal in 1975 obviously could not last forever.

Other factors made base-level organizations less than fully representative. Informal structures can be manipulated not only by talented individuals but also by tightly organized groups with hidden agendas. In the Portuguese commissions, party militants were especially likely to try to control and divert activities; the problem often became acute and was never resolved.

The fact that popular mobilization is locally based creates another problem for the popular power: it may generate parochial and competing claims rather than recognition of common interests. This may become a tactical problem; but more importantly, it may contravene the model's claims of universality. The Portuguese experience presents some favorable evidence, for by encouraging a more sweeping definition of problems, mobilization led to demands for solutions which applied to the society as a whole. On the other hand, particularly in firms in economic difficulties, people often sought the most immediate remedy for a problem rather than uniting with others to work for political responses.

Advocates claim that direct democracy, unlike representative democracy, ensures substantive equality. But the demand for participation is largely procedural. Whether greater participation actually increases material equality will depend on the historical situation from which the demand emerges. The Portuguese movement, like other movements for popular power, was encouraging in that the movement for political change grew out of the working class's material demands; workers at first mobilized to meet their immediate needs and then discovered that only political changes would enable them to assert the claims of their class.

The popular power model presents direct democracy as the appropriate form of organization both for the new socialist society and for the political struggles which will bring it into existence. The model itself claims that democratic organizations must be forged during the struggle: if democracy is to be present at the end it must be present throughout. But the structures of participation which were created during the Portuguese revolution were clearly not sufficient to serve as governing institutions of a future society, and it is not likely that institutions forged in any revolutionary struggle, even one which lasts longer than the Portuguese process, will be adequate for postrevolutionary government; the creation of satisfactory institutions will require a long period of experimentation and conflict.

Whether popular power is feasible as a system of national government remains open. The chief objection is that a nation is simply too big; some decisions have to be made centrally because they require either society-wide coordination or technical expertise. Because national-level popular power was never tried in Portugal, it offers no test of its feasibility. But the model itself posits that there can be no blueprint for the structures of the society it aims to create; they must emerge from the process.

The Portuguese experience at a minimum argues for strengthening participation at the local level—in the community and the workplace, for example. Local institutions of direct democracy enable participants to develop their political skills; at the same time their existence should make national representative structures more responsive to their constituents. If the experience of popular power does not prove that it is viable for a nation, it does demonstrate its creativity and promise.

Centralists, like those who promoted popular power, claimed to support widespread participation; they denied that they intended to proceed from the top down. But in practice the centralists discouraged autonomous mobilization and called for passive and unquestioning support. They erred in failing to recognize the empowering effect of base initiatives on the people who undertook them, believing as they did that all inequalities are due to capitalist ownership of the means of production. In a socialist society, the transformation of property relations must be matched in the consciousness and organization of the working class, a long and difficult process, and one which requires active participation of those in whose name it would be brought about.

Even in defeat the Portuguese revolution was an important test of the possibility of popular power and full democracy. Its lessons are not entirely favorable: the revolution revealed serious limits to both the democratic conduct of the popular movement and its chances of achieving power. Nevertheless, the struggle for popular power remains significant for showing that ordinary people—women and men, soldiers and civilians, in the city and in the countryside—could unite and seize the opportunity to struggle for a different kind of life. They failed, but they accomplished more than even they imagined they could.

Notes

1. Introduction

1. Portugal retained Macao for several years in deference to China, and Indonesia seized East Timor with Portugal's acquiescence.
2. For accounts of the importance of worker control in these revolutions, see for the Paris Commune, Marx and Engels 1972; Edwards 1971; for Russia, Anweiler 1974; Brinton 1975; Sirianni 1982; for Germany, Morgan 1975; for Italy, Spriano 1975; for Spain, Brenan 1943; Dolgoff 1974; and for Chile, Espinosa and Zimbalist 1978; Winn 1986; Zimbalist and Petras 1976.

2. The Fascist Regime

1. For accounts of the PIDE, see Backmann 1974; Figueiredo 1975: 128–30; *Manchete* 1974; *Repórter Sombra* 1974; and Soares 1975: 45.
2. Sources on PCP history before 1974 are fragmentary, and the party has not encouraged historians to examine it. Its own most complete account is contained in a book commemorating its sixtieth anniversary (PCP 1982) which rehabilitates some victims of past factional battles, but offers little objectivity on the party's history as a whole. Some official documents have been reprinted: Cunhal 1979 (first published 1964); Cunhal 1974 (first published 1971); PCP 1975. See also *Expresso,* May 4, 1974; *Expresso,* February 2, 1980; Guerreiro 1974; Ventura 1983.
3. There are two interesting pictures of clandestine life in the Communist Party. A novel said to be a pseudonymous work of Secretary General Alvaro Cunhal presents a romantic picture (Tiago 1975), and an autobiography by a disaffected member presents a critical view (J.A.S. Marques 1976).

3. Colonial War and the Armed Forces Movement

1. The map is reproduced on the cover of *Portugal: Fifty Years of Dictatorship* (Figueiredo 1975).
2. For full accounts of the rise of the liberation movements and the colonial war, see Marcum 1969; 1972; 1978; and Minter 1972.
3. Lourenço 1975: 49–63; Saraiva and Silva 1976: 23–30; Wheeler 1979: 194–96. After the revolution the same tradition held: not until 1986 was there a civilian president. General Antonio Ramalho Eanes held the office from 1976 to 1986, and his two major opponents for the presidency were also generals: Otelo Saraiva de Carvalho of the left in 1976 and Soares Carneiró of the right in 1980 (Carvalho only briefly, as an *ex officio* general).
4. Martins 1968: 307, 328. Wheeler argues that the independence of the military from the fascist regime has been exaggerated, and that the regime dominated the armed forces while exploiting their propaganda value (1975: 198–99). But his own evidence of the frequency of coup attempts and the relatively mild punishment of the plotters makes clear that the military was the one institution where there was a possibility, however limited, of resistance to the regime.
5. The estimate is that of Dr. José Francisco Graça Costa, director of the National Statistical Institute (personal communication).
6. Portugal's social welfare services were even less generous than those of other West European countries at similar economic levels, such as Greece and Ireland. Government propaganda pointed with pride to the regime's accomplishments in public housing, but even there (despite a few large and highly visible projects) it did less than the other two countries (Schmitter 1975a: 49–57).
7. Marcum 1978: 179. Schmitter's estimate (1975c: 17) is slightly lower.
8. Successive versions of the program appear in A. Rodrigues et al. 1976: 299–304.
9. The composition of the "middle class" (or "middle classes") which benefit from military rule is not spelled out, however (Huntington 1968: 221–22; cf. Nun 1968).

4. The Revolution of the Carnations

1. Zolberg's discussion of "moments of madness" in French history (1972) and Reed's account of the Bolshevik revolution (1960) describe similar contagious feelings of euphoria at moments of dramatic political change. In both cases, emerging from one's habitual quiet to talk to strangers was a symbol of newfound freedom and power.
2. It must be noted, however, that the word *controlo* is ambiguous in this context. It can refer to participation in management or to the right to monitor management

performance. According to M.L. Santos et al. (1976: 49–50), both kinds of demands were expressed; they do not make clear in what proportions.

3. *Freguesia:* parish, the smallest political unit, roughly equivalent to a ward in cities or a township in rural areas. Except historically, the term has no ecclesiastical significance. *Concelho:* council, a larger political unit, roughly equivalent to a county. The largest cities are coterminous with their *concelhos.* I refer to their governments, which are called "municipal chambers," as city councils.

5. Laying the Groundwork

1. With the emergence of Eurocommunism in the 1970s, the relevance of the dictatorship of the proletariat to the late twentieth century was hotly debated among Communists in West Europe; eventually, rejection of the concept became a hallmark of Eurocommunism. Although the PCP was the least Eurocommunist (that is, both the most pro-Soviet and the most closed in its internal policies) among the major parties, however, it was the first to abandon the phrase officially.

6. Housing and Neighborhood Commissions

1. The discussion of neighborhood commissions in this chapter and in Chapter 9 is drawn from the following sources, in addition to my own interviews: for Lisbon, Branco 1979; Rocha et al. 1979; Russette and Ferreira 1979; and Russinho and Costa 1976; for Oporto, A.A. Costa et al. 1979; for Setubal, Callado 1979; Downs 1980; 1983; and Downs et al. 1978; and in general d'Arthuys and Gors 1976; *Livro Branco do SAAL* 1976; and Oliveira and Marconi 1978.

2. City governments were called administrative commissions to highlight their provisional status, because no official city governments were established after April 25.

7. Seizing the Commanding Heights

1. The MDP had been part only of the first provisional government, from May to July 1974.

2. In addition, the nationalized press was both a political and an economic liability: politically, it provided the basis for accusations of government control of the

press and made the later dispute over the newspaper *República* far more significant; economically, it meant that the state had to meet the deficits of the many unprofitable papers.

3. On nationalization, see Keefe (1977: 320–31); Murteira (1979: 335–37); Pinho (1976: 742–47); and Rosa (1976: 68–89).

4. Detailed analyses of the election returns are presented by Gaspar and Vitorino (1976) and Hammond (1979).

8. Worker Control in City and Countryside

1. This cooperative was atypical. Most construction cooperatives did not grow out of old capitalist firms, but were founded by construction workers who had been laid off because of lack of work.

2. I use the term "worker-controlled firm" to include two legally recognized forms: firms operating under a Ministry of Labor credential, called "self-managed firms" (*empresas em autogestão*), and firms with a legal charter, called "cooperatives," many of which had been self-managed. I refer to the workers as "members," although the latter term technically applied only to cooperatives.

3. J. Barreto (1977: 705) reports that many worker-controlled firms immediately reduced the salary range, alienating those who had received the highest salaries.

4. J. Barreto (1977: 702) reports another case in which the recalcitrant owner of a small factory, who refused to meet with the workers' commission at the Ministry of Labor, was "escorted" there by COPCON troops.

5. These firms do not constitute a sample in any sense of the term. All are in the Lisbon area (which does have the greatest concentration of cooperatives) and my introductions came (directly or indirectly) from political contacts associated with either the Communist or the Socialist Party. All survived to 1980, while other worker-controlled firms went out of business or were taken back by their capitalist owners. Given the source of my introductions, these six can be presumed to be among the more successful worker-controlled firms. All but one were legally chartered cooperatives by 1980; the one exception was still operating under a credential granted in 1975.

6. For discussions of various issues relating to the structure and effects of worker control, see Bernstein 1976; Blumberg 1973; Braverman 1974; Hunnius et al., 1973; Jenkins 1974; Pateman 1970; Rothschild-Whitt 1979; Vanek 1971; Zwerdling 1980.

7. Only 152,000 hectares were occupied by the end of July, but a million hectares more had been occupied by the end of the year (Baptista 1978: 26; Barros 1979: 68–70).

8. The decree also established the right of owners to compensation and to retain a

"reserve" of land; but it did not define these rights. The expropriation law (406A/75) and the nationalization law (407A/75) of July 29 were accompanied by a decree allowing occupied farms to receive emergency agricultural credit, previously available only to small farmers, to purchase supplies (but not to pay their workers' salaries—that would come later).

9. Bandarra and Jazra 1976: 110–18: Baptista 1978: 76–77: A. Barreto 1984b; Barros 1979: 125–37. According to Barros there was a tendency to form cooperatives on more fertile lands, which had had a larger number of permanent workers before the occupation, and to form collectives in regions of lower fertility, where farms were larger in the first place and most occupiers were day laborers.

10. Baptista 1979: 6–8; Cardoso 1976: 58; B.H. Fernandes 1978: 76–84. Bermeo claims that cooperatives were more productive than privately owned farms (1986: 127–28). What she shows, however, is that the presence of cooperatives was associated with an increase in *total* production—to be expected, since they brought more land under cultivation and put more people to work on it. She offers no evidence about productivity per unit input (of land or labor).

11. This shows, incidentally, that it was not only the PCP and its sympathizers who adopted the centralist model, for Belo Moreira makes clear that as director he had his differences with the PCP (Moreira and Simões 1982: 141).

12. Some would argue that the PCP succeeded in imposing its centralist model by creating collectives in 1976 and later. The collectives, however, were hardly state farms; Barros argues, moreover, that the creation of collectives was due at least as much to the physical conditions and economic possibilities of the farms as to political leadership.

9. Direct Democracy and the Neighborhoods

1. According to Downs (1980: 445–47), no shantytown commissions in Setubal occupied any buildings, because there were no buildings in the shantytowns to occupy. In other places, however (e.g., Linda-a-Velha, Oeiras; Miragaia, Oporto), shantytown commissions did occupy nearby buildings for commission headquarters.

2. The exact number is unknown, but in January 1976, an employee of the *Caixa Geral de Depósitos* reported that approximately 1200 tenants were paying their lowered rent into the escrow account.

3. Neves 1975: 49. The multiple objectives of the popular assemblies are outlined in, e.g., *Regimento [regulamento?] da assembleia popular do [sic] zona do regimento de Eng. No. 1* (Pontinha), mimeo, July 13, 1975; *Projecto de Estatutos para a Assembleia Popular dos Olivais,* photocopy, undated but

evidently July, 1975; Secretariado da Comissão Política Nacional (MES), *CDR's/CRT—Falsa opção*, June 19, 1975.

10. The Hot Summer

1. Accounts of this external pressure can be found in, among others, Eisfield 1984; Hammond and Szulc 1978; Maxwell 1976: 267; *New York Times,* August 29 and September 27, 1975; Szulc 1975–76.

11. Counterattack

1. Faye 1976: 196–99. This version, based on ambiguous claims by several of the officers (*Expresso,* April 3, 1976), is also accepted by Rodrigues et al. in their first account (1976: 275–76). In a later book, however, they treat it more skeptically (1979: 149–50).
2. In an earlier article I stated that "no insurrection was made, attempted, or contemplated" (Hammond 1980: 157). Not wishing to rewrite history without acknowledging it, I will state here that I now believe that that statement is too strong. It is highly likely that the PCP participated in plans for a preventive coup or a countercoup by its supporters in the armed forces. But November 25 was not that coup and after November 25 it was clear that any such attempt would be suicidal.

12. Conclusion

1. The high point of measurable support for the popular movement was the presidential election of 1976, in which Otelo won 16 percent of the vote, a result which can best be interpreted as an endorsement of popular power. This vote is larger than the vote for a far-left candidate in a national election anywhere else; still it makes clear that the support for popular power was far too narrow to serve as the basis for a national project in the short run.
2. Sirianni makes the same error about the popular power movement, attributing insurrectionary intentions to it. His brief discussion of Portugal in his criticism of dual power strategies errs by assuming that workers' commissions sought to "centraliz[e] power against the state" (1983: 95). While some of the far-left parties which supported popular power spoke in terms of insurrection, the movement as a whole did not envision or plan for an armed seizure of power.

Bibliography

Abrahamsson, Bengt. 1971. *Military Professionalism and Political Power*. Stockholm: Göteborgs Offsetstrycken.

Almeida, Diniz de. 1977. *Origens e Evolução do Movimento de Capitães*. Lisbon: Edições Sociais.

—————n.d. *Ascensão, Apogeu e Queda do M.F.A.*, II. Lisbon: edição do autor.

Amendola, Giorgio. 1977. "The Italian Road to Socialism." *New Left Review* 106 (November–December): 39–50.

Antunes, Albertino et al. 1975. *A opção do voto*. Lisbon: Intervoz Publicidade, Lda.

Antunes, José Freire. 1980. *O segredo do 25 de Novembro: O verão quente e os planos desconhecidos do grupo militar*. Lisbon: Publicações Europa-América.

Anweiler, Oskar. 1974. *The Soviets: The Russian Workers, Peasants, and Soldiers Councils 1905–21*. New York: Pantheon Books.

As Paredes em Liberdade. 1974. *As Paredes em Liberdade*. Lisbon: Editorial Teorema.

As Paredes na Revolução. 1978. *As Paredes na Revolução*. Lisbon: Mil Dias.

Ash, Roberta. 1972. *Social Movements in America*. Chicago: Markham Publishing Company.

Backmann, René. 1974. "Los Archivos de la P.I.D.E.," *Triunfo,* September 28, 26–29.

Baklanoff, Erik N. 1976. "Spain." In Eric N. Baklanoff, ed., *Mediterranean Europe and the Common Market: Studies of Economic Growth and Integration*. University: University of Alabama Press, pp. 177–208.

—————1978. *The Economic Transformation of Spain and Portugal*. New York: Praeger Publishers.

—————1987. "The State and Economy in Portugal: Perspectives on Corporatism, Revolution, and Incipient Privatization." In William P. Glade, ed., *State Shrinking: A Comparative Inquiry into Privatization*. Austin: University of Texas, Institute of Latin American Studies, pp. 257–81.

Bandarra, Alvaro and Nelly Jazra. 1976. *A estrutura agrária portuguesa transformada?* Lisbon: Iniciativas Editoriais.

275

Bandeira, Antonio Rangel. 1976. "The Portuguese Armed Forces Movement: Historical Antecedents, Professional Demands, and Class Conflict." *Politics and Society* 6: 1–56.

Baptista, Fernando Oliveira. 1978. *Portugal 1975—os campos*. Porto: Afrontamento.

————1979. "Sobre a economia das cooperativas e unidades colectivas de produção." *Economia e Socialismo* 41–42 (August–September): 3–19.

Barata, Oscar Soares. 1972. *O factor humano no espaço português*. Lisbon: Revista Militar.

————1973. *Evolução demográfica e desenvolvimento no espaço português*. Lisbon: Revista Militar.

Barreno, Maria Isabel, Maria Teresa Horta, and Maria Velho da Costa. 1975. *The Three Marias: New Portuguese Letters*. Translated from the Portuguese by Helen R. Lane. Garden City: Doubleday & Company.

Barreto, António. 1984a. "Classe e Estado: os sindicatos na reforma agrária." *Análise Social* 20: 41–96.

————1984b. "Estado e Movimento Social na Reforma Agrária 1974–76." Paper presented to the International Conference on Modern Portugal, Durham, New Hampshire.

Barreto, José. 1977. "Empresas industriais geridas pelos trabalhadores." *Análise Social* 13 (July): 681–717.

Barros, Afonso. 1979. *A reforma agrária em Portugal: das ocupações de terras à formação das novas unidades de produção*. Oeiras: Instituto Gulbenkian de Ciência.

————1982. "Le problème du Sud au Portugal et la réforme agraire." *Révue Tiers-Monde* 23 (January–March): 115–32.

Berelson, Bernard R. et al. 1954. *Voting: A Study of Opinion Formation in a Presidential Campaign*. Chicago: University of Chicago Press.

Bermeo, Nancy Gina. 1979. "Socialist Policy Toward Worker Management in Portuguese Industry." Paper presented to the International Conference Group on Modern Portugal, Durham, New Hampshire.

————1986. *The Revolution Within the Revolution: Workers' Control in Rural Portugal*. Princeton: Princeton University Press.

Bernstein, Paul. 1976. *Workplace Democratization: Its Internal Dynamics*. Kent: Kent State University Press.

Bica, António. 1976. "Considerações sobre a reforma agrária." *Economia EC: Questões económicas e sociais* 1 (February–March): 3–27.

Blackburn, Robin. 1974. "The Test in Portugal." *New Left Review* 87–88 (September–December): 5–46.

Blumberg, Paul. 1973. *Industrial Democracy: The Sociology of Participation*. New York: Schocken Books.

Bobbio, Norberto. 1976. "Quali alternative alla democrazia rappresentativa?" In *Quale socialismo?* Turin: Einaudi, pp. 42–65.

Boggs, Carl. 1977. "Marxism, Prefigurative Communism, and the Problem of Workers' Control." *Radical America* 11 (November): 99–122.

Bornstein, Stephen and Keitha S. Fine. 1977. "Worker Control in France: Recent Political Developments." In G. David Garson, ed., *Worker Self-Management in Industry: The West European Experience*. New York: Praeger Publishers, pp. 152–91.

Branco, José Francisco do N. 1979. "Elementos para a história do movimento dos bairros de lata e bairros pobres do concelho de Lisboa (25 Abril 74—Março 77)." *Intervenção Social* 2 (September): 132–43.

Braverman, Harry. 1974. *Labor and Monopoly Capital: The Degradation of Work in the Twentieth Century*. New York: Monthly Review Press.

Brenan, Gerald. 1943. *The Spanish Labyrinth: An Account of the Social and Political Background of the Spanish Civil War*. Cambridge: Cambridge University Press.

Brettell, Caroline. 1979. "Emigration and Its Implications for the Revolution in Northern Portugal." In Lawrence S. Graham and Harry M. Makler, eds., *Contemporary Portugal: The Revolution and Its Antecedents*. Austin: University of Texas Press, pp. 281–98.

————1986. *Men Who Migrate, Women Who Wait: Population and History in a Portuguese Parish*. Princeton: Princeton University Press.

Brinton, Maurice. 1975. *The Bolsheviks and Workers' Control*. Detroit: Black and Red.

Bruneau, Thomas C. 1977. "Church and State in Portugal: Crises of Cross and Sword." *Journal of Church and State* 18 (Autumn): 463–90.

Cabral, Manuel Villaverde. 1978. "Portuguese Fascism in Comparative Perspective." Paper presented to the Institute of Latin American Studies, Columbia University.

————1987. "Portugal Since the Revolution." *Luso-Brazilian Review* 24 (Summer): 79–86.

Cabral, Manuel Villaverde, ed. 1974. *Materiais para a história da questão agrária em Portugal—Sec. XIX e XX*. Porto: Inova.

Caetano, Marcello. 1974. *Depoimento*. Rio de Janeiro: Distribuidora Record.

Calado, Luis F. 1978. "Empresas geridas por trabalhadores: Que Futuro?" *Economia e Socialismo* 32–33 (November–December): 3–20.

Callado, J. 1979. "SAAL Setúbal." *Cidade/Campo* 2: 61–101.

Calvão, Alpoim. 1976. *De Conakry ao M.D.L.P.: Dossier Secreto*. Lisbon: Editorial Intervenção.

[CAP] Confederação dos Agricultores de Portugal. 1977. *CAP: Recortes de uma luta*. Viseu: Edições CAP.

Cardoso, António Lopes. 1976. *Luta pela Reforma Agrária*. Lisbon: Diabril.

Carvalho, Otelo Saraiva de. 1977. *Alvorada em Abril*. Lisbon: Livraria Bertrand.

Castells, Manuel. 1979. *The Urban Question: A Marxist Approach*. Cambridge: MIT Press.

Cerqueira, Silas. 1973. "L'Eglise catholique et la dictature corporatiste portugaise." *Révue Française de Science Politique* 23 (June): 473–513.

Coit, Catherine. 1978. "Local Action, Not Citizen Participation." in William K. Tabb and Larry Sawers, eds,. *Marxism and the Metropolis: New Perspectives in Urban Political Economy.* New York: Oxford University Press, pp. 297–311.

Comissão do Livro Negro sobre o Fascismo. 1979. *Eleições no regime fascista.* Lisbon: Comissão do Livro Negro sobre o Fascismo.

Comissões de Delegados Sindicais do Banco Espírito Santo e Comercial de Lisboa. 1975. *Sabotagem Económica: "Dossier" Banco Espírito Santo.* Lisbon: Diabril Editora.

Correia, Pezarat. 1982. "Le Rôle de l'armée pendant la période initiale de la réforme agraire." *Révue Tiers-Monde* 23 (January–March 1982): 27–38.

Correia, Ramiro, Pedro Soldado, and João Marujo. n.d. (a). *MFA e Luta de Classes: Subsídios para a compreensão do processo histórico português.* Lisbon: Biblioteca Ulmeiro.

————n.d.(b). *MFA: Dinamização cultural, acção cívica.* Lisbon: Biblioteca Ulmeiro.

Costa, Alexandre Alves et al. 1979. "SAAL/Norte: Balanço de uma Experiência." *Cidade/Campo* 2:16–60.

Costa, Ramiro da. 1979. *Elementos para a história do movimento operário em Portugal 1820–1975,* II: *1930–1975.* Lisbon: Assírio e Alvim.

Crozier, Michel. 1975. "Western Europe." In Michel J. Crozier, Samuel P. Huntington, and Joji Watanuki, eds., *The Crisis of Democracy.* New York: New York University Press, pp. 11–58.

Cunhal, Alvaro. 1974. *Radicalismo pequeno burguês de fachada socialista.* (Orig. pub. 1971.) Lisbon: Edições Avante.

————1976. *A revolução portuguesa: o passado e o futuro.* Lisbon: Edições Avante.

————1979. *Rumo à vitória: As tarefas do Partido na Revolução Democrática e Nacional.* (Orig. pub. 1964.) Lisbon: Edições Avante.

Cutileiro, José. 1971. *A Portuguese Rural Society.* Oxford: Oxford University Press.

d'Arthuys, Beatrice and Marielle Christine Gors. 1976. "Les Commissions de 'moradores': organization ou pouvoir populaire." *Autogestion et Socialisme* 33–34 (January–March): 35–53.

Dolgoff, Sam, ed. 1974. *The Anarchist Collectives: Workers' Self-Management in the Spanish Revolution 1936–1939.* New York: Free Life Editions.

Domingos, Helena et al. 1977. *A revolução num regimento: A Polícia Militar em 1975.* Lisbon: Armazém das Letras.

Downing, John. 1984. *Radical Media: The Political Experience of Alternative Communication.* Boston: South End Press.

Downs, Charles R. 1980. "Community Organization, Political Change, and Urban Policy: Portugal 1974–1976." Ph.D. diss., University of California, Berkeley.

————1983. "Residents' Commissions and Urban Struggles in Revolutionary

Portugal.'' In Lawrence S. Graham and Douglas L. Wheeler, eds., *In Search of Modern Portugal: The Revolution and Its Consequences*. Madison: University of Wisconson Press, pp. 151–80.

Downs, Chip et al. 1978. *Os Moradores à Conquista da Cidade: Commissões de Moradores e Lutas Urbanas em Setúbal, 1974–1976*. Lisbon: Armazém das Letras.

Economia e Socialismo.1977. ''Portugal ano III: Tres anos depois, a economia.'' *Economia e Socialismo* 12–13 (March–April): 3–35.

Edwards, Stewart. 1971. *The Paris Commune 1871*. New York: Quadrangle Books.

Eisfeld, Rainer. 1984. ''Outside Influence in the Portuguese Revolution: The Western European Role.'' Paper presented at the Third International Meeting on Modern Portugal, Durham, New Hampshire.

Espinosa, Juan G. and Andrew S. Zimbalist. 1978. *Economic Democracy: Workers' Participation in Chilean Industry, 1970–1973*. New York: Academic Press.

Estrela, A. de Vale. 1978. ''A reforma agrária portuguesa e os movimentos camponeses: Uma revisão crítica.'' *Análise Social* 54 (April–June): 219–63.

Faye, Jean-Pierre, ed. 1976. *Portugal: The Revolution in the Labyrinth*. Nottingham: Spokesman Books.

Fernandes, Blasco Hugo. 1975. *Problemas agrários portugueses: estruturas, tecnologias, política agrícola, reforma estrutural*. Lisbon: Prelo.

————1978. *Reforma Agrária: Contributo para a sua história*. Lisbon: Seara Nova.

Fernandes, Jorge Almeida. 1980. ''Duas ou tres coisas que eu sei do 'República.' '' *Gazeta do Mes* 1 (May): 14–15.

Ferreira, Hugo Gil and Michael W. Marshall. 1986. *Portugal's Revolution: Ten Years On*. Cambridge: Cambridge University Press.

Ferreira, Serafim, ed. 1975. *MFA: Motor da revolução portuguesa*. Lisbon: Diabril.

Ferreira, Serafim and Arsénio Mota, eds. 1969. *Para um dossier da oposição democrática*. Lisbon: Nova Realidade.

Figueiredo, Antonio de. 1975. *Portugal: Fifty Years of Dictatorship*. Harmondsworth: Penguin Books.

Freeman, Jo. 1973. ''The Tyranny of Structurelessness.'' *Ms.* 2, no. 1 (July): 76–78.

Freitas, Eduardo de, J. Ferreira de Almeida, and M. Villaverde Cabral. 1976. *Modalidades de penetração do capitalismo na agricultura: Estruturas agrárias em Portugal continental 1950–70*. Lisbon: Presença.

Gaspar, Jorge and Nuno Vitorino. 1976. *As eleições de 25 de Abril: Geografia e imagem dos partidos*. Lisbon: Livros Horizonte.

Gombin, Richard. 1975. *The Origins of Modern Leftism*. Harmondsworth: Penguin Books.

Gomes, Francisco Costa. 1979. *Sobre Portugal: Diálogos com Alexandre Manuel*. Lisbon: A Regra do Jogo.

Gonçalves, Vasco. 1976. *Discursos, Conferências de Imprensa, Entrevistas*. Edited by Augusto Paulo da Gama. Porto: No publisher indicated.

Gorz, André. 1973. *Socialism and Revolution*. Garden City: Anchor Books.

Graham, Lawrence S. 1975. *Portugal: The Decline and Collapse of an Authoritarian Order*. Beverly Hills: Sage Publications.

Gramsci, Antonio. 1977. *Selections from Political Writings, 1910–1920*. New York: International Publishers.

Guerreiro, Fernando. 1974. "A história do PCP a través de seis congressos." *Seara Nova 1550* (December): 17–24.

Hammond, John L. 1979. "Electoral Behavior and Political Militancy." In Lawrence S. Graham and Harry M. Makler, eds., *Contemporary Portugal: The Revolution and its Antecedents*. Austin: University of Texas Press, pp. 257–80.

————1980. "Portugal's Communists and the Revolution." *Radical History Review* 23 (Spring): 140–61.

————1981. "Worker Control in Portugal: The Revolution and Today." *Economic and Industrial Democracy* 2 (November): 413–53.

Hammond, John L., and Nicole Szulc. 1978. "The CIA in Portugal." In Howard Frazier, ed., *Uncloaking The CIA*. New York: Free Press, pp. 135–47.

Hastings, Adrian. 1974. *Wiriyamu*. London: Search Press.

Hobsbawm, Eric, ed. 1977. *The Italian Road to Socialism: An Interview by Eric Hobsbawm with Giorgio Napolitano*. Westport: Lawrence Hill.

Hunnius, Gerry, G. David Garson, and John Case, eds. 1973. *Workers' Control: A Reader on Labor and Social Change*. New York: Vintage Books.

Huntington, Samuel P. 1968. "Praetorianism and Political Decay." In *Political Order in Changing Societies*. New Haven: Yale University Press, pp. 192–263.

Insight Team of the *Sunday Times*. 1975. *Insight on Portugal: The Year of the Captains*. London: Andre Deutsch.

Jackman, Robert W. 1976. "Politicians in Uniform: Military Governments and Social Change in the Third World." *American Political Science Review* 70 (December): 1098–1109.

Janowitz, Morris. 1964. *The Professional Soldier: A Social and Political Portrait*. Glencoe: Free Press.

Jenkins, David. 1974. *Job Power: Blue and White Collar Democracy*. Baltimore: Penguin Books.

Kaplan, Irving, et al. 1977. *Area Handbook for Mozambique*. 2nd ed. Washington: Government Printing Office.

Keck, Margaret E. 1984. "Armed Forces and Society." In Kenneth Maxwell, ed., *Portugal: Ten Years After the Revolution. Reports of Three Columbia-Gulbenkian Workshops*. New York: Columbia University, Research Institute on International Change. (no page numbers)

Keefe, Eugene K., et al. 1977. *Area Handbook for Portugal*. Washington: Government Printing Office.

Kolm, Serge-Christophe. 1977. *La transition socialiste: la politique économique de gauche*. Paris: Editions du Cerf.

Korsch, Karl. 1975. "What is Socialization? A Program of Practical Socialism." *New German Critique* 6: 60–81.

Kurth, James R. 1979. "Industrial Change and Political Change: A European Perspective." in David Collier, ed., *The New Authoritarianism in Latin America.* Princeton: Princeton University Press, pp. 319–63.

Legvold, Robert. 1977. "Portugal, Detente, and the Problem of Fundamental Change in Western Europe." Unpub. ms.

Lemos, Noelle de Roo. 1978. "La petite paysannerie au Portugal: à propos de 'l'orthodoxie' marxiste." *Anthropologie et sociétés* 2: 5–21.

Lenin, V.I. 1975. "The Dual Power." In Robert C. Tucker, ed., *The Lenin Anthology.* New York: W.W. Norton, pp. 301–4.

Lima, Marinús Pires et al. 1977. "A acção operária na Lisnave: análise da evolução dos temas reivindicativos." *Análise Social* 13: 829–99.

Linz, Juan J. 1964. "An Authoritarian Regime: Spain." In Erik Allardt and Yrjö Littunen, eds., *Cleavages, Ideologies, and Party Systems.* Helsinki, pp. 291–341.

————1975. "Totalitarian and Authoritarian Regimes." In Fred Greenstein and Nelson Polsby, eds., *Handbook of Political Science,* III. Reading: Addison-Wesley Publishing Co., pp. 175–411.

————1976. "Patterns of Land Tenure, Division of Labor, and Voting Behavior in Europe." *Comparative Politics* 8 (April): 365–430.

Livro Branco Do SAAL. 1976. *Livro Branco do SAAL.* [Porto?]: Conselho Nacional do SAAL.

Lourenço, Eduardo. 1975. *Os militares e o poder.* Lisbon: Arcadia.

Lucena, Manuel de. 1976. *A evolução do sistema corporativo português,* II: *O Marcelismo.* Lisbon: Perspectivas e Realidades.

————1979. "The Evolution of Portuguese Corporatism Under Salazar and Caetano." In Lawrence S. Graham and Harry M. Makler., eds., *Contemporary Portugal: The Revolution and Its Antecedents.* Austin: University of Texas Press, pp. 47–88.

Luxemburg, Rosa. 1970. *The Russian Revolution and Leninism or Marxism?* Ann Arbor: University of Michigan Press.

MacLeod, Alex. 1983. "The French and Italian Communist Parties and the Portuguese Revolution." In Lawrence S. Graham and Douglas L. Wheeler, eds., *In Search of Modern Portugal: The Revolution and Its Consequences.* Madison: University of Wisconsin Press, pp. 297–320.

Macpherson, C.B. 1972. *The Real World of Democracy.* Oxford: Oxford University Press.

Malefakis, Edward. 1980. "Two Iberian Land Reforms Compared: Spain, 1931–36 and Portugal, 1974–78." In Afonso de Barros, ed., *A agricultura latifundiária na Península Ibérica.* Oeiras: Instituto Gulbenkian de Ciência, pp. 455–86.

Manchete. 1974. "PIDE: 48 Anos de Terror." *Manchete* 1161 (July 20): 136–39.

Mandel, Ernest. 1973. "Introduction." In Ernest Mandel, ed., *Contrôle ouvrier, conseils ouvriers, autogestion.* Vol. I. Paris: François Maspero, pp. 5–54.

Mansbridge, Jane J. 1973. "Time, Emotion, and Inequality: Three Problems of Participatory Groups." *Journal of Applied Behavioral Sciences* 9 (May): 351–68.

Mansinho, Maria Inês. 1980. "O crédito agrícola de emergência: balanço de uma inovação." *Análise Social* 16: 519–86.

Marcum, John A. 1969. *The Angolan Revolution, I: The Anatomy of an Explosion (1950–1962).* Cambridge: MIT Press.

————1972. *The Politics of Indifference: Portugal and Africa, a Case Study in American Foreign Policy.* Syracuse: Syracuse University, Maxwell School of Citizenship and Public Affairs, Program of Eastern African Studies 5.

————1978. *The Angolan Revolution, II: Exile Politics and Guerrilla Warfare (1962–1976).* Cambridge: MIT Press.

Marques, A.H. de Oliveira. 1972. *History of Portugal, II: From Empire to Corporate State.* New York: Columbia University Press.

Marques, Fernando Pereira. 1977. *Contrapoder e revolução.* Lisbon: Diabril.

Marques, J.A. Silva. 1976. *Relatos da clandestinidade: o PCP visto por dentro.* Lisbon, Edições Jornal Expresso.

Martins, Herminio. 1968. "Portugal." In S.J. Woolf, ed., *European Fascism.* London: Weidenfeld and Nicholson, pp. 302–36.

————1969. "Opposition in Portugal." *Government and Opposition* 4 (Spring): 250–63.

————1971. "Portugal." In Margaret Scotford Archer and Salvador Giner, eds., *Contemporary Europe: Class, Status, and Power.* London: Weidenfeld and Nicholson, pp. 60–89.

Marx, Karl and Friedrich Engels. 1972. *The Marx-Engels Reader.* Edited by Robert C. Tucker. New York: Norton.

Matos, Luis Salgado de. 1973. *Investimentos estrangeiros em Portugal.* Lisbon: Seara Nova.

Maxwell, Kenneth. 1976. "The Thorns of the Portuguese Revolution." *Foreign Affairs* 54 (January): 25–70.

Miliband, Ralph. 1977a. *The Coup in Chile.* In Robin Blackburn, ed., *Revolution and Class Struggle: A Reader in Marxist Politics.* Glasgow: Fontana, pp. 410–37.

————1977b. *Marxism and Politics.* Oxford: Oxford University Press.

Milkman, Margaret E. 1979. "L'articulation entre la politique internationale et la politique interne au Portugal après le 25 avril 1974." Travail de fin d'études, Université de Louvain.

Minter, William. 1972. *Portuguese Africa and the West.* New York: Monthly Review Press.

Moore, Stanley. 1963. *Three Tactics: The Background in Marx.* New York: Monthly Review Press.

Moreira, Manuel Belo and António Cortes Simões. 1982. "Six mois dans les centres régionaux de la réforme agraire (juin–décembre 1975)." *Révue Tiers-Monde* 23 (January–March): 133–58.

Morgan, David W. 1975. *The Socialist Left and the German Revolution: A History of the German Independent Social Democratic Party 1917–1922.* Ithaca: Cornell University Press.

Mota, José Gomes. 1976. *A Resistência: Subsídios para o estudo da crise político-militar do verão 1975*. Lisbon: Edições "Jornal Expresso."

Moura, Francisco Pereira de. 1974. *Por onde vai a economia portuguesa?* 4th ed. Lisbon: Seara Nova.

Mujal-Leon, Eusebio. 1977. "The PCP and the Portuguese Revolution." *Problems of Communism* 26 (January–February): 21–41.

Murteira, Mário. 1975. *Textos de economia política*. Lisbon: Serv. sociais dos trabalhadores da OGD.

————1979. "The Present Economic Situation: Its Origins and Prospects." In Lawrence S. Graham and Harry M. Makler, eds., *Contemporary Portugal: The Revolution and Its Antecedents*. Austin: University of Texas Press, pp. 331–42.

Neves, Orlando. 1975. *A Revolução em ruptura: Textos históricos da Revolução II*. Lisbon: Diabril.

Neves, Orlando, et al. 1978. *Diário de uma revolução*. Lisbon: Mil Dias.

Nordlinger, Eric. 1977. *Soldiers in Politics*. Englewood Cliffs: Prentice-Hall.

Nove, Alec. 1983. *The Economics of Feasible Socialism*. London: George Allen & Unwin.

Nun, José. 1968. "A Latin American Phenomenon: The Middle-Class Military Coup." In James Petras and Maurice Zeitlin, eds., *Latin America: Reform or Revolution?* Greenwich, Conn.: Fawcett, pp. 145–85.

O PCP. 1975. *O PCP e a Luta pela Reforma Agrária*. Lisbon: Edições Avante.

OECD. 1976. *Economic Surveys: Portugal*. Paris: OECD.

————1977. *Economic Surveys: Portugal*. Paris: OECD.

Oliveira, César. 1974. *O operariado e a república democrática*. Lisbon: Seara Nova.

Oliveira, Paula de and Francesco Marconi. 1978. *Política y proyecto: Una experiencia de base en Portugal*. Barcelona: Gustavo Gili.

Paige, Jeffery M. 1975. *Agrarian Revolution: Social Movements and Export Agriculture in the Underdeveloped World*. New York: Free Press.

Palla, Maria Antonia. 1975. "As eleições foram uma festa." *Vida Mundial* (May 1): 53.

Pannekoek, Anton. 1973. "Pannekoek et les conseils ouvriers." In Ernest Mandel, ed,. *Contrôle ouvrier, conseils ouvriers, autogestion*. Paris: François Maspero, pp. 132–36.

Pateman, Carole. 1970. *Participation and Democratic Theory*. Cambridge: Cambridge University Press.

Patriarca, Maria de Fátima. 1978. "Operários portugueses na revolução." *Análise Social* 56 (1978): 695–728.

PCP [Partido Comunista Português]. 1975. *Documentos do Comité Central 1965–1974*. Lisbon: Edições Avante.

————1982. *60 anos de luta ao serviço do povo e da pátria*. Lisbon: Edições Avante.

Peoples Translation Service. 1975. *Portugal: Key Documents of the Revolutionary Process*. Berkeley: Peoples Translation Service.

Pereira, João Martins. 1974. *Indústria, ideologia, e quotidiano: ensaio sobre o capitalismo em Portugal*. Porto: Afrontamento.

————1976. O socialismo, a transição, e o caso português. Lisbon: Livraria Bertrand.

————1978. "A esquerda, a crise, e a crise da esquerda." *O Jornal* (August 11): 23.

Pereira, José Pacheco. 1980. "Atitudes do trabalhador rural alentejano face à posse da terra e ao latifúndio." In Afonso de Barros, ed., *A agricultura latifundiária na Península Ibérica*. Oeiras: Instituto Gulbenkian de Ciência, pp. 163–86.

————1982. "Des luttes du prolétariat agricole avant le 25 avril 1974 à la réforme agraire." *Révue Tiers-Monde* 23 (January–March 1982): 39–58.

————n.d. *Conflitos sociais nos campos do sul de Portugal*. Lisbon: Publicações Europa-América.

Pimlott, Ben and Jean Seaton. 1983. "Political Power and the Portuguese Media." In Lawrence S. Graham and Douglas L. Wheeler, eds., *In Search of Modern Portugal: The Revolution and Its Consequences*. Madison: University of Wisconsin Press, pp. 43–60.

Pinho, Ivo. 1976. "Sector público empresarial: Antes e depois do 11 de Março." *Análise Social* 12: 733–47.

Pinto, António Costa, ed. 1982. *O fascismo em Portugal: Actas do Colóquio realizado na Faculdade de Letras de Lisboa*. Lisbon: A Regra do Jogo.

Pinto, Mário and Carlos Moura. 1972. "Estruturas sindicais portuguesas: contributo para o seu estudo." *Análise Social* 9: 140–90.

Pires, José. n.d. *Greves e o 25 de Abril*. Lisbon: Edições Base.

Piven, Frances Fox and Richard A. Cloward. 1979. *Poor People's Movements: Why They Succeed, How They Fail*. New York: Vintage Books.

Portas, Nuno. 1978. "Prefacio." In Paula de Oliveira and Francesco Marconi, *Política y proyecto: Una experiencia de base en Portugal*. Barcelona: Gustavo Gili, pp. 9–27.

————1979a. "Depoimento." *Cidade/Campo* 2: 111–24.

————1979b. "O Programa SAAL: Um balanço provisório." *Intevenção Social* 2 (September): 85–111.

Poulantzas, Nicos. 1978. "Towards a Democratic Socialism." *New Left Review* 109 (May–June): 75–87.

Raby, David L. 1983. "Populism and the Portuguese Left: from Delgado to Otelo." In Lawrence S. Graham and Douglas L. Wheeler, eds., *In Search of Modern Portugal: The Revolution and Its Consequences*. Madison: University of Wisconsin Press, pp. 61–80.

Radical America. 1975. "Women in the Portuguese Class Struggle: The Case of Sogantal." *Radical America* 9 (November–December): 55–61.

Reed, John. 1960. *Ten Days that Shook the World*. New York: Vintage.

Relatório do 25 de Novembro. 1976. *Relatório do 25 de Novembro: Texto Integral*. 2 vols. Lisbon: Ed. Abril.

Repórter Sombra. 1974. *Dossier P.I.D.E.: os horrores e crimes de uma "polícia."* Lisbon: Agência Portuguesa de Revistas, 1974.

Revolução das Flores. 1974. *A revolução das flores: Do 25 de Abril ao governo provisório*. Lisbon: Editorial Aster.

Riegelhaupt, Joyce F. 1973. "Festas and Padres: The Organization of Religious Action in a Portuguese Parish." *American Anthropologist* 75 (June): 835–52.

————1979. "Peasants and Politics in Salazar's Portugal: The Corporate State and Village 'Nonpolitics.' " In Lawrence S. Graham and Harry M. Makler, eds., *Contemporary Portugal: The Revolution and Its Antecedents*. Austin: University of Texas Press, pp. 167–90.

Rocha, Artur et al. 1979. "Oeiras, Portugal: Citizen's Participation—Local Experiences." Paper presented at the Congress of the International Housing and Planning Federation, Gotenburg, Sweden.

Rodrigues, Avelino, Cesário Borga, and Mário Cardoso. 1974. *O Movimento dos Capitães e o 25 de Abril: 229 dias para derrubar o fascismo*. Lisbon: Moraes Editores.

————1976. *Portugal depois de Abril*. Lisbon: Intervoz Publicidade Lda.

————1979. *Abril nos quarteis de Novembro*. Lisbon: Livraria Bertrand.

Rodrigues, Edgar. 1981. *Os anarquistas e os sindicatos: Portugal, 1911–1922*. Lisbon: Editora Sementeira, 1981.

Rodrigues, Julieta E.S. de Almeida. 1979. "Continuity and Change in Urban Portuguese Women's Roles: Emerging New Household Structures." Ph.D. diss. Teachers College, Columbia University, 1979.

Rodrigues, Urbano Tavares. 1979. *As pombas são vermelhas*. Lisbon: Livraria Bertrand.

Rosa, Eugénio. 1976. *Portugal: Dois anos de revolução na economia*. Lisbon: Diabril.

Rothschild-Whitt, Joyce. 1979. "The Collective Organization: An Alternative to Rational-Bureaucratic Models." *American Sociological Review* 44 (August): 509–27.

Roux, Bernard. 1982. "Le démantèlement d'une réforme agraire prolétarienne." *Révue Tiers-Monde* 23 (January–March): 9–25.

Russete, Joaquim Augusto V.M. and Maria Graciette Ferreira. 1979. "O movimento de ocupações." *Intervenção Social* 2 (September): 48–69.

Russinho, Joaquim Augusto and Luis Costa. 1976. *Caracterização da organização das populações dos bairros de lata*. Lisbon: ISSS, trabalho do quarto ano.

Santos, Américo Ramos dos. 1977a. "Tecnocracia e desenvolvimento monopolista (1968–1973)." *Economia e Socialismo* 14 (May): 24–34.

————1977b. "Monopólios, capital financeiro e especulação: Cinco anos do Marcelismo." *Economia e Socialismo* 17 (August): 3–26.

————1977c. "Desenvolvimento monopolista em Portugal: 1968/73."*Análise Social* 13 (January): 69–95.

————1978. "Economia portuguesa: Dez anos. Cinco modelos (1969–1978)." *Economia e Socialismo* 25–26 (April–May): 15–65.

Santos, Boaventura de Sousa. 1982. "Popular Justice, Dual Power and Socialist Strategy." In Piers Beirne and Richard Quinney, eds., *Marxism and Law*. New York: John Wiley and Sons, pp. 364–75.

Santos, Maria de Lurdes Lima dos et al. 1976. *O 25 de Abril e as lutas sociais nas empresas*. Porto: Afrontamento.

Saraiva, José António and Vicente Jorge Silva. 1976. *O 25 de Abril visto da história*. Lisbon: Livraria Bertrand.

Schmitter, Philippe C. 1975a. *Corporatism and Public Policy in Authoritarian Portugal*. Beverly Hills: Sage Publications.

————1975b. "Le parti communiste portugais entre le 'pouvoir social' et le 'pouvoir politique'." *Etudes Internationales* 6 (September): 375–88.

————1975c. "Liberation by *Golpe:* Retrospective Thoughts on the Demise of Authoritarian Rule in Portugal." *Armed Forces and Society* 2 (Fall): 5–33.

————1977. "Portée et signification des élections dans le Portugal authoritaire (1933–1974)." *Révue Française de Science Politique* 27 (February): 92–122.

Schumpeter, Joseph A. 1962. *Capitalism, Socialism, and Democracy*. 3d ed. New York: Harper Torchbooks.

SICP. 1976. *Portugal: um guia para o processo*. Lisbon: Edições SLEMES.

Sirianni, Carmen. 1980. "Workers' Control in the Era of World War I: A Comparative Analysis of the European Experience." *Theory and Society* 9 (January): 29–88.

————1982. *Workers Control and Socialist Democracy: The Soviet Experience*. London: Verso Editions.

————1983. "Councils and Parliaments: The Problems of Dual Power and Democracy in Comparative Perspective." *Politics and Society* 12: 83–123.

Soares, Mario. 1975. *Portugal's Struggle for Liberty*. London: George Allen and Unwin.

Spriano, Paolo. 1975. *The Occupation of the Factories: Italy 1920*. London: Pluto Press.

Stinchcombe, Arthur L. 1961. "Agricultural Enterprise and Rural Class Relations." *American Journal of Sociology* 67 (September): 165–76.

Sweezy, Paul M. and Charles Bettelheim. 1971. *On the Transition to Socialism*. New York: Monthly Review Press.

Szulc, Tad. 1975–76. "Lisbon and Washington: Beyond the Portuguese Revolution." *Foreign Policy* 21 (Winter): 3–62.

Therborn, Goran. 1977. "The Rule of Capital and the Rise of Democracy." *New Left Review* 103 (May–June): 3–41.

Tiago, Manuel. 1975. *Até amanhã, camaradas*. Lisbon: Edições Avante.

Tilly, Charles. 1978. *From Mobilization to Revolution*. Reading: Addison-Wesley.

Trotsky, Leon. 1967. *The History of the Russian Revolution*. London: Sphere Books.

U.S. Department of Commerce. 1975. *Foreign Economic Trends and Their Implications for the United States: Portugal*. Washington, D.C.: Department of Commerce.

Vanek, Jaroslav. 1971. *The Participatory Economy: An Evolutionary Hypothesis and a Strategy for Development*. Ithaca: Cornell University Press.

Ventura, António. 1983. "Documentos sobre uma tentativa de contacto entre o Bureau Político do PCP (Júlio Fogaça) e a IC em 1941." *Estudos sobre o Comunismo* 1 (September): 23–30.

Vieira, M. and D. Oliveira. 1976. *O poder popular em Portugal*. Coimbra: Centelha, 1976.

Wallis, Victor. 1978. "Workers' Control and Revolution." *Self-Management* 6 (Fall).

Wheeler, Douglas L. 1975. "Portuguese Elections and History." Paper presented to the Conference on Modern Portugal, Yale University.

————1979. "The Military and the Portuguese Dictatorship, 1926–1974: 'The Honor of the Army.' " In Lawrence S. Graham and Harry M. Makler, eds., *Contemporary Portugal: The Revolution and Its Antecedents*. Austin: University of Texas Press, pp. 191–220.

Wiarda, Howard J. 1977. *Corporatism and Development: The Portuguese Experience*. Amherst: University of Massachusetts Press.

————1979. "The Corporatist Tradition and the Corporatist System in Portugal: Structured, Evolving, Transcended, Persistent." In Lawrence S. Graham and Harry M. Makler, eds., *Contemporary Portugal: The Revolution and Its Antecedents*. Austin: University of Texas Press, pp. 89–122.

Winn, Peter. 1986. *Weavers of Revolution: The Yarur Workers and Chile's Road to Socialism*. New York: Oxford University Press.

Zald, Mayer and Roberta Ash. 1966. "Social Movement Organizations." *Social Forces* 44 (March): 327–41.

Zimbalist, Andrew and James Petras. 1976. "Workers' Control in Chile during Allende's Presidency." *Comparative Urban Research* 3 (April): 21–30.

Zolberg, Aristide R. 1972. "Moments of Madness." *Politics and Society* 2 (Winter): 183–207.

Zwerdling, Daniel. 1980. *Workplace Democracy: A Guide to Workplace Ownership, Participation, and Self-Management Experiments in the United States and Europe*. New York: Harper and Row.

Subject Index

Author Index

John L. Hammond has studied and written about mass political movements in Europe, Latin America, and the United States. He teaches sociology at Hunter College and the Graduate Center of the City University of New York. He is the author of *The Politics of Benevolence: Revival Religion and American Voting Behavior.*